A MANAGER'S G
IT LAW
Second Edition

BCS THE CHARTERED INSTITUTE FOR IT

Our mission as BCS, The Chartered Institute for IT, is to enable the information society. We promote wider social and economic progress through the advancement of information technology science and practice. We bring together industry, academics, practitioners and government to share knowledge, promote new thinking, inform the design of new curricula, shape public policy and inform the public.

Our vision is to be a world-class organisation for IT. Our 70,000 strong membership includes practitioners, businesses, academics and students in the UK and internationally. We deliver a range of professional development tools for practitioners and employees. A leading IT qualification body, we offer a range of widely recognised qualifications.

Further Information
BCS The Chartered Institute for IT, First Floor, Block D, North Star House, North Star Avenue, Swindon, SN2 1FA, United Kingdom.
T +44 (0) 1793 417 424
F +44 (0) 1793 417 444
www.bcs.org/contactus

A MANAGER'S GUIDE TO IT LAW
Second Edition

Jeremy Holt and Jeremy Newton (Editors)

Published by British Informatics Society Limited (BISL), a wholly owned subsidiary of BCS The Chartered Institute for IT, First Floor, Block D, North Star House, North Star Avenue, Swindon, SN2 1FA, UK.
www.bcs.org

ISBN 978-1-906124-75-5

British Cataloguing in Publication Data.
A CIP catalogue record for this book is available at the British Library.

Disclaimer:
The views expressed in this book are of the author(s) and do not necessarily reflect the views of BCS or BISL except where explicitly stated as such. Although every care has been taken by the authors and BISL in the preparation of the publication, no warranty is given by the authors or BISL as publisher as to the accuracy or completeness of the information contained within it and neither the authors nor BISL shall be responsible or liable for any loss or damage whatsoever arising by virtue of such information or any instructions or advice contained within this publication or by any of the aforementioned.

Typeset by Lapiz Digital Services, Chennai, India.
Printed and bound by CPI Group (UK) Ltd, Croydon, CR0 4YY.

CONTENTS

Contributors   ix
Acknowledgements   xi
Abbreviations   xii
Glossary   xv
Useful websites   xix
Preface to second edition   xxi

1   **IT CONTRACTS – Jeremy Holt**   **1**
Introduction   1
Parts of a contract   1
Who are you going to call?   2
Checking out the supplier   3
Letter of intent   3
The supplier's terms   3
What contracts are there likely to be?   4
Appendix: Main points of an IT contract   11

2   **SYSTEMS PROCUREMENT CONTRACTS – Jeremy Newton**   **13**
The negotiation process   13
Beware the standard contract   15
Contract mechanics   15
Commercial highlights   18
Problem management   20
Enforceability of exclusion clauses   23
Conclusion   25
Appendix: The 'reasonableness' test in practice   26

3   **AVOIDING EMPLOYMENT PROBLEMS – Jeremy Holt**   **28**
Introduction   28
Computer and email usage policies   28
Avoiding health and safety claims   33
Appendix: Specimen policy for computer and email use   35

4   **INTELLECTUAL PROPERTY LAW FOR COMPUTER USERS – Jennifer Pierce**   **40**
Introduction   40
Hardware and intellectual property rights   41
Software and intellectual property rights   42
Databases and intellectual property rights   44

Websites and intellectual property rights 45
Domain names and intellectual property rights 46
The internet and trade marks 47
The internet and copyright and database right 49
Appendix: A basic guide to intellectual property and related rights 49

5   **SOURCE CODE ESCROW – Jon Leigh and Graham Wood**   **55**
Introduction 55
The importance of escrow for software users 55
When do you need escrow? 56
Technical considerations 59
Verification 59
What should be lodged? 60
The agreements 61
User's duties 62
Choosing an escrow agent 62
Advantages of escrow for software owners 62
Conclusion 63

6   **OUTSOURCING – Jeremy Newton**   **65**
Introduction 65
Defining the services 66
Design risk 67
Service Level Agreement 67
Pricing and payment mechanisms 69
The outsourcing life cycle 70
Other relevant issues 73

7   **DATA PROTECTION – Andrew Katz**   **74**
Introduction 74
What data are covered 75
Sensitive personal data 76
Who needs to notify? 76
How to notify 77
Data protection principles 80
Rights of data subjects 88
Exemptions 89
Penalties and enforcement 90
References 91

8   **DOING BUSINESS ONLINE – Jeremy Newton**   **92**
Introduction 92
Information to be provided to clients 93
Forming contracts electronically 95
Performance and cancellation 97
Jurisdiction 98
Marketing communications 99
Consequences of non-compliance 100
Other considerations 101
Appendix: Consolidated information requirements 102

9	**SETTING UP JOINT VENTURES** – Andrew Katz	**103**
	Introduction	103
	Joint ventures and IT projects	103
	Establishing a joint venture	104
	Structure of a joint venture	107
	The operating agreement	112
	Competition law	114
	Appendix: Checklists for a joint venture operating agreement	115

10	**CLOUD COMPUTING** – Stuart Smith	**117**
	What is cloud computing?	117
	The services in the cloud	118
	The evolution of cloud computing	118
	Cloud formations	119
	Silver linings and thunder clouds	119
	Data protection and security	122
	Important clauses in a cloud computing contract for services	123
	Conclusion	125

11	**OPEN SOURCE SOFTWARE** – Andrew Katz	**126**
	Introduction	126
	What is open source?	126
	The public domain	130
	Open source and communities	130
	Open source software businesses	132
	Running open source in your business	133
	Open source and licensing	134
	Software development in context	137
	Contracting open source projects	137
	Open source software and due diligence	140
	Open source policies and procedures	141
	Open source software: employees and contractors	141
	Open source software and patents	142
	Associated licences	143
	Further information	143

12	**WEEE REGULATIONS** – Andy Lucas	**144**
	Introduction	144
	The players	144
	What is WEEE and what do the regulations cover?	146
	Key obligations on IT businesses	149
	Key commercial issues	151
	Further information	152

13	**FREEDOM OF INFORMATION** – Victoria Hordern	**153**
	Introduction	153
	Transparency Agenda	154
	Public authorities	154
	A public authority's obligations	154
	Providing information to the public authority	155

The request process		156
Withholding information		157
Impact of FOIA on private companies		159
Dealing with FOIA		160
Procurement		161
Drafting a clause		162
Further information		162
14	**RESOLVING DISPUTES – Sara Ellacott**	**164**
	Introduction	164
	Overview of dispute resolution methods	164
	Key factors in dispute resolution	165
	Specific dispute resolution methods	166
	Conclusion	177
	Index	178

CONTRIBUTORS

Sara Ellacott is the Senior Legal Director, EMEA Litigation, at Oracle Corporation. Sara advises on issues arising out of IT projects. She has experience of a wide range of dispute resolution procedures, including negotiated settlements, High Court litigation, arbitration and mediation. Sara speaks regularly on issues related to risk and dispute management.

Jeremy Holt is the head of the Computer Law Group of Clark Holt Commercial Solicitors (www.clarkholt.com). He has specialised in IT and ecommerce law for over 20 years. In 2003, Jeremy helped set up, in Swindon, the first museum in the country dedicated to the history of computing. He was for 11 years the Secretary of the Law Specialist Group of the British Computer Society. Jeremy writes and lectures extensively on IT law and contracts.

Victoria Hordern is a senior associate in Field Fisher Waterhouse LLP's Privacy and Information Law Group (www.ffw.com). She advises the public sector, charities and private companies on compliance with privacy and information law, has provided tailored training on handling exemptions and exceptions under the Freedom of Information Act 2000 and the Environmental Information Regulations 2004 respectively, as well as training more broadly on data protection and privacy matters. She has assisted with responses to information access requests (both for those organisations responding to a request and for those affected by the potential disclosure) and is particularly interested in the tension between the privacy and information access regimes.

Andrew Katz is a partner at Moorcrofts Corporate Law, a niche corporate and commercial legal practice based in Marlow, Buckinghamshire, and specialises in technology, media and telecoms work. He trained in London and moved to a large Midlands firm where he became their youngest-ever partner. Andrew was previously a computer consultant and was one of the first people to advise public bodies on data storage and retrieval using optical (CD-ROM) technology, and he became an accredited developer for Steve Jobs's NEXT computer system. He is currently interested in the legal challenges of open source software and peer-to-peer networking. He has been a member of the board and council of the Telecommunications Industry Association.

Jon Leigh has been Director of Escrow Solutions at NCC Group plc since 2003 where he is responsible for the product development and sales strategies of the Group's Escrow Solutions division. Jon has been with the NCC Group for more than 20 years having joined the escrow division in 1997 as head of testing.

Previously he was project manager of several European consortium projects to establish internationally recognised conformance testing services. Jon previously worked for Ferranti Computer Systems having graduated from Hull University with a Joint Honours degree in Chemistry and Computing.

Andy Lucas is a partner in the Technology Law Group of Field Fisher Waterhouse LLP. He specialises in all aspects of non-contentious computer law. He has acted for both suppliers and customers in numerous large-scale software procurements and is currently an adviser to many government departments on some of their most high profile technology implementations. This advice includes not only the drafting and negotiation of agreements and schedules, but also expert advice on the implementation of the public procurement regulations.

Jeremy Newton is a Director of Technology Law Alliance, a specialist IT/ outsourcing law firm. He has over 20 years' experience of IT and outsourcing contracts, both in practice and in-house with Sun Microsystems and on secondment to HM Treasury. Apart from contributing to this book, he is a contributor to *Computer Law* (Oxford University Press), and writes and lectures widely on the subject. Jeremy is also the Secretary of the Financial Services Specialist Group of the BCS, and an active member of the international Technology Law Association (iTechLaw).

Jennifer Pierce, a partner in the law firm Charles Russell (www.crlaw.co.uk), advises both customers and suppliers in the UK and overseas in respect of legal issues relating to software, equipment, peripherals and other associated technology as well as internet and data usage. Her clients range from household names to private individuals. Jennifer writes and lectures widely on intellectual property and information technology. She is the joint editor and a major contributor to *Working with Technology: Law and Practice*, published by Sweet & Maxwell, a visiting lecturer of the Queen Mary Intellectual Property Research Institute, and has appeared as an expert on BBC current affairs programmes.

Stuart Smith was a solicitor in the Computer Law Group of Clark Holt Commercial Solicitors for three years before joining the Information Technology Team of Bond Pearce in 2011. He advises a range of customers and suppliers of hardware, software and IT services.

Graham Wood is a consultant with Curule Consultants Ltd providing specialist advice on intellectual property and information technology law. He spent four years with the National Computing Centre in Manchester where he was a lawyer in the Escrow department. Graham is currently project manager for the introduction of data protection legislation in Bermuda. He speaks regularly and writes for international business publications.

ACKNOWLEDGEMENTS

The authors wish to acknowledge the contributions made by the following:

Martin Bazen

Richard Folsom

Peter James

Charlotte Hanham

Dawn Holt

Daniel Hopkin

David Hudson

Nathan Hudson

Nia Hudson

Annette Leigh

Isabelle Katz

Lucy Katz

Oscar Katz

Miranda Mowbray

Antonia Newell

Melanie Newton

Adrian Phillips

Tina Pullen

Sian Rudgard

Christopher Smith

Sally Smith

ABBREVIATIONS

AATF	Approved Authorised Treatment Facility
ADR	Alternative Dispute Resolution
AE	Approved Exporter
ASP	Application Service Provider/Provision
AWS	Amazon Web Services
BIS	The Department for Business Innovation and Skills
BPO	Business Process Outsourcing
BSD	Berkeley Software Distribution
CAP	Code of Advertising Practice
CCTV	Closed-Circuit Television
CPR	Civil Procedural Rules
CPU	Central Processing Unit
CRM	Customer Relationship Management
DCF	Designated Collection Facility
DMA	Direct Marketing Association
DR	Dispute Resolution
DSE	Display Screen Equipment
DTI	Department of Trade and Industry
DTS	Distributor Take-back Scheme
EA	Environment Agency
EC	European Commission
EC2	Elastic Compute Cloud
EEA	European Economic Area
EEE	Electrical and Electronic Equipment
EEIG	European Economic Interest Grouping

EMAS	Employment Medical Advisory Service
EMU	Economic and Monetary Union
ERP	Enterprise Resource Planning
EU	European Union
FLOSS	Free, Libre and Open Source Software
FM	Facilities Management
FOIA	Freedom of Information Act
FOSS	Free and Open Source Software
FSF	Free Software Foundation
GPL	General Public License
HMRC	Her Majesty's Revenue and Customs
HSE	Health and Safety Executive
IaaS	Infrastructure as a Service
ICO	Information Commissioner's Office
IP	Intellectual Property
IPR	Intellectual Property Right
ISP	Internet Service Provider
IT	Information Technology
JV	Joint Venture
KPI	Key Performance Indicator
LLC	Limited Liability Corporation
LLP	Limited Liability Partnership
MIT	Massachusetts Institute of Technology
NDA	Non-Disclosure Agreement
NHS	National Health Service
NIEA	Northern Ireland Environment Agency
NIST	National Institute of Standards and Technology
OEM	Original Equipment Manufacturer
OFT	Office of Fair Trading
OGC	Office of Government Commerce
OIN	Open Invention Network
OSI	Open Source Initiative

PaaS	Platform as a Service
PCS	Producer Compliance Scheme
PFI	Private Finance Initiative
PI	Performance Indicator
POBA	Project Open Book Accounting
PPP	Public Private Partnership
RSI	Repetitive Strain Injury
SaaS	Software as a Service
SEPA	Scottish Environment Protection Agency
SI	Systems Integration
SLA	Service Level Agreement
SMS	Short Message Service
SSADM	Structured Systems Analysis and Design Method
TCC	Technology and Construction Court
TUPE	Transfer of Undertakings (Protection of Employment) Regulations
UCTA	Unfair Contract Terms Act 1977
URL	Uniform Resource Locator
VAT	Value Added Tax
VCA	Vehicle Certification Agency
VDU	Visual Display Unit
WEEE	Waste Electrical and Electronic Equipment

GLOSSARY

Acceptance Testing   The running of a set of programs, under designated conditions, on a computer before the acceptance of the system by the customer.

Alternative Dispute Resolution (ADR)   A method of settling disputes without resorting to the legal courts. Examples include mediation and expert determination.

Application Service Provider (ASP)   A business that rents out the use of software running on its own servers to remote customers using a web-based connection to access the service.

Business Process Outsourcing (BPO)   The subcontracting by a business of some or all non-core business activities allowing it to concentrate on its principal activities.

Change Control   The process for changing customer requirements during a project.

Civil Procedure Rules (CPR)   The rules of practice and procedure that apply to the conduct of civil litigation in England and Wales.

Claimant   The person who brings a legal action before the courts in England and Wales (formerly called the plaintiff).

Competition Law   The law relating to the abuse of market power by buyers or sellers such as price fixing, cartel and the abuse of monopolies (also called anti-trust law).

Cookie   A tag sent by a server to an internet user that is sent back to the server each time the internet user accesses that server.

Copyright   A right for the creator of an original literary, dramatic or musical work to prevent the copying of such work. The right lasts for the life of the creator plus 70 years. No registration is required in the United Kingdom.

Customer Relationship Management (CRM)   An integrated information system that is used to run the pre-sales and post-sales activities of a business.

Database Right A right under European law for the creator of a database to prevent the copying of such a database for 15 years. No registration is required.

Data Controller A person who holds information about a living individual either on a computer or in structured manual records.

Data Subject A living individual about whom another holds information on a computer or in structured manual records.

Decompiler A program that generates high-level source code from machine code.

Design Right A right to prevent the copying of the external appearance of a manufactured article. Such protection can last for 25 years from the time of registration.

Display Screen Equipment (DSE) Computer monitors and any other screens that display text, numbers or graphics.

Dispute Resolution (DR) The settling of an argument between two parties.

Distance Selling A sale where the buyer and seller do not meet face to face, for example sales via the internet, sales catalogue, fax or telephone.

Domain Name The address of an internet site, including a host name, subdomain and domain, separated by dots (e.g. www.bcs.org.uk).

Due Diligence The process of investigation into a business or intellectual property rights before their purchase or entry into a contract relating to them.

Economic and Monetary Union (EMU) The consolidation of European currencies into the monetary unit of the euro that began in 1999.

Enterprise Resource Planning (ERP) A software system designed to support and automate the business processes of medium and large businesses.

Escrow The process of an independent third party holding something in readiness for a possible event. One example is an escrow agent holding the source code of software that would be released to a customer if the supplier became insolvent.

European Economic Area (EEA) The countries of the member states of the European Union, plus Iceland, Liechtenstein and Norway.

Facilities Management The management of a user's computer installation by an outside organisation.

Force Majeure A supervening event, such as a general strike or outbreak of war, that a contract provides will validly prevent one party to the contract from carrying out its obligations to the other party.

Framing A method of including one page from the web within what appears to be another page.

Information Commissioner A government official in the United Kingdom who holds a register of data controllers and enforces data protection legislation (formerly known as the Data Protection Registrar).

Information Technology (IT) The application to information processing of current technologies from computing, telecommunications and microelectronics.

Intellectual Property Right (IPR) Legal rights for the owners of inventions, designs and other materials to control their publication or use. Examples include patents, trade marks and copyright.

Interface Software that enables a program to work with the user, with another program or with the computer's hardware.

Joint Venture (JV) An arrangement between two (or more) businesses under which they work jointly for a common purpose.

Linking In a web page, the process of using a hypertext connection or highlighted piece of text to move the reader to another page.

Metatag A tag that identifies the contents of a web page (such as a keyword for search engines).

Moral Right The right of the author of a copyright literary work to be identified as its author and for the work not to be subjected to derogatory treatment.

Non-Disclosure Agreement (NDA) A contract between two parties under which one (or both) will keep various matters confidential.

Object Code The list of machine code instructions produced by passing the source code of a computer program through a compiler or an assembler.

Original Equipment Manufacturer (OEM) A misleading term for a business that repackages material made by other businesses. Unlike a value-added reseller, an OEM does not necessarily add anything except their name to a product.

Outsourcing The assignment of tasks, such as payroll and data entry, to independent contractors outside the business.

Passing Off The action of a business giving the impression that it is (or is linked to) another business. This may be by the use of a similar name or other marketing get-up or the appearance of a product.

Patent A right granted by the state to an inventor of a new invention that, in return for a full public disclosure of the invention, the inventor will have a monopoly over the exploitation of the invention for up to 20 years.

Personal Data Information about a living individual.

Repetitive Strain Injury (RSI) Damage to the hands, arms, neck, back or eyes due to computer use.

Respondent   The person against whom a legal action is brought in the courts in England and Wales (formally called the defendant).

Sensitive Personal Data   Information about a living individual that relates to their race, political opinions, religious beliefs, trade union membership, physical or mental health, sexual life or criminal record.

Service Level Agreement (SLA)   A contract between two organisations about the quality of service to be provided by one to the other.

Source Code   A textual description of a computer program, written in a programming language.

Spam   Email that is not requested by the recipient (the word is believed to have been taken from a repetitive Monty Python song).

Specification   In relation to software, a description of the operating environment and proposed features and functionality of a new program; in relation to computer hardware, information about its capabilities and features.

Structured Systems Analysis and Design Method (SSADM)   A technology that is widely used for the analysis and design of IT systems.

Subject Access Request   The right under data protection legislation in the United Kingdom for an individual to ask a data controller what information it holds about that individual.

Systems Integration (SI)   The combining of different programs or components into a functional system.

Systems Procurement   The choice and purchase of a new computer system.

Technology and Construction Court (TCC)   A division of the High Court of England and Wales that deals with technically complex legal claims.

Trade Mark   A graphic sign that is capable of distinguishing the goods or services of one organisation from another. A trade mark can last indefinitely (including where it has been registered).

Transfer of Undertaking (Protection of Employment) Regulations (TUPE)   Legislation in the United Kingdom that preserves the employment rights of individuals upon the sale of the business in which they work.

Value Added Tax   A sales tax applied in the United Kingdom.

Verification   The process of confirming that a result is correct or that a procedure has been performed.

USEFUL WEBSITES

www.bcs.org/content/conWebDoc/1562	BCS Professional advice register
www.worklink.org.uk	Worklink service
www.bsi.org.uk	British Standards Institution
www.cedr.com	Centre for Effective Dispute Resolution
www.dma.org.uk	Direct Marketing Association
www.fpsonline.org.uk	Fax Preference Service
www.hse.gov.uk	Health and Safety Executive, Information line: 08701 545500, Publications: 01787 881165
www.informationcommissioner.gov.uk	Information Commissioner, Office of the Information Commissioner, Wycliffe House, Water Lane, Wilmslow, Cheshire, SK9 5AF, Telephone: 01625 545700, Email: mail@notification.demon.co.uk
www.iso.org	International Organization for Standardization
www.itechlaw.org	International Technology Law Association
www.mpsonline.org.uk	Mailing Preference Service
www.mca.org.uk	Management Consultancies Association
www.the-stationery-office.co.uk	Stationery Office Ltd
www.tpsonline.org.uk	Telephone Preference Service

PREFACE TO SECOND EDITION

This book is a practical guide for managers dealing with computer-related issues. The authors felt the law in England in this area should be summarised in a way that is easy to understand. Things have changed so much and so quickly since the first edition that it was felt that the book should be updated to reflect these changes.

The book is not designed to be read from cover to cover. Readers can dip into the various self-contained chapters to find the answers that they seek. It provides practical advice on the appropriate steps that should be taken.

We hope that it will be a valuable guide to managers as well as being of interest to IT professionals, legal practitioners and students.

Jeremy Holt and Jeremy Newton

1   IT CONTRACTS

Jeremy Holt

This chapter outlines the contents of a contract and lists the matters that should be covered by different types of contract. If you do not have time to read all of the chapter, the appendix to this chapter lists the main points that you should consider.

INTRODUCTION

Pity the unfortunate manager. It has been bad enough trying to get the computer project organised. Now, possibly at the last moment, the contracts have arrived, some with print small enough to make the reader go blind. The manager suspects (rightly) that these contracts are one-sided in favour of the supplier, but knows that the project will only proceed if those contracts (or something similar) are signed. How does the manager work out what needs to be done and from whom advice can be obtained? This chapter provides a practical framework of help in this situation. If you are looking for an academic guide to computer contracts, you must look elsewhere.

PARTS OF A CONTRACT

The first point to consider is the form that contracts normally take. At its simplest a contract consists of:

- the date on which the contract was entered into;
- the names and addresses of those entering into the contract;
- a short description of what the contract is about (generally entitled 'Background', 'Recitals' or even, regrettably, 'Whereas');
- definitions of terms used in the contract;
- what the supplier is going to do for you;
- what you must do for the supplier;
- what you must pay the supplier.

Do not forget we are engaged in contract first aid here. If all else fails, concentrate on what the supplier is going to do for you and what you are expected to pay. Standard terms that are not specific to this individual contract (what lawyers call 'boilerplate') are generally grouped together at the end of the contract. A list of the more important boilerplate clauses is shown in the box.

IMPORTANT BOILERPLATE TERMS

Force Majeure – this says that neither party shall be liable for any failure to perform the contract because of circumstances beyond its control such as an Act of God, fire, flood etc. This is likely to be invoked by the supplier more than the client. This clause effectively absolves the supplier from responsibility, so the circumstances in which it can be invoked should be checked carefully to ensure that they are no wider than is reasonable.

Entire Agreement – this says that the entire agreement between the parties is set out in the written contract and so no other previous representations by the supplier may be relied upon by the client. This is a reasonable principle, but the client must make sure that the contract deals with all the important points.

Governing law and jurisdiction – ideally this should be English law enforced in the English courts. An alternative is to agree arbitration, and as this happens behind closed doors then the supplier may worry less about bad publicity.

It is sensible to agree an alternative dispute resolution procedure (such as mediation), which must be carried out before any dispute is referred to the courts or to arbitration.

WHO ARE YOU GOING TO CALL?

You are not going to be able to do all this on your own. You are going to need professional advice. Computer law is a specialist area, and a rapidly changing one (it did not even exist as a field of legal practice 25 years ago). The correct advice from a lawyer experienced in this field can save a great deal of trouble later. The function of a good lawyer is to assess risk, help the client to understand the level of risk and then reduce it.

There are two directories of lawyers that you might like to consult: *Chambers' Guide to the Legal Profession* and *The Legal 500*. New versions are published each year and each has sections on lawyers who specialise in computer law (sometimes called 'information technology law'). These two books can generally be found in the reference section of a public library, and can also be searched without charge on the web. Alternatively, you can ring the Law Society or the Society for Computers and Law for suggestions of lawyers who work in this field and who could help you.

CHECKING OUT THE SUPPLIER

It may seem like an obvious point but make sure that you know who you are dealing with. This will mean, at least, doing a company search. A credit check would do no harm. As the Army maxim has it 'time spent on reconnaissance is seldom wasted'. If you discover that the supplier company was set up last year and has an issued capital of £1 you may like to consider asking for a guarantee of the contract from a more substantial body. Business is not all about making a rational decision on paper. Do you get good vibes from the supplier? On small things, do they do what they say that they will do? If, for whatever reason, you do not trust them, do not go ahead with the contract under any circumstances because this will only lead to worry and tears later.

LETTER OF INTENT

The supplier may ask for a letter of intent from you because it may need to start work on your project before contracts are signed, and because the negotiation and agreement of the contract terms may take a little while. Alternatively, you may like to suggest one so that you are not pressurised into signing the contracts before you have gone through them properly. A letter of intent is no more than written confirmation from you of your intention to enter into a contract with the supplier. What is critical, however, is that the letter of intent from you to the supplier must contain a statement that the letter is not intended to be contractually binding, otherwise you may unwittingly enter into a contract earlier than you intended. Where there is a non-binding letter of intent and the supplier, at your request and to save time, starts work on the project, it is reasonable for the supplier to ask to be paid for this initial work carried out regardless of whether the project proceeds or not. There are two important matters to agree. The first is the rate for the job (e.g. a daily rate – work normally starts under a letter of intent on a time and materials basis; the definitive contract may include a fixed price for a specified deliverable). The other is an overall cap on your liability to the supplier for this work. This obligation to pay the supplier should be contractually binding (unlike the rest of the letter of intent).

THE SUPPLIER'S TERMS

There is, of course, no obligation on you to accept that you will purchase a new computer system on the basis of the supplier's terms.

You could propose your own terms entirely – this is certainly an approach taken by large organisations with extensive experience of computer contracts. However, it is generally better to use the supplier's contract terms (unless they are completely unreasonable) as a start and amend them to your satisfaction. It is a good idea to ask for the supplier's proposed terms at as early a stage as possible. Do not wait until you have told them that they have been awarded the contract.

WHAT CONTRACTS ARE THERE LIKELY TO BE?

Any computer system will require the purchase of hardware (e.g. servers, PCs, printers etc.), software (the application software and the operating system software) and services (such as support and maintenance). When computers first started to be widely and routinely used in business life about 30 years ago the emphasis was very much on the hardware, which was comparatively unreliable. Nowadays the emphasis is much more on the software and services. It is normal to decide upon the software first and then to choose the appropriate hardware. If the contract relates to the procurement of a new system, the reader is referred to Chapter 2. The rest of this chapter deals with the purchase or licence of individual services or components.

Contracts for consultancy services

Long before the order for a new system is placed, the client may enter into a consultancy contract, perhaps relating to a feasibility study, analysing requirements, recommending a system to meet those requirements, helping select the appropriate suppliers, or assisting with preparation of an invitation to tender. A large part of the work carried out in the computer industry is under consultancy contracts. The client may need help on a one-off basis or require skills that do not exist within the client's workforce, so there is a need for an outside consultant to carry out the work. Sometimes the consultancy arrangement is dealt with by means of an exchange of letters; a formal consultancy agreement, however, is a better option for both parties.

- **Defining the deliverables** One of the most important issues that must be dealt with in such a contract is a detailed description of what the consultant is expected to do. If the description is loose or inexact, this can give rise to differences between what the client is expecting to receive and what the consultant is expecting to deliver. This can, predictably, lead to disputes. So defining the nature and quality of the deliverable is particularly important.

- **Payment arrangements** The payment to the consultant by the client may be on a time and materials, fixed price or estimated maximum price basis. It is an aspect of consultancy that the amount of work required will be uncertain. The disadvantage of a fixed price payment mechanism (as with any other contract) is that the consultant will inevitably include a contingency element in the price quoted. If the consultancy can be broken down into a series of stages, payment against milestones will allow each party to gauge how the work is going.

- **Copyright and confidentiality** Copyright will almost always be an issue. Broadly speaking, there is a simple choice as to how the parties deal with ownership of copyright in the consultant's work. Either the consultant can assign to the client all intellectual property rights in whatever is produced (provided that the consultant has been fully paid) or the consultant can grant a perpetual licence to the client to use such intellectual property rights for the purposes of the client's business (see Chapter 4 for more details). It goes almost without saying that the consultant should be obliged to keep confidential any information given by the client about its business. It is important to note that if there is no agreement with a consultant about copyright the client does not automatically get ownership of such copyright. It stays with the consultant (although there may also be an implied licence for use of the copyright by the client).

The problem is that once a consultant has carried out an assignment for one client in an industry, the consultant may be ideally placed to carry out assignments for other clients within that same industry. Sometimes, therefore, clients go further and stipulate in the contract that not only must their own information be kept confidential, but also that the consultant must agree not to carry out projects for the client's competitors for a period (perhaps a year) after the work is completed.

- **Insurance** In order to provide peace of mind to the client, the client may require the consultant to take out professional indemnity insurance. This is still relatively inexpensive because, in practice, it is rare for claims to be made under such policies.

- **Key personnel** The client will want to know the identity of the staff who the consultant will be using to carry out the work. It is normal for the client to be able to veto any staff members of whom they disapprove for whatever reason.

The client will want to retain the right to terminate the consultancy contract if the consultant is guilty of serious misconduct or any other conduct likely to bring the client into disrepute.

Contracts for hardware purchase

Computer hardware is much more reliable than it used to be, so contracts for the supply of hardware are not generally contentious. A hardware purchase contract requires the following details:

- A detailed description of the hardware (this is likely to be in a schedule).

- A warranty about the quality of hardware (normally this warranty applies for a year after acceptance of the hardware by the client).

- Delivery dates.

- Price.

- Acceptance testing.

- Future maintenance.

- Training.

Problems can arise if the hardware is not large enough for anticipated demand, and with the integration of hardware (such as servers and printers), which may have been supplied by different suppliers. In many cases the cost of the hardware is not a large percentage of the total system cost. Profit margins on hardware are relatively low, so the software supplier may be relaxed about whether the client obtains the hardware from the software supplier or from a third-party supplier. It is always worth asking the software supplier to quote for supplying the hardware because they may have better bargaining power than you would have on your own. At the end of the day, the two most important matters in a contract for hardware are to check that there is an exact description of what you are buying and that there is an obligation on the supplier to repair or replace it if it does not work properly.

Contracts for hardware maintenance

Hardware maintenance is more of a commodity than software maintenance and there are likely to be more alternative suppliers for the maintenance of hardware (and so prices are keener). There are two different types of hardware maintenance: preventive maintenance and corrective maintenance. Preventive maintenance covers the regular testing of the hardware (e.g. once every six months) before any problem is reported. Corrective maintenance deals with faults as and when they arise, normally in response to a service call from the client. With corrective maintenance the key element is the response time: how quickly will the supplier start to respond to the problem once it is reported? This is generally within a fixed number of working hours. For example, an engineer may have to arrive at the site no more than eight working hours after the problem has been reported by the client. This does not mean that the engineer will solve the problem within eight hours, merely that a start will be made to try to solve it. Sometimes online diagnosis is used: the client's hardware is linked by telecommunications to the supplier who can solve the fault at a distance. (The impetus for online diagnosis came from the USA where the distances were so great it was often not practicable to send an engineer in person.) Payment for hardware maintenance is generally made in advance on a monthly or quarterly basis. The annual amount varies but can often be between 10 per cent and 15 per cent of the list price of the hardware. Other points that will normally be covered in a hardware maintenance contract include a right for the supplier to:

- make an additional charge for frivolous or unnecessary call outs;
- increase the charges from time to time, perhaps in accordance with a recognised index (such as the Consumer Price Index); and
- refuse to cover equipment that is more than five years old or which is past its reasonable working life.

The client will be under an obligation to:

- pay for corrections that are not caused by the equipment itself (e.g. faults arising from electrical fluctuations);
- notify the supplier of problems promptly after they arise (so that time does not make them worse); and
- allow the supplier reasonable access to the equipment.

Contracts for software licences

At its simplest, any contract for software should allow you to use the software in the way that you envisaged without the risk that anyone can come along later and say either that you can not use it any more or that you have got to pay more money. It follows, therefore, that one of the first checks that you should do is to confirm that the software supplier either owns the copyright in the software or has the right to license it to you. It is a feature of the computer industry that software is often licensed to end-users by organisations other than the actual owner (for example it may be sub-licensed by a distributor or channel partner). You should not put up with oblique answers to your demand for evidence that the supplier can license the software to you. They should be able to produce it immediately.

At this point you may wonder why a licence agreement is necessary at all. Why can the supplier not simply sell you the software? The supplier is not actually selling you ownership of the software (because they would like to continue to license it to other people). The licence is only a permit for you to use the software for your own purposes. This leads onto the next important point. You must check in the licence agreement to whom the software is licensed and for what purpose. Is the software to be licensed to your particular company or can it be used by the whole of your group (in which case the software supplier will want more money)? Alternatively, is the software to be restricted to a limited number of users and, if more than that number use it, then do you have to pay an additional licence fee? This is one of the oldest tricks in the software supplier's book. They allow the client to sign up for a very limited number of users and then the supplier makes a considerable profit from the additional users who will almost inevitably be required by the client later. The supplier, of course, responds that this simply reflects the extra use (and, as a result, commercial benefit) that the client is making of the software.

It is also possible that at some time in the future the client may want to outsource its computer operations (see Chapter 6). Consequently, provision for the transfer of the licence from the client to an outsourcing company should be made in the original software licence agreement.

Contracts for software maintenance
No software of any complexity is ever free from errors. The older the system the more likely that it will need maintenance. Furthermore, if a system is installed in a rush (e.g. to meet a particular deadline), then it is likely not to have been tested properly and so require more attention after it has been installed. In some ways, future charges for maintenance are the icing on the cake for software developers. If they can generate sufficiently wide sales of the software, then support fees can be guaranteed for years to come. It is important for managers to be aware of this as three-quarters of a budget for software may be for future software maintenance. The client is well advised to check how wide the maintenance supplier's client base is (the wider the better) and to look at the offices from which the supplier will be providing the support (and how many people will be providing such support). The maintenance contract will almost certainly be prepared by the supplier. Some of the most common provisions are discussed below.

- **Charging arrangements** – Sometimes the cost of the software licence is bundled with the first year's maintenance charges. One interesting point is from when the support charges should run. Some clients argue that they should start from the end of the warranty period for the software. However, it is now generally accepted that they should begin from acceptance of the system because warranty and support are separate matters.

7

- **Scope of maintenance services** – Maintenance or support will normally cover the investigation by the supplier of errors in the system reported by the client as well as updated documentation and telephone or, more frequently nowadays, online advice. It will, in most cases, cover updates to the software (but not necessarily new versions of the software). The client may want to categorise different kinds of problems into those that could be critical for its business and those that are no more than an irritation and could be dealt with next time a new version of the software comes out. The supplier's response time will be different depending on the severity of the problem. The supplier will not normally commit to a fix within a particular period, only that they will start to fix it within a particular time.

- **Exclusions from scope** – The maintenance supplier will also be keen to list in the contract what maintenance does not cover. Most of these exceptions are reasonable. They generally include problems arising from changes to the software made by people other than the supplier, incorrect use of the software by the client or events beyond the control of the maintenance supplier such as hardware failure, fluctuation of electrical supplies or accidents. Normally, the maintenance supplier will still seek to help the client where the exceptions apply (indeed there should be a contractual obligation to do so). However, the supplier may want to make an additional charge for such work and will not guarantee any particular recovery time. From the supplier's point of view it becomes difficult to manage support if the client base is using a number of different versions of the software. Consequently, the supplier normally restricts support to the latest two versions of the software and will refuse to support earlier versions.

- **Charge increases** – The client will want to ensure that the maintenance charges will not rocket up. One means of doing this is to tie the maintenance charges to a percentage of the list price of the software (e.g. 10–15 per cent), but of course the supplier has control over the list price. Alternatively, any increase in maintenance charges can be tied to a recognised index. Clients sometimes suggest the Consumer Price Index. However, suppliers (who know that increases in salaries are generally greater than increases in retail prices) prefer to tie them to an earnings index. There is some logic in this because the bulk of the supplier's expenses are salaries.

- **Payment arrangements** – Payment is almost invariably made in advance. In the past, it was for a year, but now it is more commonly paid three months or a month in advance. This is so that if the supplier goes into liquidation the client will not have overpaid very much and the client can also swiftly withhold the payment of maintenance charges if there is a problem with the service provided.

- **Termination** – It is important for the client to look at the termination clauses of the contract offered by the supplier. The client will want to know how much notice they have to give to end the maintenance contract. This is often three or six months. It is a good idea for the client to ask the supplier to commit on its part to supply maintenance (if the client wants it) for the potential life of the software (e.g. five years).

Contracts for software development

Software will often need to be customised for the client by the supplier. However, this is really only a tinkering with the main programs. In certain circumstances, it may be necessary for the client to commission new software because there is no existing software that meets the client's needs. Contracts for software development are complex and it is wise for the client to seek professional advice both about the specification for the software and the contract under which the software will be written. This is all the more important because software development projects have a reputation for taking longer, and for costing more, than originally forecast. Consequently background research by the client into the proposed supplier is particularly worthwhile. Pricing for the project will be either fixed price or time and materials. Payments will normally be made conditional upon project milestones being reached. The client will seek to ensure the quality of the software product delivered by the supplier by requiring acceptance tests of the software and a warranty from the supplier that the product will be in accordance with the agreed specification. A thorny question is whether the client should own the copyright in the software program produced. At first glance, it might be thought that this should obviously belong to the client who has paid for it. However, all the client needs is to use the software; the client needs neither to own it nor to develop it further. There is a benefit to the client in the supplier having an incentive to carry out further development of the software program and license it to other clients. The original client does not then pay the total cost of all the subsequent fixes and has the benefit of the faults reported by other users. If the supplier becomes insolvent, then the client needs access to the source code of the software in order to maintain it. For this reason the client should require the supplier to put a copy of such source code in escrow with an independent third party so that it is available if required (see Chapter 5). The supplier will normally provide a warranty that defects in the software reported within a particular length of time after the start of its use will be rectified. This is frequently 90 days after acceptance of the software by the client.

Service level agreements

Service level agreements (SLAs) are critical to the computer industry, but they are rarely fully understood. Under an SLA, a supplier undertakes to supply a service to a client at a particular level.

Perhaps because so few lawyers have a reasonable working knowledge of the computer industry, SLAs are often drawn up by the participants without legal advice.

A service level agreement should cover the following:

- The service required (i.e. what the client wants and what the supplier is prepared to commit to supply).
- Quality standards (i.e. the standards or levels the supplier must achieve), such as host/terminal response times, batch processing times, 'uptime' or processor availability, by specifying what? when? how? and by whom?
- Deliverables (e.g. regular reports).

- The consequences of failing to meet service procedures or standards (e.g. compensation in the form of service credits).

- Procedures for the client to monitor performance of obligations by the supplier.

- Procedures for change control (i.e. changing part of the service that is being provided by the supplier under the agreement).

- Terms dealing with access to, and security of, the client's site and data.

- A procedure for disaster recovery (either upon a system failure or a catastrophe).

- The agreed frequency of meetings between the client and the supplier to review the supplier's performance of the agreement, properly minuted with subsequent action plans and awards of priority.

Ideally, an SLA should be a self-enforcing agreement within a continuing relationship. There should be no need for either side to litigate and changes required should be dealt with through a change control procedure. In some ways, the process of creating the SLA is as valuable as the agreement itself. SLAs can be between different businesses or between different parts of the same organisation (such as the IT department and its users). Facilities Management Agreements, Software Maintenance Agreements and Managed Data Network Agreements are all examples of SLAs. Alternatively, the SLA may be one aspect of a larger agreement for services, that is it may be the schedule that stipulates how well the services have to be provided and what happens if the supplier does not provide this.

What form should a service level agreement take?
At its weakest, an SLA may be a simple oral understanding, documented by an exchange of letters. The best form is a formal legal agreement with the technical procedures and specifications annexed as separate schedules.

What happens if the terms of a service level agreement are broken?
If the breach is fundamental, the party not in breach will be entitled to terminate the agreement and sue for the loss suffered as a result of the breach. In other circumstances there will be a system for measuring breach and apportioning cost. These systems range from an event-based system (i.e. if... then...) to a more sophisticated system of 'failure points' (i.e. if there are more than five examples of... then...). The functions of such compensation systems vary from simply drawing attention to a problem to compensation for loss. Compensation for loss is difficult to quantify and, if it is excessive, will be unenforceable by a court. In practice, the right to withhold payment is a valuable weapon. The end (or slowing down) of payments by the client into the supplier's accounts department is likely to put pressure on the supplier. Escalation clauses are undervalued and should be more widely used. These provide for a problem to be escalated up the various tiers of management on both sides if it cannot initially be resolved. Even the best SLA does not last for ever and there must be a procedure for orderly termination and (if necessary) migration from the supplier's system to another system.

The failure to include such clauses was a frequent weakness of early SLAs. Migration is critically important in relation to facilities management contracts and, as a rule of thumb, a year is generally allowed for this. The supplier should also be required to provide all reasonable assistance to the client with the migration to another system.

Contracts relating to cloud computing

Cloud computing is sometimes called software as a service. It appears set to revolutionise the computer industry over the next few years. See Chapter 10 for a description of what cloud computing is and the contracts that you are likely to need.

APPENDIX: MAIN POINTS OF AN IT CONTRACT

Read this on its own if you have not got enough time to read the rest of this chapter. But read it carefully.

- Make sure that you know exactly what you want and what is achievable because if you do not know, then you are not going to get the contract right. (Among the most common causes of computer project failure are unclear client requirements and unrealistic client expectations.)

- Make sure that all the prospective suppliers sign a confidentiality agreement with you. If you are going to give them a detailed functional specification of what you want and information about your business you do not want there to be any question of that confidential information being obtained by your competitors.

- Beware of falling into the trap of entering into a contract before you intend to. There are no legal formalities in this country about entering into a computer contract, so make sure that all pre-contract correspondence is headed 'subject to contract'. If you leave discussions about a written contract incomplete (e.g. lots of draft contracts sent between you and the supplier but nothing ever signed), then a court is likely to take the last undisputed draft as being the basis of the contract between you and the supplier.

- If a particular point is important to you make sure that you get it in writing from the supplier. It may well be that an aspect that is critical to you is not dealt with in the supplier's draft contract at all. If so, you must, for evidence's sake, get it in writing from the supplier. An ordinary letter from the supplier is sufficient provided that it is either referred to in the main contract or, possibly, included as a schedule or as an attachment. If the supplier drags its heels and, despite repeated requests from you, refuses to confirm a point in writing, you should write to the supplier saying that you are only entering into the main contract on the basis that this point is agreed. If the matter ever goes to court the production of your letter will be of great assistance to your case.

- Make sure that you get the supplier to agree to supply support and maintenance for the products purchased for a decent length of time (e.g. five years). You do not want the supplier cancelling support after a couple of years just when your new system is working well. Note that you do not have to commit to take the support and maintenance for five years: ideally your commitment should be on a year by year basis. It is just that the supplier agrees to make the support available to you for at least five years if you want it.

- Make sure that you order enough training. One of the most common reasons for the failure of a computer project is inadequate training. It is sadly all too common that, if there is an overspend in other areas, the amount budgeted for training is cut. As a rule of thumb, roughly 20 per cent of a project's cost should be spent on training. If it is substantially less than that you should ask why.

- Make sure that the procedure for acceptance testing is known and agreed. If this has not been sorted out in the contract, how are you going to stop a bad system from being installed? In the past, the test data were generally supplied by the client; nowadays it is more acceptable for it to be provided by the supplier.

- Make sure that you can get access to the source code of the software programs supplied if the supplier either goes into liquidation or stops supporting the software. Ideally, this source code should be deposited with an independent third party (see Chapter 5) and kept updated by the supplier as each new version comes out.

- Finally, never forget that the contract is a delivery mechanism for ensuring that a project is completed in the right way at the right time by the right person and for the right price. No more, no less.

2   SYSTEMS PROCUREMENT CONTRACTS

Jeremy Newton

Terms like 'computer contract' or 'system procurement contract' cover a broad range of commercial transactions, from the purchase of a single CD-ROM from a high street retailer through to multimillion pound agreements for consultancy or outsourcing services. This chapter outlines the legal issues that need to be addressed in any contract of this type, using examples from actual case law to illustrate the kinds of dispute that commonly arise in relation to systems procurement, and discusses how the process of drafting and negotiating the agreement can be used to prevent some of the most common problems.

THE NEGOTIATION PROCESS

The function of a written contract is to record the terms governing the supply of goods and services. In the absence of a clear, express understanding between the parties, certain terms may be implied into the contract as a matter of law, for example, that products will be delivered within a 'reasonable' time and that they will be of 'satisfactory' quality. The main terms that can be implied into a contract as a matter of law are summarised in the box.

TERMS IMPLIED BY LAW

Certain terms may be implied into a contract as a matter of law: this means that the contract will include these provisions automatically, unless the parties expressly agree to exclude them. The main implied terms are summarised below.

Title – All contracts of sale include an implied term that the seller has the right to sell the goods in question (Sale of Goods Act 1979 s.12(1)). If the seller fails to transfer ownership (e.g. because the goods are subject to the rights of some third party, such as a bank), then it will be in breach of this term and the buyer may reject the goods and recover the price, plus damages.

Quiet possession – This right is, in effect, a promise by the seller that no person will in the future acquire rights over the goods and enforce them against the buyer (Sale of Goods Act 1979 s.12(2)). If this should happen (e.g. because the use of the product turns out to infringe some third-party intellectual property right), then the buyer will be entitled to claim damages. In the worst case, where the third party exercises its rights in such a way as to prevent the buyer using the goods at all, the

---

buyer's damages will be assessed as the cost of buying a replacement, in effect returning the original purchase price.

Correspondence with description – Goods must correspond with the description given by the seller (Sale of Goods Act 1979 s.13). This description can take many forms: a standard printed specification, an agreed user requirements specification, and even claims made by the sales force or set out in the manufacturer's publicity material.

Quality and fitness for purpose – Goods must be of satisfactory quality and reasonably fit for their purpose (Sale of Goods Act 1979 s.14). 'Satisfactory quality' means that the goods meet the standard that a reasonable person would regard as satisfactory, taking account of any description of the goods, the price (if relevant) and all the other relevant circumstances.

Reasonable care and skill – The law also implies a term into contracts for services (such as consultancy, development or support), to the effect that the services will be provided with reasonable care and skill (Supply of Goods and Services Act 1982 s.13).

Apart from the above terms, which are implied as a matter of statute law, terms may also be implied from the facts and circumstances of the particular contract, if they are necessary to give 'business efficacy' to the contract.

However, given the vagueness of the implied terms and the unpredictability of their legal interpretation, any prudent buyer or seller of IT systems will prefer to ensure that the parties' intentions are recorded as clearly and unambiguously as possible.

The negotiation process that leads to the written contract should help ensure that the parties understand each other's expectations and commitments.

Many IT projects fail precisely because the parties do not exercise sufficient care to ensure that their expectations match, and often because of an uncritical acceptance by the customer of the supplier's standard terms of business (or indeed, by the supplier of the customer's standard procurement contract).

Any well-drawn contract will have provisions relating to three broad categories of expectation. The aim of the negotiation process is to ensure that no essential terms are missing from the final agreement, and this chapter will address each of the categories in turn:

- **Contract mechanics** – who delivers what, and when?
- **Commercial highlights** – what is the price, who owns the resulting intellectual property rights, and what warranties are given in respect of the system?
- **Problem management** – what happens if the project goes wrong and what remedies are available?

BEWARE THE STANDARD CONTRACT

The dangers of agreeing unquestioningly to the standard supply terms (or, for that matter, to a client's standard terms of procurement) are illustrated by the case of *Mackenzie Patten* v. *British Olivetti*.

A law firm bought an Olivetti computer system to run their accounts. They discussed their needs with the salesperson and signed up to Olivetti's standard terms. These dealt only with the system's technical performance: they did not address certain other important issues that had been discussed between the parties.

In the event, the system proved unsuitable for the firm's purposes: it was slow, difficult to use, and could not expand to cope with new business, but none of these matters was dealt with in the written contract. Even though a court found that Olivetti was bound by its salesperson's claims that the system would be suitable for the law firm's needs, the firm had by that stage expended significant time and money in the litigation and still had to find a replacement system.

Put another way, 'standard' forms are only suitable for entirely 'standard' transactions, and will often fail to address some essential point that the parties had in mind for their particular deal.

CONTRACT MECHANICS

Principal obligations

An IT contract need not be a complex document. It does not even need to be in writing, though a written document is clearly desirable to record fully each party's commitments to the other. In the simplest case, however, a written contract need say no more than this: that the supplier will provide a system X computer to the client; and that the client will pay £Y to the supplier.

That is the essence of the commercial relationship and there is nothing else (from the strict legal point of view) that requires to be said. However, if the aim of the contract process is to ensure that the project goes ahead smoothly and with the minimum scope for disagreement between the two sides, the contract should be considerably more specific in terms of what is being delivered, when and how.

Specification

A clear specification is the foundation stone of a successful systems supply contract. Although the law implies a term into a contract that the system will conform to its description and be of satisfactory quality, this is no substitute for ensuring that the supplier and the client agree (and document, in as detailed a manner as possible) exactly what is to be provided and the performance and quality standards to be achieved.

Every system supply contract should, accordingly, include a detailed specification setting out:

- the required functionality (what the system is required to do);
- performance targets (how well it is supposed to do it);
- compatibility requirements for interfaces with other systems.

The need for a formal system specification
The legal implications of not developing a proper specification are illustrated by the case of *Micron Computer Systems Ltd* v. *Wang (UK) Ltd.*

One of Micron's complaints against its supplier was that the Wang system did not provide 'transaction logging'. The judge observed that 'the acknowledged absence of a transaction logging facility is not in reality a fault in the system that was sold. Micron can only complain about its absence if Micron can establish a contractual term … to the effect that the system included such a facility. In order to make good its case in transaction logging, Micron must therefore establish that they made known to Wang that they required such a facility'.

The judge found that Micron had not made its requirement for transaction logging clear to Wang and accordingly that part of Micron's case failed.

Timetable
The process of preparing the specification should enable the parties to assess the likely timescale for the project and to prepare a project plan setting out key deliverables (or 'milestones') and their expected dates. In almost all major systems implementations, staged payments will be triggered by the achievement of individual milestones. It is, accordingly, essential that these are identified with as much precision as possible and generally reflect the terminology of the contract.

The buyer will usually have in mind a timescale within which the system should be provided, although the sophistication of the timetable will vary according to the complexity of the project and how closely the payment arrangements are tied into the achievement of specific milestones.

Delivery
Although the law provides for an implied term that goods will be delivered 'within a reasonable time', delivery arrangements should always be dealt with expressly. From the point of view of contractual certainty, the ideal approach is for the contract to set out specific delivery dates, but it should also go on to deal with the 'mechanics' of delivery and installation. The contract should address:

- the date on which delivery is to be made;
- whether all the elements of the system are to be delivered at one time or whether it is to arrive in instalments;
- who has responsibility for installation and testing;

- the implications of late delivery or non-delivery (e.g. an express provision permitting cancellation of the contract, with or without compensation to the buyer, if the goods are not delivered by some cut-off date or if some other key milestone is not achieved by the required date).

Acceptance testing

Formal acceptance testing arrangements are a crucial aspect of any successful procurement. The system is required to meet the functions and performance targets set out in the specification, but until it is tested the parties can not determine whether those requirements have been met.

The nature of acceptance tests varies widely between projects. Where a major piece of development work is involved, the parties may negotiate and document detailed testing arrangements as part of the contract. At the other extreme, the acceptance procedure may simply be that if the buyer uses the system 'live' for, say, 30 days without rejecting it, then it is deemed to have been accepted.

From the point of view of creating contractual certainty, then, the acceptance procedure should:

- provide for an objective and measurable 'yardstick' as to the standards of performance and functionality to be demonstrated;
- address all those elements that are necessary to demonstrate, to the buyer's satisfaction, that the system meets its requirements; and
- be clear as to the consequences of both the passing and failing of the acceptance test.

Acceptance will generally trigger payment of the whole or the final instalment of any lump sum charges, or the start of periodic charges, and following acceptance the buyer's remedies will be limited to a claim under the warranty provision.

In the event of failure of the acceptance tests, the contract will typically provide for a period during which the supplier may rectify problems and then retest; but further failure will signal the premature end of the contract, with the buyer able to return the hardware and software in exchange for a refund of any money paid.

Client obligations

The successful implementation of a complex IT system normally requires the performance of obligations not just by the supplier, but also by the client. Although primary responsibility for providing a system rests with the supplier, the client may well have obligations in relation to providing information about its business, testing the software, providing employees to be trained and so on.

These obligations need to be spelled out in the contract every bit as clearly as the supplier's commitments.

Change control

Client requirements may change frequently over the lifetime of a project. The parties need to agree a procedure for specifying and agreeing changes to the scope of work. The proper management and documentation of these changes will help to avoid disputes about what each party's obligations actually were.

The contract should include a formal 'change control' clause, setting out a mechanism whereby the client can request (and the supplier can recommend) changes to the specification, the project plan, or any other aspect of the deal. Any such change needs to be considered from the point of view of:

- technical feasibility;
- impact on the respective obligations of the supplier and client;
- cost implications;
- impact on the timetable.

As a general rule, no change should take effect unless it has been formally agreed and documented by both parties.

Termination

Provision has to be made for termination of the contract, setting out the circumstances in which the contract may be brought to an end and the consequences of that action. These provisions will vary according to the nature of the contract and the deliverables.

Apart from a general right to terminate the contract in the event of material breach or the insolvency of the other party, the following points should be considered:

- The client may wish to reserve a right to cancel or terminate the contract for convenience (say, because its business requirements change). In that event, the parties will need to discuss what compensation (if any) should be payable to the supplier.

- Contracts for development services are typically terminable by the client if specific time-critical milestones are significantly overdue. Provision should be made for treatment of the developed software on termination, including delivery of all copies (and source code) and certification that no copies have been retained.

- Contracts for continuing services (consultancy, support and maintenance services, bureau services) should be terminable on notice. The length of the notice and the earliest dates on which it may be effective are matters of negotiation in each case.

COMMERCIAL HIGHLIGHTS

Pricing and payment

There are as many pricing and payment structures as there are types of IT deal, and there is little to be gained from making generalisations about pricing and payment terms. The one point worth making is that, where payments are tied into specific targets (such as system acceptance or other milestones), the terminology and structure of the payment schedule should accurately reflect that of the timetable.

There are several payment-related mechanisms that are commonly used to ensure that both parties have incentives to perform their obligations:

- The client may wish to provide for payment by instalments as the various parts of the system are delivered, retaining a proportion of the price until the complete system has been tested. The retention of a significant proportion of the charges will give the buyer some assurance that the supplier will finish the job.

- In respect of periodic fees, specifically, the buyer will be concerned about the supplier's rights to increase the fee and may seek to limit rises by agreeing to, for example, only one increase a year or by tying increases to an appropriate index.

- It is common for hardware suppliers to retain title in the goods they supply as security for payment. This means that although the buyer gets possession of the goods, ownership remains with the seller until certain conditions (normally payment in full) are met. If the buyer fails to comply with the conditions, the seller can repossess the goods and sell them to recoup its losses.

Intellectual property rights (IPRs)

System supply contracts generally entail the transfer of technology and information from one party to another, for example, specifications, software, data and confidential business information. The lawful use of technology and information depends on compliance with the laws relating to copyright, confidentiality, database rights and other forms of intellectual property (see Chapter 4), so system supply contracts must deal comprehensively with IPR issues. There are two key IPR aspects to consider: ownership, and warranties and indemnities in respect of third-party IPRs.

In relation to ownership, the contract should specify what IPRs are to be created or used, and precisely who owns them (including identifying the owners of any third-party IPRs that are to be used or licensed). Copyright law contains a common trap for the unwary in relation to contracts for software development or consultancy work. The IPR in work undertaken by a contractor (as opposed to an employee) will normally vest in the supplier rather than the client. This means that an express, written assignment of copyright is needed if the aim is for the client to own these IPRs outright.

In relation to warranties, most system supply contracts will contain an assurance that the client's use of the system will not infringe third-party rights and an indemnity in respect of any claims that may arise against the client. The contract should set out any express warranties required by the client as to the supplier's ownership or entitlement in respect of the IPRs comprised in the system, together with a process for addressing any breach of those warranties.

In relation to the possible infringement of third-party IPRs, the client will typically impose a formal obligation for the supplier to deal with any such allegations, especially if the system is a critical part of the client's business and merely rejecting it and claiming back the purchase price would be insufficient. A typical IPR indemnity clause will provide:

- a right for the supplier to take over, litigate and/or settle any such action;
- a right for the supplier to modify the system so that it does not infringe the alleged right, provided that it still conforms with the specification; and
- an indemnity given by the supplier against the client's losses in the event of a successful third-party claim.

Supplier warranties

The client will normally require the supplier to give certain other express assurances in respect of the system to be delivered. Ideally, the client will want to obtain a warranty that the system will comply with its specification and/or meet specified performance criteria.

Such warranties are often subject to time limits or other restrictions. It is not unusual for the supplier to seek to limit the warranty to, say, six months from acceptance: after that point, any defects are rectified under maintenance and support arrangements (paid for by the client) rather than under warranty.

PROBLEM MANAGEMENT

Contractual remedies

The parties must consider at the negotiation stage what happens if a contract does not go according to plan, for example if the supplier fails to deliver a working system within the contracted time frames. Although damages and other remedies may be available as a matter of general law, it is preferable to spell out expressly the remedies that each party may have in particular situations.

One common mechanism for managing such disputes is to provide for payment of 'liquidated' damages for certain breaches. This involves setting out in advance the precise sum to be paid as compensation for certain breaches (e.g. late delivery at £X per day). Provided that the sum is a genuine estimate of the likely losses and not a penalty to force the other party to perform, the clause will be enforceable.

If the breach in question persists for a specified time or reaches a specified level of severity, the innocent party may also want a right to terminate the contract outright.

Limitations and exclusions of liability

IT suppliers generally seek to restrict their potential exposure to actions resulting from breach of contract or defects in the system. This is treated by some as purely a 'legal' issue, but in fact is a major question of commercial risk assessment and allocation, and these provisions can be amongst the most hard-fought in any contract negotiation.

A typical standard exclusion clause may take the following form:

- The supplier does not exclude liability for death or personal injury caused by negligence.
- The supplier seeks to exclude liability altogether for certain kinds of loss, often termed 'special', 'indirect' or 'consequential'.
- The supplier accepts a limited degree of liability for certain other classes of loss.

From the legal point of view, exclusion clauses need to be considered from two broad angles. First, suppliers will often argue that they should have no liability for 'consequential loss', on the basis that the nature of IT products means that their uses (and so the potential losses resulting from failure) are not easily foreseeable at the time the contract is made and the potential exposure is in any case disproportionate to the contract value. Whether this is an acceptable commercial stance depends on the nature of the system and the extent of the client's dependence on it. However, the courts have exercised considerable ingenuity in manipulating and interpreting expressions like 'consequential loss' in ways that the parties may not originally have intended.

CONSEQUENTIAL LOSS: THE SEMANTIC LABYRINTH

Although they are commonly used in all sorts of commercial agreements, the meaning of the expressions 'special', 'indirect' and 'consequential' in the context of contractual claims is open to interpretation by the courts, and there is often a resulting lack of certainty as to the precise effect of an intended exclusion.

The usual starting point for any discussion of consequential loss is the case of *Hadley* v. *Baxendale*. In that case, the court distinguished two classes of loss that could be recovered for breach of contract. These are:

- Such losses as may fairly and reasonably be considered either as arising naturally, that is according to the usual course of things ... or such as may reasonably be supposed to have been in the contemplation of both parties at the time they made the contract as the probable result of the breach of it.

- If the parties were aware of special circumstances at the time the contract was made, the losses which they would reasonably contemplate would be the amount of injury which would ordinarily flow from a breach under these special circumstances.

That basic distinction has been reworked several times over the years, but the terminology that is widely used in IT contracts does not fit neatly into the *Hadley* v. *Baxendale* rules and in fact means different things to different people. Indeed, the courts are repeatedly restating the meaning of these expressions in an effort to bring clarity to the concepts, but two cases will illustrate the kind of semantic problems that can arise.

In the 1999 case of *British Sugar Plc* v. *NEI Power Projects Ltd*, NEI had supplied some defective power equipment, with a headline value of about £100,000, to British Sugar. The sale contract expressly limited the seller's liability for 'consequential loss'.

As a result of breakdowns, increased production costs and resulting loss of profits, British Sugar put in a claim of over £5 million. British Sugar argued for the narrowest construction of the term 'consequential loss', interpreting it to mean 'loss not resulting directly and naturally from breach of contract'; whereas NEI argued that the term meant 'all loss other than the normal loss which might be suffered as a result of the breach of contract, negligence or other breach of duty'. The court found for the claimant and approved earlier authorities that 'consequential damages' means the damages recoverable under the second limb of *Hadley* v. *Baxendale*.

By this analysis, where loss of profits or loss of business (commonly regarded as typical examples of 'consequential loss') arise naturally from the breach of contract, they should be recoverable by the user: a result that may surprise many IT suppliers.

More recently, in 2009, British Gas brought a claim against Accenture in relation to a failed project to design and build of a new billing system (*GB Gas Holdings Ltd* v. *Accenture (UK) Ltd*). The new system was supposed to replace the utility company's existing Customer Relationship Management (CRM) and billing systems for residential customers, and was accordingly critical to its business. The contract stated that neither party would be liable for 'loss of profits or of contracts arising directly or indirectly; loss of business or of revenues arising directly or indirectly; [or] any losses, damages, costs or expenses whatsoever to the extent that these are indirect or consequential or punitive'. The High Court found that this exclusion did not prevent British Gas from recovering losses like overpaid gas distribution charges (which resulted from its own suppliers being given incorrect information about gas usage) and additional borrowing charges (resulting from the late billing or non-billing of customers). The court found that all these losses were foreseeable as 'the very likely consequence' of the breach; and that they were accordingly 'direct' losses and should be recoverable.

Similar confusion applies in relation to other commonly used terms. The term 'consequential' has at one point been defined simply to mean 'not direct'; but there is also judicial authority to suggest that 'direct loss' could include 'consequential loss' in certain circumstances. Likewise, the term 'special damages' has no fewer than four possible meanings, including past (pecuniary) loss calculable as at the trial date (as opposed to all other items of unliquidated 'general damages'); and losses falling under the second rule in *Hadley* v. *Baxendale* (as opposed to 'general damages' being losses recoverable under the first rule).

Secondly, there is an extensive body of law relating to the enforceability of exclusion clauses generally: if the exclusion clause is found to be unreasonable or defective in some other way, then the party seeking to rely on the exclusion may nevertheless be exposed to a greater degree of legal and financial risk than it originally envisaged.

The combined effect of the enforceability rules and the uncertainty about the meaning of commonly used language is that clarity is of the utmost importance in the wording of exclusion clauses: it is not in anybody's interest for the effect of the exclusion to be uncertain and indeed it is surprising that businesses should continue routinely to use some of the terminology that regularly crops up.

Instead of debating abstract concepts like 'consequential loss', suppliers and clients alike should focus on the specific risks associated with the particular system. The client will generally accept that the supplier has a legitimate concern about exposure to unspecified types of liability, but the kinds of loss that will flow from a breach of an IT supply contract can be classified, at least in general terms:

- Loss of cost or salary savings, or other expected benefits.
- Costs of repairing or replacing the defective system.
- Costs of additional IT staff and consultants required to make the system work.
- Loss of profits resulting from non-performance.
- Costs of wasted management time.

These categories of loss are not intended to be definitive: there is no 'definitive list' as such, and each client and supplier will have its own specific concerns.

However, the starting point for constructing an effective provision must be to identify the categories of loss that are foreseeable, and to state explicitly how the parties intend to allocate these risks between themselves. Any unspecified types of loss will then fall to be determined by the court according to normal legal principles.

ENFORCEABILITY OF EXCLUSION CLAUSES

The *contra proferentem* rule
An exclusion clause will only operate to limit a party's liability if it covers the breach that has occurred. The rules of interpretation are complicated, but in general the more serious the breach of contract, the more clearly worded the clause must be if it is to exclude liability for that breach: it is interpreted against the person who seeks to rely on it.

One illustration of this rule at work is the case of *Salvage Association* v. *CAP Financial Services Ltd*. In that case, a contract to supply bespoke software contained a warranty from the supplier under which it promised to remedy certain types of defect, and also provided that a limitation of liability would apply 'if CAP fails to perform its obligations under [the warranty]'.

The wording of the warranty was sufficiently ambiguous that the court could interpret it as meaning that the warranty did not come into effect until after acceptance of the system by the client. Acceptance had never in fact occurred because the dispute began before the contract's acceptance procedures were reached, so the court decided that the warranty never came into effect and so the exclusion of liability never came into effect either. The result was that the supplier's liability for breach of contract was completely unlimited.

The 'reasonableness' test

Under Section 3 of the Unfair Contract Terms Act 1977 (UCTA), where the buyer deals either as a consumer or (if the buyer is a business) on the seller's written standard terms, any exclusion clause favouring the seller must satisfy a test of 'reasonableness' in order to be effective.

The measure of 'reasonableness' is whether it was fair and reasonable to include the clause at the time the contract was made. The court will take account of matters such as the following:

- The relative bargaining position of the parties.
- Whether the buyer received some benefit (e.g. a lower price) for agreeing to the clause.
- How far the buyer knew or ought to have known of the existence and extent of the clause.
- If the exclusion is contingent on compliance with some condition (e.g. regular maintenance), whether it was reasonable to expect the condition to be complied with.
- Whether the goods were 'off the shelf' or were specially made or adapted to the client's order.

The courts have also held that the question as to which of the parties can most readily insure against the loss is a relevant consideration and that a limitation of liability is more likely to be reasonable than a complete exclusion.

The appendix to this chapter outlines the way in which the courts have applied the UCTA reasonableness test in practice.

Special considerations in software contracts

Computer programs are governed mainly by the law of copyright, which requires that the user of a program has a licence from the copyright owner. (Note that the term 'licence' is synonymous with 'permission' or 'consent'.)

There are no particular legal formalities with regard to the form of the licence, but it is desirable for the licence to be in writing to ensure that there is complete clarity as to what may and may not be done with the software.

The type of licence depends on the nature of the package:

- Standard software is often supplied by retailers or distributors under a 'shrink-wrap' licence: the disk is wrapped in a clear plastic film, through which the terms of the licence granted by the copyright owner are clearly visible, along with an instruction that breaking the seal on the package will amount to acceptance of those terms.

- Contracts for bespoke software tend to be entered into on a more formal basis because of the need to agree a specification and to address other issues arising out of the development process. (It may also be the case that the client wishes to own the program outright rather than use it under licence, in which case see the warning in the section on IPRs as to the need for an express assignment of copyright from the contractor.)

The term of the licence may be perpetual or for a fixed period. Again, it is desirable for the term to be spelled out expressly because, in the absence of any express contractual provision, the normal rule is that an intellectual property licence is terminable by 'reasonable notice'.

The licence will often impose restrictions on the use that the client may make of the software. Common restrictions include:

- limiting the number or class of users who may access the software;
- restricting use to the 'internal purposes' of the client (to prevent the client depriving the supplier of potential licence fees by using the software to provide bureau services to third parties);
- prohibiting the client from transferring the software to any third party, on the basis that the supplier has a right to know precisely who is using its software.

These are all legitimate concerns on the face of it, but the client should check the wording carefully to ensure that the permitted uses reflect all its present and anticipated future requirements. Exceeding the permitted use may leave the client exposed to a claim for copyright infringement or to being charged additional licence fees. At the very least, consider:

- Does this wording prevent the client processing data on behalf of other companies in its group?
- Does the clause operate in such a way as to allow the supplier to impose undefined conditions (such as additional licence fees) in the event of a transfer of the software?
- Might the restriction operate to prevent the client getting a third party to run the system as part of an outsourcing arrangement?

CONCLUSION

The delivery of a working system that meets the client's needs is a difficult enough task, but it is even more difficult to achieve in a contractual vacuum.

Clearly recording each party's contractual obligations and setting up appropriate mechanisms for resolving potential disputes will help to ensure the project stays on track. Defining those obligations and mechanisms is the principal purpose of the contract negotiation process.

APPENDIX: THE 'REASONABLENESS' TEST IN PRACTICE

St Albans City and District Council v. International Computers Ltd

ICL had developed a complex package (COMCIS) to calculate and administer the community charge (or 'poll tax') system of local taxation. St Albans used COMCIS to calculate the number of community charge payers in its area and used that figure to set its community charge rate. The software contained an error, so that although the St Albans database contained all the necessary details, the population figure reported was too high, the per capita charge was therefore set too low and, as a result, St Albans suffered a financial loss.

The contract contained a clause limiting ICL's liability to the price or charge payable for the item of equipment, program or service in respect of which the liability arose or £100,000 (whichever was the lesser) and completely excluding liability for any indirect or consequential loss or loss of business or profits sustained by the client. Liability turned on whether this clause was reasonable under UCTA.

ICL contested that UCTA applied at all, arguing that the contract had not been on standard terms. However, the judge held that UCTA did apply. Even though many elements of the contract were negotiated at length (e.g. delivery dates and specification), ICL's standard terms (which contained the limitation and exclusion clauses) 'remained effectively untouched in the negotiations', and indeed were referred to by ICL staff as 'Standard Terms and Conditions' in witness statements and letters.

The court then went on to consider whether the exclusions were 'reasonable' and concluded that they were not. Although St Albans knew of the limitation and had attempted to negotiate it, the following factors operated to render the clause unreasonable:

- ICL had substantially more resources than St Albans.
- ICL held product liability insurance in an aggregate sum of £50 million worldwide.
- ICL called no evidence to show that the limitation to £100,000 was reasonable, either in relation to the potential risk or the actual loss.
- The contract had mistakenly been made on an outmoded version of the General Conditions; in the then current version, the standard limitation had been increased to £125,000.
- Local authorities are not in the same position as private sector businesses: their operations are constrained by statute and financial restraints and they cannot necessarily be expected to insure against commercial risks.
- St Albans received no inducement to agree to the limitation and there was evidence that all ICL's competitors imposed similar limitations of liability.
- When St Albans tried to negotiate the limitation, albeit at the last moment, ICL in effect said that this was not possible because it would delay the provision of the software to St Albans beyond the date for implementation of the community charge.

The judge accordingly found that ICL had not discharged its burden of proving that the term was fair and reasonable and also that, financially, ICL was better placed to bear a risk of this kind through insurance and to spread it across its client base.

South West Water Services Ltd v. International Computers Ltd

SWW and ICL had entered into two contracts (a turnkey agreement and a project management agreement) under which ICL was to deliver a client service system to SWW. After ICL accepted that it would be unable to deliver the system to specification and in accordance with a planned timetable, SWW sued for breach of contract, claiming that ICL had failed to deliver the system as agreed, and for misrepresentation.

Both agreements had contained a clause based on a standard ICL contract and purporting to limit ICL's liability for any claim for loss or damage.

The evidence was that, during the negotiations, SWW had originally submitted its own standard procurement conditions to ICL and that ICL had rejected them.

The question then arose whether, in these circumstances, the ICL limitations could be regarded as ICL's 'standard terms'. The court followed the St Albans decision in finding that, even though SWW originally offered its own terms in negotiations, in the event ICL had dealt on ICL's standard terms that had been only slightly adapted. The fact that one fairly predictable eventuality, that is failure to progress the project to a point where there was a system in place for SWW that was capable of being tested, had not been addressed in the documentation also tended to suggest that the contract should be regarded as 'standard terms'.

The judge went on to note that the extent to which a party has had discussions and has freely entered into a contract on the other party's standard terms may be relevant as an important circumstance in considering whether those terms are reasonable. ICL argued that its standard limitation clause should be treated as reasonable in this case because its terms had been subject to arm's length discussion and negotiations, but this was found not be the case on the evidence.

This contribution is based on the author's chapter on System Supply Contracts, in the 6th edition of Computer Law (2007), published by Oxford University Press.

3   AVOIDING EMPLOYMENT PROBLEMS

Jeremy Holt

This chapter discusses policies for the use of email and computers by employees and the health and safety requirements with which an employer must comply. Each section ends with an action plan, and the appendix at the end of the chapter contains a specimen computer use policy.

INTRODUCTION

Employees can cause their employers all manner of problems in their use of computers and email. For example:

- misuse of computer systems can waste staff time and leave businesses (and their management) exposed to claims for discrimination, harassment, defamation or worse;

- failure to include proper business information in electronic communications can result in criminal liability under the Companies Act;

- stringent health and safety requirements about the quality of screens and other computer equipment used by staff must be met.

COMPUTER AND EMAIL USAGE POLICIES

An employer can be held responsible for wrongful actions carried out by employees in the course of their employment. This is the case even if the act is done in a way that has not been authorised by the employer. For example, an employer can be held responsible for employees' acts involving racial and sexual harassment, downloading pornography, defamation of management, customers or competitors, breach of confidence, copyright infringement, hacking and breaches of the Data Protection Act.

Employers have adopted computer use and email policies to provide staff with some guidance to avoid these problems. Every business is different and no single policy will suit all.

Employers should also remember that, in certain cases, both the employer and the employee are liable for the employee's wrongful action. It can be useful to remind employees of this in order to encourage them to comply with rules forbidding particular conduct.

The problem with email

Users adopt a more relaxed manner when using email, similar to a telephone conversation rather than a letter. However, the form of the communication is much more permanent and it can be stored and passed on very easily. The thoughts of an employee expressed in an email could be critical later when used to defend, or damage, their employer in legal proceedings. Two graphic examples of what can go wrong come from large firms of solicitors in London (who should really know better). In one, a male solicitor received an email from his (then) girlfriend commenting favourably on their most recent sexual encounter. The explicit content of the email ensured that copies of it were passed on in a chain reaction to millions of people within weeks. In another case, which involved a race discrimination claim, a throwaway comment from the employer about the ideal physical attributes of any new secretary (which was somehow passed on to the claimant, a former secretary, who did not have such attributes) brought a great deal of unwanted publicity to the firm concerned.

Two points should be emphasised. First, if these comments had been spoken (or even expressed in a written letter, which would have been much more difficult to copy and pass on to a large number of people), they would not have caused the trouble that they did. Secondly, the damage to the employer is more likely to be to their public reputation than financially, particularly if the comments expressed are sexual or discriminatory in some way.

The problem that the storage of emails can cause was highlighted in the celebrated Oliver North case in America. Although Oliver North had thought that he could completely delete certain computer data, such data were retrieved by the authorities and used as evidence against him. It is surprising how effective a good computer forensic company can be. In another case a drug dealer was convicted because he had stored details of his drug transactions on his handheld computer and, although he believed that they had been deleted, they were retrieved by the police.

An email message is stored in a number of places: the sender's machine, the recipient's machine and (because of the technical manner in which email messages are transmitted across the internet) the machines of any other people to whom it may have been copied. As a result, it is extremely difficult to destroy all records of a message sent.

Staff should be discouraged from commenting by email on any legal dispute in which their employer is involved, in case such comments are used against the employer later in legal proceedings.

Monitoring emails and internet use

Employers sometimes wonder whether they have the right to monitor voice calls or email messages and there are a number of myths about this. For a start, there is no legal distinction between phone calls, faxes and email messages for these purposes; all telecommunications are treated the same and the same rules apply to each medium.

The basic principle (set out in the Regulation of Investigatory Powers Act 2000) is that telecommunications may not be intercepted by employers unless both the sender and the recipient have consented to the interception.

Indeed it is a criminal offence for employers to carry out unauthorised interception and, if they do, they face up to two years' imprisonment and/or a fine, as well as the possibility of an injunction or damages claim.

However, under a separate set of regulations (snappily entitled the Telecommunications (Lawful Business Practice) (Interception of Communications) Regulations 2000), businesses are allowed to intercept communications without consent for certain limited purposes, as long as the messages relate to the business and are on a system provided in connection with the business. The purposes include:

- establishing the existence of facts (e.g. recording transactions in case there is a contractual dispute);
- compliance with regulatory standards;
- detecting crime (e.g. fraud or corruption);
- investigating unauthorised use of the system (e.g. to check that company rules on emails or internet use are being followed);
- checking on the standards of people using the system (e.g. for quality control or staff training);
- protecting the system from viruses or other threats to the system;
- backing up or re-routing emails when a member of staff is on holiday or off sick.

Employers are required to take all reasonable steps to notify users that interception may take place. This is relatively easy with employees because it can be stated in a staff policy. However, it is much more difficult with outsiders sending inbound emails. One method of notification is in outbound email and fax disclaimers. Employers should remember that even if interception of messages is carried out by them in a legitimate manner, any use by them of the information gathered must be proportionate and in accordance with the Data Protection Act (see Chapter 7).

The Information Commissioner has published a code on monitoring at work. Although this code does not have the force of law it will be used in any enforcement action by the Information Commissioner and may be referred to in employment tribunal proceedings. The code emphasises that monitoring of messages should only take place when there is a real business need and the methods used should not be unduly intrusive into an employee's privacy. Employees have a right to expect that they can keep their personal lives private, which means that they are entitled to some privacy at work. It is recommended that employers should wherever possible avoid opening emails, especially ones that clearly show that they are private or personal. Employees should be aware that monitoring is taking place and told the reasons for it and the means used. Covert monitoring will only be legitimate in the most exceptional of circumstances such as the detection of crime or equivalent wrongdoing. It is good practice for the monitoring to be carried out by someone other than the employee's line manager (e.g. Security or Human Resources personnel). In this way, personal information that is picked up can be sifted so that only the most relevant information becomes known to those who work with the employee.

Laying down a policy for staff

All businesses should draw up a policy for staff on their use of computers (and access to the internet, if applicable) and notify all staff of it. Unless it is wildly unreasonable, staff cannot argue about such a policy. Their use of the employer's equipment is conditional upon their following the policy laid down, otherwise they can be in serious trouble. The policy should be emphasised during the induction of new staff. A specimen staff computer use policy is shown in the appendix at the end of this chapter. Note that this policy should not just be restricted to employees; it should also be given to outside contractors and agency staff.

The policy can be backed up by reminders on computer screens and regular training. Internal audits should check that security policies are being followed and the side should not be let down by senior management (it frequently is). The aim should be that no user of the firm's computers could reasonably argue that they were not aware of the rules for the use of them.

Private email

It is unrealistic for employers to ban completely the private use of email by employees. No doubt the same discussions took place when the telephone first started to be used widely within business.

If private email use is allowed, it is critical that such messages be sent in an appropriate format and that they not appear to be official messages from the company. The best way to do this is in the signature section of the message.

There should be two different formats for the employee to use depending on whether the message is official or private, and private messages should be accompanied by a heading or signature block that states, for example, 'This message is from Jeremy Holt and is sent in a private capacity'. The next section discusses the signature for business emails. The importance of differentiating between the two kinds of messages, official and private, can be seen if employees send messages to newsgroups or bulletin boards.

Some employers allow employees to set up private web-based email accounts for private emails. In this case, the employer can not monitor such messages and the messages sent do not use the employer's return address.

Website access

The policy prohibiting staff visits to unauthorised sites (e.g. pornographic or recruitment agency sites) can be reinforced by the use of filtering systems and blocking software (which is surprisingly inexpensive). In the writer's experience, just the knowledge by the staff that such blocking software is being used is enough to reduce significantly visits to unauthorised sites during work time. Obviously, staff may visit them from their home computers, but this does not waste valuable working time.

It is surprising how tough Employment Tribunals are prepared to be about the dismissal of employees for the downloading of pornography, particularly if there is a policy in force forbidding this. One question that is often asked in these circumstances is whether employers are required to notify the police. Generally the police are not interested unless the pornography is being sold by the employee or it involves children.

There is no doubt that employers can dismiss staff for excessive surfing of the web during working hours. A computer manager at a firm of management consultants was dismissed fairly for using the office computer to do 150 searches for cheap holiday deals. Whilst it may not be practical for employers to check what sites employees have been visiting, peer group pressure does work. If other employees are having to work harder because one is surfing the web, the employer is soon likely to hear about it.

Hacking
Some astute employers give new employees a copy of the Computer Misuse Act 1990 when they start. The Computer Misuse Act makes it a criminal offence to use, access or alter another person's computer without prior permission, and providing a copy of it underlines to the employee that the company's systems should not be used other than as permitted in the course of the employment.

Disclaimers on business emails
Businesses sometimes believe that all their ills can be cured by a well-drafted disclaimer at the foot of an email. Email disclaimers are of little value other than to notify the recipient that the contents of the email are confidential and to offer a method of reporting any misdirection. Email disclaimers are no substitute either for a proper staff email policy or for the legal information that must be shown in an email, which is the same as must be shown on a business letter (see box).

INFORMATION REQUIRED ON BUSINESS EMAILS AND LETTERS

The following information must appear on company emails and letters:

- The full name of the company.
- The registered number of the company.
- The address of the registered office and an indication that that address is the registered office.
- The country of registration of the company.

For partnerships of 20 or fewer partners, the names of the partners and an address for service must appear. Partnerships of more than 20 may simply say that a list of the partners is available at a particular address.

Sole traders must have their real name (i.e. not just a trading name) and a geographical address on their business letters.

Businesses who do not abide by these rules risk looking amateur or newly started (or both).

There is no reason to differentiate between a letter sent by post and a letter sent by email. Some businesses still fail to follow these rules fully in relation to emails at the moment. This is all the more surprising when the vast majority of business messages are now sent by email rather than by formal business letter. There are a number of consequences of failing to abide by the law in providing the required information in company letters or emails:

- It is a criminal offence both by the company concerned and by the person who authorises the communication on behalf of the company.

- If the communication relates to an order for goods and the company's name is not mentioned in the email, the individual who sent it can be personally liable for the order.

- Difficulties can arise in bringing legal proceedings to enforce a contract made where the appropriate information has not appeared on the company's note-paper or in the company's email.

Action plan on computer use

- Introduce a computer use and email policy. If there is no policy, an employer cannot monitor what is happening except in very limited circumstances.

- Make sure that such a policy is notified to all employees and contractors and that they are reminded of it from time to time (e.g. by banner warnings when logging on to the system), otherwise it will not be possible to rely on it later just when it is needed.

- Ensure that all emails contain the correct business information.

- Devise a system whereby personal emails from members of staff are clearly differentiated from emails on company business. (This might be as simple as requiring the employee to put the word 'Personal' in the subject line of any outbound emails that are of a private nature.)

AVOIDING HEALTH AND SAFETY CLAIMS

Health and safety legislation rears its head in relation to the use of computers by staff. Most businesses use computers now and it is critically important to be aware of the health and safety aspects. Failure to abide by such rules can lead to imprisonment or a fine, in addition to the inevitable bad publicity. It also leaves the door open for personal injury claims from present (or, more likely, past) employees. For example, there are well over 200,000 repetitive strain injury (RSI) claims in the UK each year. RSI is now known as 'upper limb disorders in the workplace'.

The law on health and safety at work

There are general duties on all employers under the Health and Safety at Work etc. Act 1974 and the Management of Health and Safety at Work Regulations 1999 that require the risks to health that may be associated with work to be addressed. In addition, the health risks in relation to work with display screen equipment (DSE) are covered by the Health and Safety (Display Screen Equipment) Regulations 1992 as amended by the Health and Safety (Miscellaneous Amendments) Regulations 2002. The Health and Safety Executive (HSE) publishes specific guidance on the subject. Duty holders must comply with the DSE Regulations and guidance.

The DSE Regulations

The DSE Regulations apply to anyone who regularly uses display screen equipment (which includes screens that display text, numbers or graphics) whether at the work site, off site or in a home-based office. An evaluation of display screen use must be carried out, including an assessment of all workstations.

The requirements are in the form of general targets rather than technical specifications:

- Screens should be flicker-free as far as is possible; brightness and contrast should be adjustable. The screen height and angle should also be adjustable allowing operators to avoid glare and maintain a natural and relaxed posture.

- The keyboard should be designed to allow operators to locate and use keys quickly, accurately and without discomfort. (Some employers offer staff a choice of keyboards such as the Microsoft® ergonomic or 'Cherry' styles.)

- The height of the work surface, the work chair and, if necessary, the foot rest should all be adjustable to allow the user to achieve a comfortable position.

- Lighting should be appropriate for the tasks performed and reflections and glare reduced to a minimum.

- Background noise should be kept at a level that does not impair normal conversation. Normal conversation is regarded as the ability to hold a conversation up to two metres apart without raising the voice.

- Ventilation and humidity should be maintained at levels that prevent discomfort and problems of sore eyes.

- Software must be suitable for the task, easy to use and display information in a format and at a pace that are adapted to users.

- Software must not contain quantitative or qualitative checking facilities of which the user is unaware.

The Regulations give users the right to eye tests for display screen work, at the cost of the employer. A user can request a test when they first become a user and at regular intervals afterwards. If the tests show that the user requires spectacles or contact lenses for VDU work, then the employer is responsible for the cost of providing one pair of basic spectacles or contact lenses.

Action plan on health and safety

Employers should do the following to stay out of trouble:

- Assess which workstations require analysis and conduct an appropriate audit to ensure compliance with the minimum requirements.

- Consult with employees to discuss health and safety issues as well as their working environment and set up a reporting procedure to respond to any problems.

- Inform staff of their rights concerning eye tests and the provision of glasses or contact lenses.

- Arrange appropriate training for staff in their use of their workstations and equipment.

- Keep a 'paper trail' of all the actions taken by the employer in order to provide a defence against any future personal injury claims by employees.

- Carry out pre-employment health screening, effective sickness absence management and exit health screening to ensure employees' fitness and capabilities for work.

- Be aware of the requirements of the Disability Discrimination Act 1995 (e.g. providing modifications and adaptations for staff deemed disabled). (The Disability Employment Advisor from the local Placement and Counselling Team in the Employment Service can assist in this.)

- Vary work activities and ensure adequate breaks from work and between tasks.

There is no antidote for employers against an RSI claim, but employers can reduce the risk of successful claims by meeting health and safety obligations, in particular concentrating on posture, ergonomics and working methods.

If you find all this rather tedious and you would like help, ask an occupational health professional. They can provide you with useful advice (beyond simply the minimum legal requirements), such as ways to help staff to avoid back problems. To find an occupational health professional, ring the HSE Information Line to get the details of your local HSE office and the Employment Medical Advisory Service (EMAS). Although they cannot make individual recommendations, they can provide you with details of providers in your area. Occupational health professionals are more likely than lawyers to know the Health and Safety regulations and they are far cheaper.

APPENDIX: SPECIMEN POLICY FOR COMPUTER AND EMAIL USE

We do not wish to restrict in any way your use of our computer system – indeed we encourage it. However, we regard the integrity of our computer system as key to the success of our business. All employees must abide by the following policies to avoid misunderstanding and confusion. Breaches of this policy will be taken seriously and could amount to gross misconduct. You should direct any queries about this policy to the Human Resources Department.

Licensed software
Only properly licensed software may be loaded onto our system. You are not allowed to use within the company any material that you either know, or suspect to be, in breach of copyright. In addition, you are not allowed to pass

such material on to anyone else. It is important to bear in mind that breach of copyright for business purposes can be a criminal offence both by the company and by the individual concerned. No software may be loaded onto our system without first obtaining the express permission of the IT Department. Software includes business applications, shareware, entertainment software, games, screensavers and demonstration software. If you are unsure whether a piece of software requires a licence, please contact the IT Department. The copying of software media and manuals is also prohibited.

Networks
You are not allowed to make any change to the connection or configuration of your PC. None of our PCs may be connected to a customer's network without permission from the IT Department and written permission from the customer concerned. In addition, none of our PCs may be connected to a public network (e.g. the internet) without permission from the IT Department.

Disks
You must not use disks from unknown sources or from home computers.

All data disks must be virus-checked before they may be used on our computer system.

Viruses
Generally, more damage to files is caused by inappropriate corrective action than by viruses themselves. If a virus is suspected you should do nothing more until instructed. The matter must be reported immediately to the IT Department. The most likely way that our computer system will be infected by a virus is from an external message. Any outside material must be properly virus-checked before being loaded on to our computer system. Many viruses are now spread by email messages and use the address book of the recipient to pass it on to other people. Some of these viruses are activated when an attachment to the message is opened. Creators of these viruses frequently encourage the user to open the attachment simply by using a header such as 'You must read this!' You should not open any attachment of this type and must generally be suspicious of any message that is received from an unknown source. In other words, only open mail when you know it is from a reliable source. If you receive email warnings about viruses please ignore the instructions they contain. In the majority of cases they are hoaxes and the instructions, if followed, will damage our computer system.

Customer procedures
If you use a customer's computer system you must observe the customer's rules relating to their computers. In the absence of any such rules, our rules should be followed.

Access
You are only allowed access to those parts of our computer system that you need in order to carry out your normal duties.

Inappropriate material

You must not view or download or pass on any pornographic material on our computer system or place obscene or offensive screensavers on your PC. In line with the normal rules that apply to you as an employee, you are not allowed to send racist, sexist, blasphemous, defamatory, obscene, indecent or abusive messages on our computer system, either internally or externally. Do think carefully before sending any questionable messages that could reflect badly on us as a company.

Use of the internet at work

The primary reason for our providing you with internet access to use websites and/or email is to assist you in your work for us. You are allowed to send personal emails in a similar way to the way that minor incidental personal telephone use is allowed. Such activity should not be excessive and must not affect your ability to work properly for us during normal working hours. Personal emails should be kept to a minimum and the company's footer **must not** be shown on a personal email.

You are not allowed to send unsolicited emails or emails to multiple recipients or to use email for personal gain. You are also not allowed to use the company's internet access and email system to sign up for online shopping, internet membership schemes or chat rooms.

Business emails

You must not order anything on our behalf by email without proper authorisation.

You should always bear in mind that an email from the company has the same legal effect as a letter from the company on the company's notepaper. This under-lines the importance of being careful with what you say in an email in case it is misunderstood. All company emails must contain our standard footer, which will be notified to you from time to time. As stated above, personal emails must not contain the company's standard footer.

Confidentiality

Before sending any confidential information by email consider carefully whether appropriate steps have been taken to maintain such confidentiality.

Email is not inherently a more secure medium of communication than traditional means, and emails can be easily copied, forwarded and stored.

Security

Do not give internal passwords to anyone outside the company. In addition, you must not give any customer-related security information to anyone other than the customer unless specifically authorised in writing by the customer in advance.

Records

Keep proper records of our dealings with outsiders. It is always possible that what appears to be a relatively trivial point could be of immense significance later. It is not possible to foresee what will subsequently need to be checked so keep a complete record of all transactions.

Data protection
If you have access to data about individuals you must bear in mind at all times the provisions of the Data Protection Act 1998. Guidance on these may be obtained from the HR Department.

Passwords
Use passwords at all times and change them at the intervals notified to you.

Do not select obvious passwords. All passwords must be kept confidential.

Backups
Regular backups must be carried out in accordance with the rules laid down from time to time. Critical information should not be stored on the hard disk of your workstation in case it is lost.

Misuse
Misuse of computers is a serious disciplinary offence. The following are examples of misuse:

- Fraud and theft;
- System sabotage;
- Introducing viruses and time bombs;
- Using unauthorised software;
- Obtaining unauthorised access;
- Using the system for unauthorised private work or game playing;
- Breaches of the Data Protection Act 1998;
- Sending abusive, rude or defamatory messages via email;
- Hacking;
- Breach of the company's security procedures or this policy.

This list is not exhaustive. Depending on the circumstances of each case, misuse of the computer system may be considered gross misconduct, punishable by dismissal without notice. Misuse amounting to criminal conduct may be reported by us to the police.

Breaches
All breaches of computer security must be referred to the IT Department. If you suspect that a fellow employee (of whatever seniority) is abusing the computer system you may speak in confidence to the HR Department. You are responsible for any actions that are taken against us by a third party arising from restricted and/or offensive material being displayed on, or sent by you through, our computer system.

Monitoring
The company reserves the right to intercept and monitor your communications, including email, internet use and telephone calls. This right to monitor may be

exercised, for example, to decide whether communications are relevant to the business, to prevent or detect crime or to ensure the effective operation of the system. In addition, the company reserves the right to monitor communications in order to determine the existence of facts, to detect unauthorised use of the system and to decide the standards that ought to be achieved by employees using the system.

Improvements
We welcome suggestions from you for the improvement of this policy. These should be directed to the HR Department.

4 INTELLECTUAL PROPERTY LAW FOR COMPUTER USERS

Jennifer Pierce

Intellectual property law is a relatively complex subject. This chapter concentrates on the more important aspects for users, so that you are aware of the pitfalls and know when to seek professional advice. The appendix at the end of the chapter provides a basic guide to intellectual property and explains the terminology in use.

INTRODUCTION

Intellectual property is an inescapable element of modern business, especially in the field of information technology. It protects both suppliers' rights in the systems that they provide and users' rights in aspects of their usage. Everybody needs to know roughly who owns each part of a computer system and how that impacts on its use. They also need to know what not to do with the equipment on the internet, so as to avoid being sued.

There are five main types of intellectual property in the UK:

- **Patents** – protect inventions, which could be found in any part of a computer system. Software as such is not technically patentable, but if it has other features that fulfil the criteria for patentability this will not prevent the grant of a patent.

- **Design** – there are, technically, four different types of right, which also overlap with copyright. They cover items that are as diverse as semiconductors and computer graphics.

- **Copyright** – protects literary, artistic and other works. Software is a literary work and graphical user interfaces are artistic works.

- **Database right** – covers collections of data that are accessible by electronic or other means.

- **Trade marks** – broadly, protect brands, such as 'Microsoft®' and 'Intel®'.

For those who are not familiar with intellectual property, at the end of the chapter there is a further explanation of these rights. Rights in other territories, even European Union (EU) territories, may be different, although some rights are harmonised throughout the EU.

HARDWARE AND INTELLECTUAL PROPERTY RIGHTS

Hardware is a bit of a misnomer because much hardware contains systems software too. From an intellectual property perspective, the distinction is very important because the real hardware element is sold but the systems software is usually licensed (see the next section), although there is a current legal debate over whether this is appropriate. If hardware is protected this is generally by patents and/or designs, although brands are extremely important in this sector.

The non-software element is treated like any other gadget. If it is protected, you need authority from the person who owns the intellectual property to manufacture, sell or import it, and so on. However, after the first authorised sale of the hardware in the European Economic Area (EEA), all those rights are 'exhausted' in the EEA, unless there are special conditions on the sale. This means that if the equipment comes from an authorised source you can do what you like with it, unless there is a special arrangement or you export it from the EEA or do drastic repairs that amount to remaking it (or bits of it).

Authorised sales
So everything is fine if you buy from an authorised source, but how do you tell who is authorised and who is not? There are plenty of people who call themselves 'authorised dealers'. Some will be fully authorised under all of the necessary rights, some will have limited rights, and others may not be authorised at all.

You can always check the status of a dealer with the equipment manufacturer. Unfortunately, even reputable dealers appointed by equipment manufacturers may not have all the necessary rights because it can be very difficult to check who has relevant rights. The reason for this is that registered intellectual property, such as patents, gives the owner a monopoly. This means, broadly, that anybody making and selling equipment within the specification of registered intellectual property without permission can be infringing that property, even if they are unaware that the rights exist.

Currently, the amount of registered intellectual property is increasing rapidly, so it can be difficult to search for it. As a result, even the larger computer manufacturers may sell infringing hardware without knowing about it, although this is less likely because they have considerable facilities for searching.

Technically, the owner of intellectual property can seize infringing equipment, so it is a serious matter. However, in practice it is rare for an intellectual property owner to seize equipment from end-users.

So what should you do? There should be a relatively low risk if you buy hardware from a reputable supplier who gives you a full indemnity (see Chapter 2) to cover the situation where the hardware infringes somebody else's intellectual property. You should also pick a supplier with a 'deep pocket' who will be sure to meet its obligations under the indemnity.

Special conditions

Some intellectual property owners attach special conditions to the sale of their equipment. This is not the technical terminology, but is an easy way of describing what happens. For example, they may insist that you do not take it outside a particular territory or that you only use it with another piece of equipment. Some of these conditions are unenforceable because they breach trade laws, but others may be enforceable. Most restrictions on exporting goods that have been brought in one EEA country to another EEA country are unenforceable.

Repairs

When you have bought equipment you generally have a right to repair it, although repairs by somebody who is not authorised by the manufacturer may affect your warranty and maintenance contract. If the repair entails replacing parts that are covered by intellectual property, the same rules apply to repairs as applied to the original sale, so this sort of repair must be made by an authorised person.

SOFTWARE AND INTELLECTUAL PROPERTY RIGHTS

Copying and adapting – the general rules

Copyright is the main form of intellectual property protecting software so it is treated differently from hardware. Software can also be protected by some of the rights protecting hardware, including registered rights. So all of the rules relating to hardware may apply, but there are additional things to think about.

Copyright protects against copying, adapting, distributing and communicating copies of the protected material to the public. It can protect against other things, but these are the main types of protection in this context. You cannot do any of these things unless you own the copyright or have the authorisation ('licence') of the copyright owner.

It is fairly unusual for a user to own copyright because most software houses want to grant licences to several users in order to reduce costs and to make maintenance both cheaper and more profitable. However, if a supplier is making a bespoke program and you are to pay the full economic costs of this, there are strong arguments that you should own the copyright if the program is stand-alone. If you are to own the copyright you need a document that transfers the rights to you.

Simply running software involves copying it, so if you do not own the rights you need a licence to run it. You also need a licence if you are going to alter it because that amounts to adaptation. In practice, few software houses will simply allow you to copy and adapt their software. They tend to specify precisely what you can do with it.

You also need a licence if you are going to rent, lend or broadcast copyright material. The average software user does not want to do any of these things, so they are not covered in this book.

Backup copies

Whatever the licence says, there are some things that the supplier cannot stop you from doing. So if you have a licence, the supplier cannot stop you from making backup copies if you need them for your permitted use of the software.

Maintenance

As a general rule, you can copy or adapt software if that is necessary for you to use the software, provided that the licence doesn't stop you. So, for example, you can adapt software to correct errors, unless the licence specifically says that you cannot do it.

Decompilation and interfaces

You can decompile a program if you want to create an interface with another program, provided that you do not use the information that you glean from this to do anything else and do not give it to anybody who does not need it to build the interface. Similarly, if you can get the information from another source (such as the supplier) or if you use it to build a copycat program, the decompilation is not permitted.

What does all this mean in practice?

In many cases, it is just not feasible to change the printed terms that you will be offered. The terms may not be enforceable if they are unreasonable, but that is a hard call for you to make without advice and you should never depend on it.

Have a good look at the scope of the licence and look for anything that you would want to do that is left out. If it says 'copy and adapt' you will have no problems, unless you want to sell copies, and most suppliers only allow professional distributors to do that. If it is of more limited scope and sets out a list of things that you can do, you need to scrutinise the list.

Many users cannot and do not want to maintain software, but they may want to know that they can go to another supplier if something goes wrong. This is precisely what many suppliers want to avoid because they do not want anybody else meddling with their trade secrets or depriving them of maintenance fees. So some clients ask for maintenance rights, whilst many suppliers try to avoid granting them; in the end, it is a matter for discussion, although the supplier will often win the argument.

You will encounter similar problems with decompilation, but in that case the supplier can only prohibit decompilation if it provides sufficient information to allow you to build an interface. So this is less of a problem.

In any event, the right to adapt for the purpose of maintenance may well be of limited use unless you have a copy of the source code. This topic is dealt with in more detail in Chapter 5.

Transferring a licence

Many licences prohibit the transfer of rights to somebody else and sometimes the consent of the licensor is required before the rights can be transferred.

This may limit the scope for selling on systems. Before you sell or transfer a computer, you need to check that you can pass on rights in the software and possibly rights under maintenance contracts, depending on the circumstances. This can be crucial in the context of outsourcing.

Non-compliance

Needless to say, if you do something outside the scope of your licence, which is prohibited by copyright, technically you are infringing copyright and the copyright owner may sue you and seize the software. In practice, if you do something accidentally and no real harm is done, the copyright owner may give you a warning, without taking the matter any further.

DATABASES AND INTELLECTUAL PROPERTY RIGHTS

Taking a licence of somebody else's rights

The intellectual property rights protecting databases are relatively easy to understand provided that you can envisage the constituent parts of a database.

Databases are usually manipulated by software. Then there is the form of the actual database, the collection of data to populate it, and finally individual items of data.

From a legal perspective, the software is no different from any other software. The form of the database is protected by copyright in a similar way to software. The collection of data may be protected by copyright, to a certain degree, if the selection or arrangement of the contents constitutes the author's own intellectual creation. There is also database right, which can protect the contents of the database against substantial extraction and re-utilisation. In order to qualify for protection there must be a substantial investment in either obtaining, verification or presentation of the contents of the database and the resulting database must be arranged in a systematic and methodical way, accessible by electronic or other means. The right does not protect the individual items of data. Individual items of data, such as photographs, may also be protected by copyright.

So what does this add up to in practice? It means that you need a licence to use any of the rights protecting a database that you do not own. You need to ensure that the licence covers the way that you envisage using the database in terms of extraction and re-utilisation of data. In particular, if you are using a database to extract large amounts of data, you need to watch out for any limits on usage.

Protecting your own rights

It also means that in setting up your database and populating it you will acquire rights in the data that you assemble provided that you or your employees do this, or you acquire the rights under a written contract with the person who does.

If you ever need to enforce your rights you will need to prove that they are still current. This entails keeping records of the dates when the database is finished or made available to the public (if earlier), together with a copy of the database at that time. You need to do the same thing each time that it is substantially updated, because major updates may qualify for further protection.

You also need records of the nationality of the person, company or partnership that took the financial risks of making it. The database will only qualify for protection if the maker is from the EEA. If it is a company it must be incorporated in the EEA with either its central administration or principal place of business in the EEA or its registered office and a firm base in the EEA.

It is worthwhile marking all copies of the database with the name of the owner. This may deter infringers and will help you to claim damages from them. It could also, potentially, be used as evidence of the origin of any pirate copies.

WEBSITES AND INTELLECTUAL PROPERTY RIGHTS

Make sure that you own your website

Many people spend a great deal of money on websites, but allow the designer to own rights in them. It is a bit like buying something and leaving part of it in the shop on a permanent basis. Nonetheless, appreciable numbers of people do this, probably because they are now used to somebody else owning the software that they use.

The contents of a website are protected by copyright, which arises automatically when it is created, provided that it is first published in the UK (or another country, such as an EU state that is party to the same treaty as the UK) or fulfils certain other criteria. It is also possible to apply for registered designs in respect of specific graphics such as icons. This is a registered right, so it gives monopoly protection, which means that anybody else using a design within the scope of the registration will infringe.

Trade mark protection may be available for signs that are used on your website. These can overlap with registered designs in this context. As a very general rule, in the UK, trade mark applications are more expensive to process than ones for designs. However, trade marks can give broader protection and they can last indefinitely if you pay the renewal fees.

Many websites are dependent on software to assist in navigation and to process data that are input. The same rules apply to this software as to any other software. Similarly, there may be a facility for accessing and searching a database and that database should be treated in the same way as any other database.

Look after your rights

Copyright, registered designs and trade marks can all be valuable assets of a business, and can be used to protect it against imitators, so you should aim to own rights in your website. Consultants who build websites are likely to use certain generic material on each job. They would be foolish to give this to you, but anything that is specific to your project should be yours and you should protect it.

Before your designer starts work, you should have a written agreement, transferring rights in the material he creates to you and obliging the designer to keep the designs confidential in case you want to register them. Otherwise, the designer may be able to argue that he owns the copyright, and you just have a licence or somebody else may try to register the design before you do.

If you own the copyright in your website, it is worthwhile marking it to deter infringers, to ensure that you can claim damages from them and to take advantage of protection under international copyright treaties. You should put the © symbol followed by the name of the copyright owner and the date of first publication on the website.

If you put material onto a website, visitors are entitled to assume that they can use it in some way, so you need to be clear about what they can do. For example, if they can make copies solely for domestic use, but not for a business or any other purpose, you must state that specifically. Similarly, if they may not adapt it or give other people copies, you need to say so and the notices must be prominent so that they cannot miss them.

It is easy to catch infringers on the web

The second thing to remember about websites is that they are very public. Some people think that infringement of intellectual property goes unnoticed on the web. The truth is that sophisticated software has been developed to search for infringers, especially trade mark infringers. It is also easier to prove infringement because the evidence is recorded. See the sections below on internet use for further information on infringement.

DOMAIN NAMES AND INTELLECTUAL PROPERTY RIGHTS

Why there are problems

In the 1990s one of the more memorable rackets was buying up domain names that corresponded to famous trade marks and then holding the trade mark owner to ransom by demanding vast sums to transfer the domain name to them. Courts in many jurisdictions have now put a stop to this by holding that the 'cyber-squatters' are infringing trade marks.

Unfortunately, that is not the end of the story. There are still problems with domain names and trade marks. Trade marks are registrable in 45 different classes of goods and services and it is possible to subdivide each class by specifying only some of the goods or services within that class. So a great many businesses with the same trade mark may co-exist without problems.

This is not so with domain names because it is only possible to register a name once. So, for example, if the BCS has registered 'BCS.org' nobody else can register 'BCS' with the top-level domain of '.org'. The situation has improved with the creation of further top-level domains, such as '.biz', but the old ones like '.com' are still the most popular.

Opposing a registration

Domain names are generally allocated to the first person to register (although there maybe special arrangements for trade mark owners to have priority when top-level domains are allocated). This means that if somebody has already registered the name that you are seeking to register, you will only be able to oppose the registration in limited circumstances.

You can complain if a name within the top-level domains, such as '.com', '.net', or '.org':

- is identical or confusingly similar to your trade mark; and
- the person using the domain name has no right or legitimate interest in that domain name;
- the person using the domain name registered it and is using it in bad faith.

The domain name registry may cancel the domain name or transfer it. In some circumstances it is unclear whether there has been bad faith but in others, such as cyber-squatting, this has been relatively easy to decide. This also applies to certain country-code top-level domains. In the case of other top-level domains, the grounds for opposition will depend on the rules of the domain name registry concerned.

In addition to using the procedure in the relevant domain name registry, it is also possible to bring an action for trade mark infringement in a conventional court, although this may be difficult if the domain name owner is in a different business and the trade mark is not well known.

Avoiding disputes

If a domain name is not used or is not commercially important, and where there are no grounds for opposing its continued registration, it may be possible to purchase the domain name for a relatively modest sum.

In practice, the best way to avoid disputes is to register a domain name early and, if you can afford it, registering a corresponding trade mark in the same jurisdiction as the domain name registry can help too. If you think that there are grounds for opposing a domain name registration, it is best to seek professional advice.

It goes without saying that if you are registering a domain name you need to be careful to avoid infringing somebody else's trade mark (see the next section).

THE INTERNET AND TRADE MARKS

Infringement

The international trade mark system has historically been divided by national boundaries or by trading blocs. Internet use is international by its very nature, so if you use a trade mark on the internet there is a technical possibility of infringing separate trade marks in a large number of territories. Registration in one or more jurisdictions will not protect you from infringement in others.

In order to infringe a trade mark, it is usually necessary to use at least a similar mark for the same or similar goods or services as the trade mark is registered for. In Europe, if the mark or services are similar but not identical, and you want to claim infringement, you must show that people would be confused about where the goods or services come from.

Well-known marks are a special case because it is possible to infringe them by trading in different goods or services and, in the EU (including the UK), if without due cause the use would take unfair advantage of the mark or be detrimental to it. In the USA, use of marks that blurs their distinctiveness or tarnishes their reputation may also amount to trade mark dilution. Some uses, such as referring to the owner's goods and services in an honest way, will not infringe in some territories.

In practice, it is most likely that somebody will take action if you are actively using a mark in a particular jurisdiction, more especially if you trade there or have assets in that jurisdiction, because the trade mark owner then has a more realistic possibility of suing you successfully.

What should you do?
There is no easy answer to this because laws and trading methods are still being developed. Full international searches are prohibitively expensive for many companies. However, it should be possible to search for trade marks in the major jurisdictions before using a mark on the internet. If you cannot afford a professional search by a trade mark attorney, some patent offices, such as the UK, provide limited internet searching facilities. Nonetheless, a professional search is always preferable.

Examples of infringement
In addition to using a trade mark on a website, or as a domain name, the most likely ways in which trade marks can be infringed on the internet are through linking and framing, and metatags.

Linking and framing
There are two types of links on web pages: hypertext links and inline links.

With a hypertext link, you click on an icon and your browser retrieves material from a second website. With an inline link, material from a second website is automatically retrieved by and shows as an integral part of the first website.

Framing is an extreme form of linking where material from the linked site is framed by advertising and other material from the first site, so that it appears as if it is all on the same site. Linking technologies allow people to pretend that somebody else's content is theirs. Links that bypass the home page of another site can bypass valuable advertising.

In terms of intellectual property, linking can lead to confusion over whose products are being displayed under which marks. So, for example, the marks from the linked site may appear with products from the first site and the products of the linked site may appear under the trade marks of the first site.

Legally this may amount to trade mark infringement, unfair competition or passing off, depending on the jurisdiction, so it is safest not to skip home pages and to inform users that they are entering another site.

Metatags
Search engines find and classify websites by reference to keywords. Website owners assist the engines by embedding keywords, to increase use of their sites. Some unscrupulous people have embedded competitors' trade marks and well-known marks as keywords to try to divert business to their sites. In the UK, this usually amounts to trade mark infringement or passing off if there is a likelihood that those using the search engines would think that the site with the metatag is the site of the trade mark owner. There are similar remedies available in other jurisdictions.

Keyword advertising, where banner advertisements are linked to keyword search terms, presents similar problems, although in many cases generic words will be used so there will be no trade mark infringement or passing off.

THE INTERNET AND COPYRIGHT AND DATABASE RIGHT

Publishing literature, art and music on the internet, as well as other forms of broadcasting, merit a separate book, so they are not included in this chapter. Basic copying from websites is dealt with in the section on websites.

The aspect of ordinary usage that deserves further mention is the copyright aspect of linking. Creating links may not infringe copyright because the material on the other website is not copied or otherwise affected when the link is created.

However, there is a possibility of copyright infringement through linking because the owner of a copyright work has the exclusive right to communicate that work to the public and linking may infringe that right, more especially if the site to which the link is made prohibits linking.

Similarly, it is possible to infringe database right through linking if the material on the site that is linked qualifies for protection by database right.

APPENDIX: A BASIC GUIDE TO INTELLECTUAL PROPERTY AND RELATED RIGHTS

Copyright
What is copyright?
Copyright protects the means of expression of concepts, including literary works, fine art, crafts, music, films, broadcasts, and so on. In order to qualify, works

must be original; that is to say that they have not been copied, although EU law for both software and databases states that in order to be original the material must be the author's 'own intellectual creation'. There is usually a requirement that a work is recorded in some permanent form.

Three-dimensional works are not protected by copyright, except for artistic works, such as sculpture or architecture, and works of artistic craftsmanship.

Duration
In the case of literary, dramatic, musical and artistic works, protection generally lasts for 70 years after the end of the year in which the author dies. There are exceptions, notably for computer-generated works, which are only protected for 50 years after the end of the year in which they were created.

No registration
Copyright arises automatically on creation, and in the UK and many other jurisdictions there is no need for registration. There are exceptions, most notably in the USA for certain purposes. As an unregistered right, copyright does not protect against independent creation of the same or a similar work, provided that there is no copying involved.

Computer software qualifies for copyright protection as a literary work. This stretches the right somewhat and produces a rather unsatisfactory result. It means that copyright protects the way that code is written, as opposed to the underlying concepts, which are often more valuable. There is a certain amount of overlap between concept and expression, but not much.

Copyright also protects manuals (in whatever form they are produced), the structure, the collection of data and certain items of data in databases, and the contents of websites.

Moral rights
With certain notable exceptions, authors of copyright works have moral rights. These rights are, broadly, the right to be identified as the author; the right to object to derogatory treatment of a work; the right not to have a work falsely attributed; and the right to privacy of certain films and photographs. Exceptions to these rights include computer programs and computer-generated works. Employees have limited moral rights. Moral rights cannot be transferred, but they can be waived.

Database right
Database right protects the collection of data in a database, provided that the data are arranged in a systematic and methodical way and are individually accessible by electronic or other means. The right lasts for 15 years from the end of the year in which it is completed or the end of the year when it is made available to the public, if that happens before completion.

Databases must be original. The database must be sufficiently original to 'constitute the author's own intellectual creation'. There is a further requirement that there has been a substantial investment in obtaining, verifying or presenting the contents of the database.

Database right is another unregistered right, which arises automatically and can be circumvented by independent creation of a similar database (see section on databases above).

Patents
What is patentable?

Patents protect new inventions that make an inventive step beyond the current technology and which are of use to industry. Some types of invention, such as software and business methods, are unpatentable as such, but they can still be patented if there is another facet of the invention that is patentable.

So, for example, word-processing software is generally viewed as plain software, but software that has a technical effect, such as control software used in a car, may still be patentable. An appreciable amount of software is now patented, and some of the large software providers have a considerable number of patents.

As a registered right, a patent can be exceedingly powerful, so there are strict requirements for validity. In industrialised countries, inventions are unpatentable if they have been disclosed to anybody, with limited exceptions such as certain confidential disclosures. As regards the inventive step, it must be something that would not be obvious to a skilled but unimaginative worker in the field.

Patents and applications contain a description of the invention together with 'claims' that set out the features of the invention that merit protection. They generally last for 20 years from the date when the application was filed, subject to payment of renewal fees. Patents are always subject to revocation on the grounds that they do not meet the requirements for patentability. In the territories where they are granted, they provide a monopoly within the scope of the claims.

Formalities

Applications for patents must be made for each territory where protection is required. There are international filing systems that assist with delivering the applications and it is possible to postpone dealings with national and regional patent offices for around 30 months.

After patents are filed there is usually a search to determine whether the invention is novel. This is followed by examination of the application in each patent office where the application is made, to see whether the invention meets the requirements for patentability. At this stage the scope of the claims may be reduced during negotiation with the examiner.

As a result of this procedure and the requirement for translations, patenting can be costly, especially large-scale international filings. However, a patent is the best means of protection for a great many inventions and can be very valuable.

Confidential information

In England, it is possible to protect confidential information, such as secret formulae and sensitive commercial information. Protection arises automatically if the information is genuinely confidential, but it is lost if the information ceases to be confidential. It is possible to get an injunction to prevent disclosure, but after information has become widely known you can only claim damages for the unauthorised disclosure.

Proving that information is confidential and that disclosure is unauthorised can be difficult, but it is much easier if you have a contract that says that it is confidential and that it must not be disclosed.

Strictly speaking, confidential information is not intellectual property.

Trade marks
What is registrable?
In the UK and the EU, trade marks protect signs that indicate the origin of goods and services. They are not confined to word marks and logos. Provided that they can be represented graphically, they can even be shapes and smells, although many such applications have been refused.

In principle, anything may be registered provided that it is capable of distinguishing the goods of the trade mark owner. However, if a mark is descriptive of the goods themselves it may be refused registration.

Registration may also be refused if a mark is too close to a mark that is already registered or if use of the mark could lead to passing off (see below).

Infringement
Trade marks provide a limited monopoly. They can be used to prevent others from using the same mark on the same goods or services, or, if there is a possibility of confusion, a similar mark with similar goods or services. Well-known marks can also be infringed if they are used on different goods that would not be confused where, without due cause, the use would take unfair advantage of the mark or be detrimental to it.

Formalities
As with patents, an application needs to be made in each territory where protection is required and there are international conventions that assist with this. In addition to national marks in the EU, there is a separate Community mark that covers the entire EU. In the UK, trade marks are renewable every 10 years, and may last indefinitely with continued renewal. Like patents, they are always subject to revocation on the grounds that they no longer meet the requirements for registration.

Passing off
Passing off is a right that protects goodwill. Technically, there must be a misrepresentation made in the course of trade to existing or prospective customers that is calculated to injure the goodwill of an enterprise and is likely to cause damage.

This is not as complicated as it sounds. It usually involves one business trying to persuade customers of another that they are one and the same so that the clients of the first business will buy from the second. Selling lemon juice in a plastic lemon that was suspiciously similar to another trader's packaging has been sufficient to give rise to a claim for passing off.

Like confidential information, it is not, strictly, an intellectual property right, but it can be very useful for protecting unregistered trade marks and get-up, and there are no formalities. However, lesser-known enterprises may have difficulty in demonstrating sufficient goodwill to take action.

Designs

Currently there are so many rights protecting designs that it can be confusing.

There are two types of right under UK law that are valid in the UK only: design rights and registered designs. Under European law, which is applicable throughout the EU including the UK, there is a new registered community design and a community design right.

UK registered designs

- **Scope** – This protection is similar to the registered Community design that is described below.

  Registered designs protect the appearance of the whole or part of a product resulting from features of lines, contours, colours, shapes, textures and/or materials, and/or ornamentation in particular. They cover graphic symbols such as computer icons, typographic typefaces, packaging and get-up.

  This right does not protect parts of objects that are dictated solely by their technical function, are hidden from view during normal use, or are features of objects that fit mechanically around other objects so that either object may perform its function.

- **Novelty and individual character** – Designs must be 'new' and have 'individual character' in order to qualify for protection. For these purposes 'new' means that it has not been disclosed prior to the previous 12 months in such a way that it would become known to specialists in the industry sector within the community. It is unwise to take advantage of this 12-month period, in case somebody else makes a similar design during that period.

- **Formalities** – Registered design rights may be granted on application to the UK Patent Office. Rights last for a maximum of 25 years provided that they are renewed every 5 years. In common with patents and trade marks, registered designs are subject to revocation on the grounds that they do not fulfil the requirements for registration. As a registered right, the protection provides a monopoly within the registered specification, although the scope of that monopoly may well be interpreted narrowly, more especially in very popular forms of design. Registered design protection is available in many other territories.

UK design right

A design right is an unregistered right that is peculiar to the UK. It protects aspects of shape and configuration (whether internal or external) of the whole or part of an article. It does not protect surface decoration, parts of articles that are designed to fit around other objects, or which are designed to match other objects, or principles of construction.

In the context of computers, a modified form of this right protects semiconductor topographies (i.e. chip designs). It can also protect the shape of new equipment, such as a mouse with an unusual shape.

The right lasts for 15 years from the end of the year in which the design was first recorded in a design document or an article was made to the design, whichever happened first. This 15-year period is reduced if articles made to the design are legitimately marketed in the first 5 years, in which case the right lasts for 10 years from the date of the first sale or hire.

Anybody can apply to the Intellectual Property Office for a licence during the last five years of the right.

Community designs
There is a registered Community design, which covers the same scope as UK registered designs (see above) but which extends across the entire EU.

Unregistered Community designs, which also apply throughout the EU, are similar to the registered variety, although they only last for three years from the date when they are first made available to the public within the Community. If the design becomes known to specialists in the design sector concerned, then for these purposes, it is deemed to be available to the public.

The unregistered right is intended to protect designs that are short-lived. Like the registered right, designs must be new and have individual character.

An unregistered design does not qualify for protection unless it is made available to the public. So the first person to disclose a design is entitled to any unregistered design right, although somebody who develops the design independently and not by copying can still use the design.

Taking advice
You will need to take advice from a specialist intellectual property practitioner. If you do not know of one, the Law Society should be able to help you to find one. There are other sources of this information, but they are not always reliable.

5   SOFTWARE ESCROW

Jon Leigh and Graham Wood

As businesses become more dependent on technology they also become more reliant on third-party suppliers who provide and support such technology. This chapter explains how you can mitigate this dependency through the use of escrow arrangements. Details covered include a description of what escrow is, when you should consider using escrow, the legal and technical considerations of setting up an escrow arrangement and how to choose an escrow agent.

INTRODUCTION

The word 'escrow' is a legal term meaning 'money, goods or a written document, held by a trusted third party, pending the fulfilment of some condition'.

This type of arrangement has been used for hundreds of years to facilitate deals where there is a time lag between the initial stages and completion of a business transaction.

Property transfers are a good example of this. The seller wants to know that the purchaser's funds are sufficient and available before completing and handing over the relevant documentation. By placing the funds with a 'trusted third party' who guarantees the amount and that it will be transferred upon receipt of the property transfer documents, this requirement is satisfied.

Whilst escrow is used by the software industry in the manner explained below, there are numerous applications of this process. For example if a company provides services to a business using proprietary financial models developed to assist in its decision-making process, it may well be prudent to request that these models be placed in escrow in the event that the services terminate abruptly.

THE IMPORTANCE OF ESCROW FOR SOFTWARE USERS

Escrow has been used in the IT sector for over 35 years to provide users of software with long-term security. The service is built upon the split between source code and object code.

Programmers write software in source code (a form of computer program that is understood by humans and is required in order to maintain and update the software). When a program is ready, a compiler converts it into executable or object code (the machine-readable form of the computer program) that is licensed to users. The compiler may be available commercially or the owner may develop it especially for the program.

Software owners normally grant users a licence to use the executable code of their programs. Only very rarely will access to source code be provided. This is normally guarded jealously by the owner because the intellectual property of the source code makes up most of the value of the owner company. The reason why owners wish to keep their source code secret lies with the limitations of the legal protection provided for software infringement.

International protection for software is provided by copyright. Copyright provides owners with the right to copy the 'work' and enables them to take action against any infringement. This right depends upon the copy being 'materially' the same as the original. If the source code was to be made public any competitor would be able to see how the code was created and may be able to use this information to create quickly (and cheaply) a similar program.

Having to prove in court that this new version is a copy of the original would be expensive and time-consuming. It is therefore far better to keep the source code secret and never to allow this situation to arise.

Source code is necessary in order to maintain and update the software, so by ensuring that it remains confidential, the owners prevent users from doing this work themselves. This creates a business risk for the users because they are then reliant upon the owner for the correct and continuing operation of the software. If the package is key to their business and the owner for some reason is no longer able to support the package, operations may be critically affected.

Software escrow agreements provide for the placing of the source code with an independent trusted third party, known as the escrow agent. This agreement, which is made between the owner, the licensee and the escrow agent, states the events under which the source code will be released to the licensee and what the licensee may do with it once he receives it.

WHEN DO YOU NEED ESCROW?

Software escrow is not necessary for every software package that you purchase. A company needs to assess the criticality of the software package and the financial or operational loss that would occur in the event of its failure. This ideally needs to be done when procuring a new software package because it is far easier to request escrow during the negotiations leading to the purchase of a licence.

Looking at software you already use or waiting for a problem to occur before trying to enter into an escrow agreement is more problematical because owners are usually reluctant to enter into escrow arrangements after the licence has been signed (see below).

You should address the following points when considering escrow:

- The software owner:

  o Is the owner a substantial company that is highly unlikely to cease trading or is it a small start-up that could find itself in difficulties very quickly?

  o Do you have concerns over the software owner's commitment to supporting the software package?

  o If it is a smaller company, is it backed by a large organisation that will step in and pick up the pieces in the event of a problem?

- The software:

  o If you do not accept the latest version of the software from the owner will the one that you have continue to be maintained?

  o Is there an alternative software package on the market that you could quickly switch to with little difficulty and cost?

  o Are there regular maintenance issues with the software?

  o What is the intended lifespan of the software?

- Your business:

  o Is the software key to your business? Would your business still be able to function effectively if the software suddenly becomes unavailable?

  o Would revenues be affected if the software became unavailable?

  o Will it cost a large amount to switch software in the event of a problem with the owner?

Table 5.1 When do you need escrow?

Type and scope of software	Type of supplier	Stability of software	Need for escrow
Standard package used across the company	Large multinational software company	Very stable: no maintenance is required and new versions and upgrades appear as a matter of course.	Little risk of the owner going out of business; the owner is unlikely to agree to an escrow arrangement.

(Continued)

Table 5.1 *(Continued)*

Type and scope of software	Type of supplier	Stability of software	Need for escrow
Standard package; medium criticality – used daily	Successful specialist software company	Stable: but could be acquired and is reliant on few customers; upgrades required to address business issues.	Medium risk of the owner going out of business; and ownership of package may change. Should check if owner has existing escrow arrangement in place that you can join.
Specialist package; critical to your business	Large specialist software company	Stable: no maintenance is required and you do not use the infrequent upgrades; the owner will not give assurances that the version you use will continue to be maintained.	Important: high risk to your business if the owner goes out of business or fails to maintain the package. Ensure escrow is addressed prior to entering into a licence agreement so that you have sufficient leverage to require escrow as part of the arrangements.
Specialist package; critical to your business	Small software start-up company	Unstable	Essential: high risk that the owner may go out of business or cease to be able to support and maintain the software.
Bespoke package developed specifically for your company	Software consultancy or contractor	Unstable and untested	Essential: you own the code, so should have copies of it in case you need to continue the development yourself or with a new contractor. Software escrow offers a solution if you do not wish to manage the receipt and checking of source code from the contractor.

TECHNICAL CONSIDERATIONS

Merely being able to access the source code may not be sufficient. Software source code is often immensely complex and completely unintelligible to the layman. Even an expert will usually find it difficult to understand the source code of a complex program if he is not familiar with it. So the question arises as to what you can do with it when it has been released to you?

The two main options available are to contract with a new software supplier to maintain the software package for you or to take over the maintenance in-house.

Almost all software releases under escrow agreements are made due to the insolvency or cessation of trading of the owner. In these circumstances, the people who wrote the source code will usually be looking for work and it is likely that they would be willing to be contracted to provide support.

During this period of support you will be able to ensure that your own staff become familiar with the package so that self-sufficiency is finally attained.

As stated, source code is often immensely complex and even for a relatively straightforward program can run to thousands of pages. For anyone to understand the code (other than its author), it is essential that certain quality controls are used by the owner in maintaining the software such as proper indentation and notes. Failure to do this can make a huge difference if someone new, either your own staff or a new software supplier, has to try to work with the package.

VERIFICATION

During the early days of software escrow, no checks were made on the material deposited with the agents. Eventually it was realised that this was a substantial area of risk because it meant that the effectiveness of the escrow arrangements relied upon the honesty and efficiency and full understanding of the software owner.

As mentioned earlier, software owners are highly protective of their source code and therefore if their technical staff are asked to deposit the source code with an escrow agent they may often deposit the object code by a mistake because they have been told never to let the source code out of the building. Mistakes can be made when putting the deposit together that cannot be rectified if you only find this out when the code is released to you and the software owner has gone out of business.

Verification addresses some of these issues. Verification takes a number of forms. At a basic level, a check is made to ensure that:

- each item of media deposited can be read without error and contains no viruses;

- if the data have been encrypted or password protected in any way that the data can be accessed using the decryption key or password provided by the software owner;

- if compression has been used that the data can be decompressed;

- the deposit contains source code.

You will note that at no stage does this basic level of verification provide any assurance that the code provided is the correct and complete source code for the package that you are using.

The most effective way to ensure that the code lodged is the required code is to ask the escrow agent to work with the software owner to go through a process of building the application through compiling the source code into the executable code. You should agree on the testing that should be carried out on the executable software package and ask that you are involved in this process. The escrow agent will be able to fully document the build process and ensure that all information and files required to build the software package are included in the escrow deposit.

WHAT SHOULD BE LODGED?

The source code alone is not normally sufficient to be able to support and maintain software. You should also ensure that the following items are considered:

- Full details of the material deposited including the name and version number and the number of items.

- The owner will have used a compiler to compile the source code into executable code. In order to reproduce the executable code, you must identify the exact version of the compiler. If it is not commercially available (it may have been developed specifically for the licensed software by the owner), you will need to have it lodged in escrow as well. The escrow agreement should cover the terms under which such third-party software is held and released.

- The technical details that will enable someone to access and understand the contents of the media including the file and archive format and the retrieval commands. The type of hardware necessary and the operating system details should also be provided.

- Names and versions of development tools.

- The names and contact details of the people who wrote the original code. If the developer ceases to trade they may then be contacted to provide support on a contract basis.

- Supporting materials, such as design notes, flow charts, written documentation etc. Anything that will assist a trained programmer in understanding the code that is lodged.

- Code developed by third parties and used in the software. Often third-party developers are used to provide specialist elements of packages. If this occurs, then the appropriate source code for this element should also be provided and the consent of its owner obtained to the escrow arrangement.

THE AGREEMENTS

There are many different types of escrow agreement that have been developed over the years in order to deal with different licensing situations and different types of material being protected. The simplest one is the three-party agreement involving the owner, the user and the escrow agent. Agreements have also been developed to deal with multiple licensing situations where a standard software package is used by many users. Whatever parties are involved in the ownership and support of the package need to be included in the escrow agreement along with the end-user, such as distributors and outsourcers.

Notwithstanding the many types of agreement, most escrow agreements contain the same elements:

- Statement of ownership or right to enter into the agreement by the owner. This is key to any escrow agreement. Ownership of the copyright in software belongs to the person creating it unless an assignment has been completed. Many software owners do not realise this and it is not unusual for them to bring in outside contractors to complete specialist parts of a package. Unless the rights have been assigned, those contractors could cause problems at a later date if they find out that a third party has access to their source code.

- The release events. These may be anything that the parties agree upon although most standard agreements contain the following:

  o The liquidation of the software owner;

  o The software owner ceasing to trade;

  o A material failure under any maintenance agreement;

  o An assignment of the software to a third party who does not provide the licensee with similar protection to the current escrow agreement within 14 days of such assignment.

- Confidentiality. Strict obligations of confidentiality should be entered into so that the source code remains a trade secret of the owner. Notwithstanding that the user has access to the source code this does not mean that it can be made available to the whole world. For example, it will still be of value to a liquidator in the event of a liquidation and should therefore be rigorously protected.

- Limitations on use. Strict limitations are normally placed upon the user so that the code may be used only for their own maintenance and support. The user should not be able to start licensing the code and making competing packages.

- Time-bound release process. If there is a dispute about release or some other critical provision a rapid resolution is essential. The user is not going to want to wait months for release at a time when his business may be in jeopardy.
- Title. Unless there are special circumstances, ownership of the source code will not change merely due to a release of the package to the user. A statement confirming that ownership remains with the original owner is found in most escrow agreements.

USER'S DUTIES

An escrow agreement is only as good as the efforts made by the user to ensure its effectiveness. For example, the owner may issue new versions on a regular basis. The escrow agent has no knowledge of these new versions unless the user tells it that they have been received. If this is not done then the agent will hold an out-of-date, and potentially unusable, version of the source code.

The user must also spend some time ensuring that the material placed in escrow is everything that is needed for support and maintenance of the software. This can be helped by asking the escrow agent to carry out high levels of verification. It is too late to correct matters if this is left until after a release event.

CHOOSING AN ESCROW AGENT

It is vital to choose an appropriate escrow agent. Many companies have used a bank or a firm of lawyers as their agent. This is not good practice because these organisations do not usually have the administrative capacity to maintain correctly an escrow deposit over a period of years. Neither do they usually have the skills to provide any level of verification. An agent should have the in-house legal, technical and administrative personnel to back up the services it offers.

There are professional escrow agents that provide a suitable level of service and these should be used wherever possible. The largest escrow agent in the world is NCC Group plc who are based in Manchester in the UK, but have offices throughout Europe and in the USA. The geographical situation of the escrow agent is often unimportant. Code can be delivered worldwide on almost a 24-hour basis. The software industry is truly global. Decisions on agents should be made on the quality of the services provided and, inevitably, cost.

ADVANTAGES OF ESCROW FOR SOFTWARE OWNERS

Software owners are increasingly seeing the advantages of actively offering escrow to all their customers.

- **Confidence.** Providing escrow protection shows a commitment to their customers. It gives customers confidence in their dealings with the software owner and can be a motivation for the customers to deal with them rather than another supplier. This is particularly true if the owner is dealing in a new market or is a start-up company.

  A number of software companies when attempting to break into a new geographical market have used escrow in their marketing literature to convince companies that there is a low business risk in dealing with them and that they are committed to such customers in a tangible long-term manner.

- **Off-site storage of the complete source code.** Whilst off-site storage should be a basic business continuity measure for all owners it is surprising how many do not do this. There have been a number of examples of owners requesting their code back from an escrow agent because they have 'lost' their own copy, especially for older versions of the software.

  Furthermore it is common to find that owners do not have a complete copy of the latest source code stored anywhere because different persons in different parts of the company will hold the source code that they are working on. Placing the source code for a package in escrow can be seen as a useful quality measure to ensure that internal standards are complied with, particularly if verification is carried out to prove that the code is correct and complete.

- **Proof of ownership.** Software is protected by copyright and one of the main issues concerning proof of ownership is the date the 'work' was created. By placing the code in escrow, the trusted third party can provide evidence of the date that the code was lodged.

CONCLUSION

There have been some notable examples where organisations have obtained release of source code from an escrow agent and been able to support and maintain it after the respective software owners have gone out of business. There have also been a number of companies that have suffered greatly because a key software owner was unable to continue providing its usual service and they have had no escrow protection in place.

Software escrow provides an 'insurance policy' against the unpredictable IT market through enabling continuing maintenance of critical applications in the event of release of code. They should therefore form an essential part of business continuity and disaster recovery planning.

Software escrow also provides users with leverage in the event that the software owner defaults on maintenance obligations because the threat of release under the escrow agreement will often result in the maintenance issues being resolved. This is also true in the case of change of IPR ownership where the users protected under a software escrow agreement are in a good position to be top priority for the new IPR owner.

Decisions concerning software escrow should not be made without a careful consideration of the surrounding circumstances. A risk assessment should be carried out on each new software package procured and then repeated on a regular basis to determine if escrow protection is required and what level of testing should be carried out. Once escrow protection is in place the arrangement needs to be managed to make sure that the source code for the correct version of the software being used by the end-user is held at all times.

6   OUTSOURCING

Jeremy Newton

This chapter outlines some of the basic concepts relevant to business process or technology outsourcing. It also considers some of the common jargon and acronyms that are used in the course of outsourcing transactions.

INTRODUCTION

Outsourcing means different things to different people. Expressions like 'facilities management', 'application service provision', 'cloud computing', 'offshoring' and 'near-shoring' are also used to describe a range of commercial arrangements, and they are frequently lumped together under the heading 'outsourcing'. In terms of their subject matter, though, these expressions all mean subtly different things.

A 'pure' outsourcing relationship involves two key elements: a transfer of assets (for example, computer systems or a property portfolio) from the client to the supplier; and the provision of services from the supplier to the client (which may be done using the transferred assets or any other resources that the supplier chooses to use, so long as it can deliver the contracted service to the client).

- **A facilities management (FM)** contract is one where the client's own systems are used by the supplier to deliver services to the client, but without any change of ownership. The assets remain under the ownership and at the premises of the client, with the supplier merely granted access to those systems to the extent necessary to provide the managed service.

- **Business process outsourcing (BPO)** involves the transfer to the supplier of an entire business process, such as finance, accounting or payroll. In other words, it is the running of the entire business function that is transferred, not merely the operation of the technology that supports that function.

- **Application service provision (ASP)** involves the delivery of an IT service by a provider who remotely hosts and manages the applications for its clients. Rather than the client buying a software package and then transferring it to the service provider (as part of a traditional outsourcing arrangement), the supplier purchases large volumes of equipment and software licences and allows its clients to use and access those applications remotely, either over the internet or via dedicated lease lines. (It is similar to the concept of 'bureau services', which has been around since the 1950s.)

The list of specific technologies or business processes that can be outsourced is endless. Common IT functions for outsourcing include telecommunications; application development, support and maintenance; desktop support; helpdesk; and training. Looking at it from the broader BPO angle, though, means considering contracts for the outsourcing of human resources functions, finance, payroll processes, and any other business function.

DEFINING THE SERVICES

The starting point for drafting an outsourcing contract is to define the services to be provided to the client. This service description or specification, together with the setting of the service levels to be achieved, lies at the heart of the outsourcing relationship, so it needs to capture all of the services to be provided by the supplier.

It is difficult to generalise usefully about the drafting of service descriptions: there are heavy academic books written on how to go about writing them and the nature and structure of the service description will of course vary substantially from contract to contract. However, there are a number of points of terminology that may be of assistance in understanding how the service description develops:

- **Statement of requirements:** this document sets out the client's requirements in detail. It is created unilaterally by the client (probably in conjunction with its technical and commercial advisers) and can be included in the tender documentation against which the contractor will propose its 'technical solution'.

- **Technical solution:** this is the contractor's proposal for the technology that is to be used to deliver the services, as opposed to the essential description of the services themselves.

- **Output specification:** service descriptions are commonly expressed in terms of an output specification: a statement of the 'outputs' or deliverables that arise out of the service, rather than a description of the 'inputs' of how that service is to be delivered.

OUTPUTS AND INPUTS

By way of illustration of the distinction between outputs and inputs, imagine that you are negotiating a BPO agreement to outsource your company's accounts department. The services you are looking for may include, say, credit checking and debt collection. As the user, you want to know that credit checks and debt collection are carried out to certain standards. However, as long as the supplier meets those standards and provides the information required in the agreed form and within agreed timescales, the outsourcing purist will say it is of no interest to you (as the user) whether the supplier performs those functions using the latest high-end servers and the fastest available networks, or whether it does so by scribbling calculations on the back of an envelope.

As long as you are getting the outputs you need, when you need them, and in the correct format, who cares how the supplier gets them to you?

DESIGN RISK

There is often a degree of overlap between outputs and inputs. The client will probably specify the management reports it wants, but also how it wants to receive them (e.g. using the interfaces between its own internal systems and the technology used by the supplier to provide the service). However, there is a sound legal reason for the client to separate outputs and inputs: if the client goes into too much detail about the technology, it may thereby approve the technical solution that the contractor has come up with (in other words, it takes back the 'design risk' that the supplier would normally bear). If the technical infrastructure fails completely, the supplier will argue that the client had approved the solution and accordingly has to live with the consequences of its non-performance.

It may be that certain inputs in the technical solution are important enough to form a mandatory part of the service description, but these are normally limited to those parts of a solution that the client considers to be so crucial to the delivery of the services that they have to be stated expressly.

Of course, the intention of transferring the design risk will vary from contract to contract. That is certainly the orthodox approach in relation to many public sector contracts, for example, but it may be different in relation to outsourcing agreements involving, say, defence companies or banks. In these cases, there are very sophisticated IT departments who want to retain a significant degree of control over the way the contractor delivers the services to the business.

SERVICE LEVEL AGREEMENT

Once the parties have defined what the services are, they can then move on to the next big commercial issue: how well are the services to be performed? This is defined in a Service Level Agreement (SLA). The SLA part of an outsourcing agreement has four main aspects:

- It defines the service levels to be achieved.
- It sets out targets for those service levels.
- It prescribes the mechanism for monitoring and reporting actual service levels against those targets.
- It addresses the consequences of failure to meet those targets (which may include, for example, payment of rebates or service credits).

SLAs are discussed in more detail in Chapter 1; but the following terminology crops up frequently in the specific context of outsourcing:

- **Performance points:** An SLA usually combines a variety of service levels and many agreements have literally dozens of performance indicators, all of which may have implications in terms of financial compensation or termination. One of the ways of handling the (potentially very complicated) arithmetic is to set up a system of 'performance points': instead of stating that the remedy for a particular breach consists of a service credit of X per cent of the charges, you say that the defect attracts Y performance points. Other service levels similarly attract performance points, and of course the number of points attributable to a particular deficiency can be weighted to emphasise the more important service levels and reduce the impact of the minor ones. At the end of the relevant measurement period, the total number of performance points is calculated and the service credit is based on the number of performance points (so N performance points amounts to a rebate of X per cent of the periodic charge). A further refinement would be that if the number of performance points in a given period exceeds a given figure, then the matter is escalated between the parties and may give rise to termination.

- **Performance indicators** and **key performance indicators:** The number of service levels to be achieved will vary from contract to contract. It is important that complexity is not built into the SLA for its own sake: just because a particular metric **can** be measured does not mean that it **need** be measured. In some contracts, the parties undertake to comply with unbelievably complicated performance regimes that are likely to be totally unworkable in practice because of the number and frequency of reports, the complexity of the arithmetic and so on. For this reason, a distinction is often drawn between performance indicators (PIs) and key performance indicators (KPIs) to clarify which measures of service need to be reported on just as a matter of interest or good management practice, and which give rise to contractual exposure in the event of failure.

- **Ratchet mechanisms:** A simple ratchet mechanism increases the number of performance points awarded for a particular failure if the defect occurs too often within a specified period. For example, if X points are awarded for a failure to achieve a particular output, then if that failure recurs more than three times in the relevant period, each subsequent occasion attracts 2X points. The aim is to encourage the contractor to rectify service defects by increasing the stakes for successive occurrences of a defect. A ratchet mechanism may be used in connection with a non-key performance indicator, where the level of financial impact from failure to perform is not sufficient to encourage the contractor to improve but is potentially inconvenient for clients or users.

ELEMENTS OF AN SLA

The performance regime needs to be built from the ground up. Start by defining what you are trying to measure and work from there to set the targets, the means of measuring performance and the consequences of failure. In a contract for the provision of call centre services, for example, the parties may agree that a relevant service level is 'time to connect to an operator'.

With that service level agreed, the parties then need to go on to define:

- the target for that service level (e.g. 8 seconds for peak and 4 seconds for off-peak calls);

- the mechanism for measuring and reporting (e.g. random sampling or continuous monitoring of all calls, averaged over a four-week period);

- the consequences of failure (e.g. some form of service credits, perhaps on a sliding scale, with credits increasing according to the severity of the deterioration in service, or termination of the agreement).

There needs to be a clear 'read-through' from one part of the SLA to the next, with the various obligations expressed in common terminology and according to an agreed structure. Too often, disputes arise out of ambiguities in the wording of an SLA, which in turn derive from the fact that different members of the team have taken responsibility for the various elements, without anyone taking overall control of the drafting across the SLA as a whole.

PRICING AND PAYMENT MECHANISMS

Pricing and payment mechanisms are the commercial heart of the outsourcing contract, but there is little that can be said by way of useful generalisations about these aspects. Basic charging structures may consist of:

- a fixed price for the service per quarter or per year;

- a fixed price per unit of utilised resource (such as £1 per 100 transactions processed);

- 'cost plus' charges, where the supplier is entitled to recover its costs of providing the services, plus an agreed percentage profit margin.

Whatever the general charging arrangements, though, a greater proportion of the time in negotiations is usually spent in devising the mechanism for price variations. Any IT contract should include a change control mechanism (see Chapter 2) as a matter of course. In the context of a 10-year outsourcing agreement (in which the technology itself is likely to change dramatically over the lifetime of the contract, even if the client's business does not), how do you build a mechanism that allows the parties sufficient flexibility to improve the delivery of the services without having to stop and renegotiate the pricing at every turn?

Project open book accounting

Project open book accounting (POBA) principles can be applied to ensure that there is transparency in relation to the accounts and costings for a project. It tends to lead to a better understanding between the parties about the level of costs incurred in delivering the services and so tends to reduce the scope for surprises or debate when changes are being priced under the change control mechanism. POBA can also assist in fostering better, more open, working relationships, which tend to be necessary in the context of the 'partnering' or 'partnership' type of outsourcing agreement.

Naturally, there is some resistance on the part of suppliers about opening their books to the client's scrutiny. It is important to ensure that the use of this information is limited strictly to the scope of the project and also, to avoid the obligations on the contactor becoming too onerous, to limit the client's right of access to its books to once or twice per year.

However, giving access to this information will allow the client to undertake its own assessment in relation to estimating the cost of changes and will also provide it with some security against unreasonable estimates for changes.

Benchmarking

Benchmarking is a process by which the contractor compares its charges with the prices for which the client could obtain the same services elsewhere in the market. If the relevant costs are higher than market costs, then the contractor makes a reduction in the price charged to the client, subject to some agreed cost-sharing ratio. If costs are lower than market costs, the contractor may seek to come back to the client and try to raise its prices.

Market testing

This is a process that applies particularly to any part of the services that are subcontracted by the contractor to a third party. The aim is that the contractor re-tenders on the market for the service, in order to test that everybody is getting value for money from that service. If a new subcontractor does the same work at a lower price, this reduction may be passed on to the client.

Problems with benchmarking and market testing

Benchmarking and market testing are common mechanisms, particularly in large-scale public contracts, but they are unpopular with contractors because one of the reasons for outsourcing is to take advantage of economies of scale. Those economies of scale will often be factored into the initial price and the contractor will argue that as long as the client is happy with the initial price, why should it be concerned whether the supplier's profit is greater, or less, or indeed whether it makes no profit at all?*

The mechanisms can also be very complex, so unless value for money is of overwhelming importance to you, it may be better to steer clear of them. These mechanisms tend to work better in the context of projects like construction or roads rather than the more subtle (and faster moving) world of IT, where costs tend to drop from year to year.

THE OUTSOURCING LIFE CYCLE

The outsourcing relationship can be a long-term arrangement, involving a number of phases, each of which gives rise to slightly different issues, and all of which need to be provided for in the contract paperwork:

- The initial transfer of assets from the client to the service provider;
- The transition of services (and perhaps staff) from the client's organisation to the service provider;

---

*Of course, if the contractor cannot make a profit, it will lose interest in performing the services properly. Regardless of the contractual rights and wrongs, this can seriously impact the client's business, for example if all the best contractor staff are moved onto a new and more profitable job.

- The service delivery phase and continuing service management;
- Exit arrangements and/or transition to another service provider.

Initial asset transfer

In terms of the contractual paperwork (as opposed to the commercial discussions), the starting point is the initial transfer of assets. Asset transfer agreements are very commonplace: any commercial lawyer can draft one.

Typically, the agreement identifies the assets to be transferred, includes some warranties as to their ownership and condition, and sets out the mechanism for paying the price. However, there is an extra dimension to the asset transfer in the context of outsourcing because the transaction is not just a one-off.

In the normal contract for the sale of an asset, the main aim of the seller is usually to get the highest price (with the lowest ongoing exposure in terms of guarantees about the condition of the asset). A good example is the sale of a car: the seller is not concerned with the use the buyer makes of the asset and if the buyer does not make proper use of it, there is normally no adverse impact on the seller.

In the case of outsourcing, however, the buyer is buying the assets for the specific purpose of providing services to the seller, so the price allocated to any asset will be reflected in the charges payable by the client for the services. So the asset transfer has to be seen in the context of the overall outsourcing deal.

The core of the asset transfer is the asset register, which is the list or schedule of assets that are to move across to the service provider. In the context of technology outsourcing, these will typically include:

- Hardware (which can be identified by reference to manufacturers' names, serial numbers and locations);
- Software licences (which can similarly be identified by reference to the package names and version numbers, and the contract numbers of the licences under which the software is used);
- Other contracts related to the use and support of those assets, like support and maintenance agreements, equipment leases, disaster recovery contracts, and employment contracts for the individuals involved with the assets to be transferred. (Most IT operations are underpinned by a web of such contracts and the service provider will want to be assured that it has the benefit of all these contracts on a continuing basis, at least until it has completed a transition of the services from the existing infrastructure to its own.)

As part of gathering this information and ensuring it is complete and correct, the parties will often undertake what is known as a due diligence exercise. This involves identifying all the relevant assets, tracking down any relevant contract paperwork, reviewing all this information (from technical, commercial and legal points of view) and then addressing any problems that come to light. For example, a common problem area is in relation to the assignment of software licences: the standard terms of most large software houses provide that the licensee may only assign the licence if the consent of the software house has been obtained. Even if the software house does not object to the proposed transfer, getting that consent in writing can be very time-consuming, so it is essential that the parties embark on this due diligence exercise at the earliest opportunity, to build up as complete a picture as possible of the assets to be transferred and the risks associated with them.

Transition of services

During the transition phase, the responsibility for the provision of the services moves across from the client (who is effectively 'self-providing' as at the contract date) to the service provider. On the day that the contract is signed, it is unlikely that the service provider will immediately be able to meet the contractual target service levels, so there is often a period (which may be up to a year in contracts requiring major business process re-engineering) during which the SLA does not 'bite' to its fullest extent. During that period, the client and the supplier will need to collaborate to ensure that the supplier has built up a full understanding of the client's business requirements. It may be that the client has to change its business processes to bring them into line with the recommendations by the supplier in order to achieve promised business benefits. The contract should include a detailed transition plan that states clearly each party's rights and obligations with regard to getting the systems and the services up and running, the timetable for achieving full service delivery, and so on.

Service delivery phase

At the end of the transition phase, the supplier should be in a position to deliver the services to meet the contracted service levels. The contract then moves into a new phase that concerns ongoing service management.

Typically, the outsourcing contract will include a governance model that describes how the relationship between the parties is to be managed during the service delivery period and includes periodic service reviews to consider both historic performance and any service improvements that may be required. Note that these review arrangements need to be dovetailed closely with the change control procedures.

Exit arrangements

The final stage of the outsourcing life cycle is termination. Whether the contract expires because it reaches the end of its agreed term or is terminated before that point, the client must ensure that there is an agreed and contractually binding exit plan. This will typically require the service provider to assist the client in getting the services (and any relevant assets) transferred either to a new service provider or back to the client. The exit plan should be reviewed periodically throughout the service delivery phase to ensure:

- that the supplier maintains an up-to-date register of all the assets it uses to provide the services;

- that all relevant documentation is kept in an orderly fashion, so that the supplier can easily verify matters like ownership of equipment and the transferability of software licences in the event of termination of the outsourcing agreement;

- that any assets that are not freely transferable to the client can at least be used by the client (or a new contractor) for a sufficient period to enable them to move the services over to new assets.

OTHER RELEVANT ISSUES

This chapter has outlined the general shape of a typical outsourcing contract and explained some of the terminology that is often heard in the course of the commercial negotiation. However, there are a couple of important legal areas that it is possible only to touch on in this book.

One issue is the sensitive matter of staff transfers and the Transfer of Undertakings (Protection of Employment) Regulations (TUPE). This law is intended to protect staff when the 'undertaking' they work for is transferred to another organisation, as will commonly be the case in outsourcing contracts.

Where TUPE applies, the current employment contracts of the staff in that 'undertaking' (which is not necessarily a company or a self-contained business unit) are automatically transferred across to the new organisation.

In the context of outsourcing, for example, the service provider may become responsible for honouring the contracts of certain client employees, whether it needs them or not. It is essential that TUPE matters are considered as part of the outsourcing discussions and contractual arrangements, but it is not proposed to say more about them here, except that it is essential to obtain specialist legal advice.

Secondly, there is considerable interest at present in offshore outsourcing, for example moving call centres or back-office functions to India or Eastern Europe. There are often sound economic reasons for making this move, but doing business in a different jurisdiction and time zone is a major step. Common problem areas in international outsourcing include the need to adopt complex corporate or tax structures; difficulties with international dispute resolution and the enforcement of judgments; and unfamiliar laws about ownership and licensing of intellectual property rights. It is essential to obtain specialist legal advice from an adviser with expertise in the relevant field (and jurisdiction) before taking such a significant step.

7   DATA PROTECTION

Andrew Katz

Data protection is a complex area. It is notoriously difficult to summarise because the legislation is so full of exemptions, provisos and exceptions. This chapter aims to give the reader a working knowledge of the overall scheme of the legislation and highlight the areas where there are potential pitfalls, so that specialised advice can be sought.

INTRODUCTION

The law in this area is primarily contained in the Data Protection Act 1998, although various other Acts and Regulations are also relevant, particularly in relation to electronic marketing. Data protection compliance in the UK is overseen by the Information Commissioner, and the website of the Information Commissioner's Office (ICO) is always a useful jumping-off point to get to grips with the law and what is considered good practice in this area. Although the information it gives may occasionally be misleading, it is a good reference source, and if any dispute arises the ICO should be receptive to the argument that a data controller should not be found to be in breach of the Act where it is following advice published on the ICO website.

New powers in 2010 for the ICO to impose fines of up to £500,000 on organisations that commit deliberate or particularly serious breaches of the Act have underlined how important it is for organisations to have a proper understanding of their obligations in relation to personal data.

TERMINOLOGY

The words 'data' and 'information' have venerable well-established meanings to those who study information theory and computing. Unfortunately, when Parliament drafted the legislation, it chose to ignore these and almost perfectly interchange the established definitions of 'data' and 'information'. If you have any grounding in information theory, try to ignore what you have been taught when reading this chapter!

WHAT DATA ARE COVERED

The Data Protection Act requires that any 'personal data' are only obtained, processed and held by entities (called 'data controllers') that have registered ('notified' in the language of the Act) with the Information Commissioner. 'Data subjects' have a right to know who holds data about them, what those data are, that the data are used properly and for specified purposes, and (by and large) they are not used in a way that can harm them. In addition, the data controller is obliged to take steps to ensure that the information is secure and is not disclosed to unauthorised persons.

Data subjects have various rights, including the right to compensation should a data controller fail to comply with obligations under the Act.

The starting point for any discussion of data protection law is understanding what is meant by 'personal data'. The definition in the Act says that personal data means data that relate to a living individual who can be identified from those data, or from those data and other information that is in the possession of or is likely to come into the possession of the data controller. Names are personal data. Names and addresses together are personal data (although the addresses themselves are probably not). Email addresses in the form andrew.katz@moorcrofts.com are personal data, but 12345@hotmail.com may not be.

Information about George V is not personal data because he is dead.

Information about companies (as long as it does not refer to members of staff, directors or other individuals) is not personal data because companies are not individuals.

These definitions raise issues that have caused a great deal of uncertainty and debate: much of it centred on the 2003 case of *Durant* v. *Financial Services Authority*. Take, for example, the proviso about data being personal data if they identify a living individual in conjunction with other information that is in the possession of or is likely to come into the possession of the data controller. Every office has a set of telephone directories. A telephone directory is a catalogue of names, addresses and telephone numbers: clearly personal data. If someone in the office holds an address or a telephone number in isolation, it may be a phenomenally difficult task to go through the telephone directory searching for the telephone number or the address to see whose name tallies up with it, but it is possible. Does this mean all email addresses, street addresses and telephone numbers should be regarded as personal information, even if their connection with a living individual cannot immediately be identified? Until *Durant*, the Information Commissioner would have said 'Yes', but the latest guidance on the ICO website is that the relevant consideration is whether there is a system in place that allows the organisation in question to find information, applying a standard search procedure, without searching through every item in a set of information.

Images (photographs and videos) of people are also capable of qualifying as personal data, which means that closed-circuit television systems (CCTV) are essentially personal data gathering and storage devices, so organisations employing them have to comply with the provisions of the Data Protection Act. This whole topic is complex and further guidance is available on the Information Commissioner's website, including a helpful flowchart intended to give a structured approach to deciding whether a given category of information constitutes personal data.

Do not fall into the trap of assuming that if you do not keep the information on a computer (or if you do not have a database), the Act does not apply to you. Manual data can be covered by the Data Protection Act and with few exceptions any data held in a 'relevant filing system' are covered by the Act. In a nutshell, if a filing system is any use (i.e. if it is ordered alphabetically by name, or if you can otherwise find information relating to a given individual without a general trawl of the whole system), then it is a 'relevant filing system'. So a filing cabinet containing personnel files ordered alphabetically is a relevant filing system, as is an alphabetical address book.

SENSITIVE PERSONAL DATA

One category of personal data, sensitive personal data, is treated more stringently by the Act. Sensitive personal data consist of information that relates to:

- the racial or ethnic origin of the data subject;
- their political opinions;
- their religious beliefs or other beliefs of a similar nature;
- whether they are a member of a trade union;
- their physical or mental health or condition;
- their sexual life;
- the commission or eventual commission by them of any offence;
- any proceedings for any offence committed or alleged to have been committed by them, the disposal of such proceedings or the sentence of any court in such proceedings.

In general, the data controller has to take particular care when dealing with sensitive personal data. There are obligations under the Act that are more stringent when relating to sensitive personal data, than when they relate to other (non-sensitive) personal data.

WHO NEEDS TO NOTIFY?

Unless a specific exemption applies, it is an offence to process personal data without an appropriate entry in the Information Commissioner's register (called 'notification'). The exemptions include individuals who process personal data for personal, family or household affairs (which also exempts domestic data controllers from most of the other provisions of the Act) and, in the context of business:

- staff administration;
- advertising, marketing and public relations;
- accounts and records.

There are also various exemptions from notification for certain non-profit making organisations, including clubs.

There are two important points:

- Exemption from notification does not (by itself) mean exemption from the other provisions of the Act.
- The exemptions are fairly narrow and it is often difficult to interpret the exemptions and decide whether they specifically apply.

Experience shows that, when most businesses are examined in any detail, they are almost invariably undertaking activities that are outside the scope of the exemptions, so they are required to notify.

There are, in any event, some advantages to notifying voluntarily, even though it will cost you £35 each year (or £500 for large organisations) and take a little bit of administration time. It removes the obligation on the data controller (Section 24 of the Act) to supply, free of charge, to anyone requesting it basically the same information that they would have to supply in the notification. It accordingly makes more sense to compile this information once for notification purposes, rather than having to do it each time somebody makes a request.

Typical examples as to why the exemptions do not go far enough are as follows:

- The administration of company pensions (including stakeholder pensions) will necessarily involve holding personal data and passing it on to pension trustees: something that is not dealt with in the employee administration exemption.
- Employee records will frequently contain information about an employee's next of kin. Our view is that next-of-kin data relates to a living individual other than the employee him or herself, and is accordingly covered by the exemption (there is some guidance from the Information Commissioner that contradicts this, but in the end it is for the courts, not the Information Commissioner, to determine the question).

HOW TO NOTIFY

You can notify on the Information Commissioner's website, by email, by post or by telephone. The information that is required to undertake a notification is:

- the data controller's name and address;
- the name and address of any representative of the data controller;
- a description of the personal data being or to be processed and the category of data subjects to which they relate;
- a description of the purpose of processing;
- a description of any intended recipients of the data;
- a list of any countries outside the European Economic Area (EEA) to which the data may be transferred by the data controller;
- answers to a standard list of questions about data security; and
- a statement (if relevant) of the fact that certain data processed by the data controller are of a type excluded from notification.

You must notify under the correct name of the data controller (e.g. if you are a limited company, the proper company name including 'Limited') as well as any names you trade under. If you are a partnership, you should notify under the partnership's trading names as opposed to the names of the individual partners. If you have more than one company in your group processing data (in practice, this is likely to be all non-dormant companies) then they each have to notify separately. Remember that they may be undertaking different processing, so the notifications may need to be different, and ensure that there is an entry in the notification allowing for the transfer of personal data between companies in the group.

As noted above, the notification form requires you to summarise the steps you have taken to ensure data security. If you have taken measures to guard against unauthorised or unlawful processing of personal data and against accidental loss, destruction or damage, do the methods include:

- adopting an information security policy (i.e. providing clear management direction on responsibilities and procedures in order to safeguard personal data)?
- taking steps to control physical security (e.g. locking doors of the office or building where computer equipment is held)?
- putting in place controls on access to information (e.g. introducing password protection and encryption on files containing personal data)?
- establishing a business continuity plan (e.g. holding a backup file in the event of personal data being lost through flood, fire or other catastrophe)?
- training your staff on security systems and procedures?
- detecting and investigating breaches of security when they occur?
- adopting the relevant international information security standards from the ISO/IEC 27000-series? (These standards are not a statutory requirement but a business-led approach to best practice on information security management.)

The Commissioner has made it easy to notify by drawing up a set of templates for a number of different types of business that contain the elements of notification most likely to apply to that business. These are available on the Commissioner's website and are by far the simplest way to commence a notification. Be careful, however, because they are not comprehensive and it is unlikely that any specific business fits precisely within a template. They are very useful as a guide but do not use them without thinking through the issues and, especially, about whether there are other areas not contained within the template that need to be covered. For example, none of the templates contains a notification relating to the issue of personal data to potential investors or successor businesses of a data controller. In practice, many businesses are in the market for acquisition or wish to raise finance; as part of that process they will have to undergo due diligence. This due diligence will almost certainly result in personal data being made available to a potential successor business or investor but, in the absence of a specific notification permitting that disclosure, it would be a criminal offence to release the information to them. The Information Commissioner's office has suggested that data provided in due diligence can be made anonymous but, in the context of most small- to medium-sized businesses, this would not be feasible. As a result, it is important to think through the processes involved in your business and potential business developments to determine the scope of an appropriate notification.

Many businesses make the mistake of thinking that once they have notified, they can go ahead and process data in whatever way they like. Notification is just the first step. Businesses still have to comply with the data protection principles in relation to the data that they hold, process and disclose, and, in particular, this may mean that they may need to obtain the consent of the data subjects before undertaking that processing.

You are required to renew your notification annually and if the nature of the business changes in such a way as to necessitate changes to your notification, you are under an obligation to notify the Information Commissioner of those changes.

Although in practice many businesses change their notifications, if necessary, at the time of annual renewal, there is an obligation to update as and when the change happens, so businesses that wait until annual renewal to do this will technically be in breach during the intervening period.

THE PRINCIPLES OF DATA PROTECTION

Personal data must be:

- fairly and lawfully processed;
- processed for limited purposes;
- adequate, relevant and not excessive;
- accurate;

- not kept longer than necessary;

- processed in accordance with the data subject's rights;

- secure;

- not transferred to countries without adequate protection.

The full text of the principles is set out in Schedule 1 to the Act, together with some additional interpretation.

DATA PROTECTION PRINCIPLES

Fair and lawful processing

'Processing' includes almost any activity involving data: obtaining them, possessing them, retrieving them, analysing them, performing actions on them and disclosing them. That means that for the processing to be lawful, the data must have been obtained fairly and lawfully in the first place. Where you are obtaining the data from the data subject him or herself, you must ensure that the data are obtained fairly (i.e. you disclose who you are, why you need the data, and what you are going to do with them). If you are obtaining data from a third party, things are more complicated.

When you obtain data from a person other than the data subject, there are essentially two scenarios. Either you have obtained the information from a person providing information about someone else (e.g. an airline obtains personal data about a passenger from the travel agent booking the ticket) or you have obtained the information from a third-party database (e.g. a mailing list broker).

In each case, you must (so far as is practicable) as soon as possible after obtaining the data, provide the data subject in question with certain details (i.e. who you are, why you have the data, and what you are going to do with them). 'So far as is practicable' are the words used in the legislation and there is as yet no guidance from the courts as to how that will be interpreted.

In practical terms, though, this means that if you are harvesting data from individuals, you should always ask them whether they are the data subject in question (e.g. if your call centre takes calls from customers over the phone and a caller gives a credit card in the name of Annabel Smith, you should ask the caller if they are Annabel Smith, and challenge them if they appear to have a male voice or sound too young to have a credit card; but this is good security practice anyway). If the person providing the data turns out not to be the data subject, you should ensure that you provide the actual data subject with the necessary information.

If you get the data from a mailing list, you will need to satisfy yourself that the list broker obtained the data fairly and lawfully, that it can lawfully pass the data on to you and that you can lawfully use the data you obtain for the purposes you want to use them for. If the list broker did not obtain the data fairly and lawfully, you cannot make use of them without breaching the Act, so you need to be absolutely sure that you can use the list and build strong protection (e.g. indemnity clauses) protecting you against any claims that the list cannot be used lawfully.

You should ask the list broker some difficult questions about how they obtained the data:

- Did you obtain the data yourself or from a third party?
- Do you know that the data subjects themselves provided you with the data and not someone on their behalf?
- Do you have the consent of the data subjects to release their details to me? How was that consent obtained? Were any of the consents given by minors? (Particular issues arise in relation to the protection of children's data; the ICO has guidance on its website.)
- Do you have the consent of the data subjects to use their names for the purposes I am contemplating?
- How do you handle updates and corrections to the list? Can I have access to your updates and corrections for the period of the list hire?
- How do you handle requests from the data subjects for their names not to be used for marketing purposes?

Any reputable list-broking firm should be able to provide answers to these questions to your satisfaction.

Schedule 2 of the Act describes a number of circumstances under which the processing of data may be considered fair even though the express consent of the data subject has not been obtained. These include processing where necessary in connection with a performance of a contract to which the data subject is a party, or where it is necessary to comply with a legal obligation (other than one imposed by contract).

These Schedule 2 conditions may enable processing to be carried out without express consent, but they should generally be approached with caution, and, as a general rule, consent is always preferable.

Processing for limited purposes

Data should be processed only for the purposes that you have notified the Information Commissioner and, where you need consent for processing, only for the purposes for which you have consent. For example, if you have obtained data from customers for billing purposes, you must not, in the absence of consent from those customers, use the data for marketing to them. It is accordingly important, when you are harvesting data, to convey to data subjects the purposes for which you want the data, and to obtain their consent to the use of the data for those purposes.

When is consent not consent?

One of the characteristics that makes processing 'fair' is that you have the data subject's consent to the processing. Where the data involved are 'sensitive personal data' then the Act says that 'explicit consent' is required. This means that the data subject must agree, in some unequivocal way, to the processing taking place and, logically, that they are fully informed as to what they are consenting to.

In other words, the data subject must be made aware of the purposes for which their sensitive personal data are to be processed; and must indicate that they give their consent. The consent can be in writing, or spoken, or even a tick in a box. However, giving the data subject the right to opt out (as opposed to opting in) in these circumstances is not sufficient. For example, a box saying 'tick here if you do **not** want your sensitive personal data processed for marketing purposes' would not be sufficient to ensure that the processing was fair.

Express consent is required for the processing of sensitive personal data, so lawyers generally assume that for other, 'non-sensitive' personal data, the consent required does not need to be explicit, and accordingly can be implicit. What is implied consent? If someone leaves their name and address details after telephoning a 'catalogue order line' voicemail, then clearly they have implied consent to use their address details to send them a catalogue. It is questionable whether they have implied consent to anything else done with those data, however.

It is arguable, but it is probably implied consent if a data subject fails to tick the box on a reply form that says 'tick here if you do **not** want us to make your details available to other companies for marketing purposes'. In other words, for non-sensitive data, opt-outs are (probably) permissible. Specific opt-ins are invariably the safer approach, though, from the legal point of view.

The question of whether implied consent has been given will depend in each case on the circumstances. Another consideration is that in addition to data protection law, separate legislation applies to restrict unsolicited electronic communications (email, phone, SMS etc.), as explained below.

Adequate, relevant and not excessive

This principle is self-explanatory. You must obtain the appropriate data you need to carry out your job properly (e.g. as a credit reference agency you would need to ensure that you have adequate data about a data subject to be able to make a decision about their creditworthiness). You must only collect relevant data (it is not necessary, for example, to collect data on the inside leg measurement of your customer if you are in the business of pizza delivery). However, it is very easy for you (or your web designers) to ask irrelevant questions when harvesting data from websites, for example.

Think whether it is necessary for you to know the age, gender or marital status of your customers. In many cases, the answer will be 'yes', but at least give the data subjects a chance to opt out of providing that information; organisations commonly mark 'essential' information with an asterisk. In practice, so long as the data you hold is relevant, then it is difficult to see how it would be 'excessive'.

Accurate

Keeping your data accurate makes good business sense. The amount of effort you invest in keeping your data accurate should be balanced against both the importance to you of keeping your data accurate and the potential harm that the data subject could suffer. For example, if you hold medical records, an incorrect reference that the data subject is not allergic to penicillin could clearly be disastrous. Likewise, if you are a credit reference agency holding incorrect data showing a data subject to be an undischarged bankrupt, you could be liable for damages to the data subject for any loss or distress caused by a bad credit rating. If, however, you are the proprietor of a pop singer's website, then you may be able to argue that the data subject's favourite colour needs somewhat less care. In practical terms, the data most companies will think about in the context of data protection are marketing and contact data and employment records; in both cases, it is sensible to have a regular review of the data you hold to ensure that it is kept up to date and accurate. In this respect, as with most issues relating to data protection, making a serious effort to comply with the Act is likely to count for a lot with the Commissioner, even if technically your organisation may not strictly be complying with the law.

The Commissioner is likely to be less sympathetic to data subjects' claims that your data was inaccurate if you make it easy for data subjects to correct any errors: for example, providing a page on the website for reviewing and amending details, or sending out an update form with the data subject's details and inviting them to amend any errors. In the latter case, do not be tempted (as several financial institutions have done recently) to send out a letter along the lines of 'We know you have opted out of marketing so we are writing to ensure that we are holding accurate details about you and to remind you of what wonderful services we can offer you'.

THE RIGHT TO OPT OUT OF MARKETING

The Act provides that data subjects can opt out of the use of their details for direct marketing purposes. In practical terms, you should ensure that you have a mechanism available to log any objections by data subjects to the use of their data for direct marketing purposes and either delete their names from your database or, if you need to keep the data for other purposes, make sure you have a flag on the database that marks those records that must not be used for direct marketing. There is also an argument that you should maintain a database of people who have objected to direct marketing, so that you can cross-check it against any data you obtain subsequently, to ensure that you do not start processing a data subject's details for direct marketing after they have sent you a notice requiring you to stop (and you have removed their name from the main database).

There are a number of stop lists (such as the Mailing Preference Service) to which data subjects may submit their names. Companies may obtain copies of these lists by signing up with the appropriate bodies and use them to purge their databases of the details of people who do not want the data used for direct marketing purposes. The Mailing Preference Service is a voluntary (i.e. non-statutory and non-compulsory) scheme, but good business sense suggests using such a service (on the basis that sending direct mail to someone who has subscribed to the list will be a waste of a stamp and may lead to a vocal opponent of your company). The service has been available since 1983, well before the advent of any data protection legislation in the UK. The Direct Marketing Association (DMA), which runs the Mailing Preference Service, also runs the Fax Preference Service and the Telephone Preference Service.

These last two schemes are statutory and operate under the Privacy and Electronic Communications (EC Directive) Regulations 2003. Prior to undertaking any unsolicited telephone marketing (or fax shots), you must remove from your target list any names that appear on the appropriate stop lists maintained by the DMA or be at risk of committing a criminal offence. Copies of the lists are obtainable from the DMA (a fee is payable). Note that it is illegal to contact private individuals by fax for direct marketing purposes without their consent, irrespective of whether they are on the stop list.

The 2003 regulations also limit the use of unsolicited text messages or emails. If you propose to send commercial text or email messages to an individual subscriber (including a partnership), you need to ensure either that you have a pre-existing business relationship with them (i.e. you are responding to an enquiry or you have supplied them with similar goods or services to the ones about which you are emailing) or that they have expressly consented (i.e. opted in) to receiving marketing information from you. Unsolicited commercial emails should always be clearly identified as such and should allow the recipient an easy way to opt out of receiving them (i.e. an effective 'unsubscribe' option).

It is also worth bearing in mind the Code of Advertising Practice (CAP), which makes it a necessity for corporate bodies, as well as individuals, to opt in to receiving unsolicited commercial emails. Although not legally binding, failure to comply with the CAP can lead to a business being blacklisted and accordingly unable to advertise in participating media. Taking this into account together with the difficulty in determining whether a 'subscriber' is an individual, a partnership or a company, many commentators are saying that the best advice is only to send unsolicited commercial emails where there is a positive opt-in, irrespective of whether the recipient is a company, a partnership or an individual.

The 2003 regulations also regulate the use of cookies. A cookie is a small piece of data that is stored on a user's computer at the request of the web server hosting a website that the user is viewing. They are designed to have a benign purpose: to enable the web server to retrieve the state of the website when the user last visited, for example. They are often used to store shopping carts, details about favourite items and to enable a web server to identify who a particular user is without them having to log in. Used in this way, they improve the user experience significantly. However, they can also be used to track a user's movements around the site and to gather various other pieces of information. The 2003 regulations require a website to alert the user to the use of cookies and to allow the user to disable them.

A recent European Directive means that as of 26 May 2011, cookies must only be used where the user has given consent, having been provided with clear and comprehensive consent about the use of the cookies (which logically can only mean 'prior consent'. Current standard practice is for websites to advise users of the use of cookies only in the websites' privacy policies, which most users don't read, and which in any case they won't have had an opportunity to read until after the cookies have already been downloaded. The new law will make this practice unlawful. At the time of writing, the Information Commissioner's Office has indicated that it will enforce with a light touch for an initial period. The explosion in the use of behavioural advertising, which uses information gathered by cookies to display 'personalised' (i.e. focused) ads to web users, means this topic is likely to receive a great deal more attention before the new provision comes into force.

Not kept longer than necessary

This heading is, at first sight, self-explanatory, but it raises some difficulties. Your auditors will no doubt insist that you keep financial data for at least seven years (and it is an obligation under the self-assessment tax regime to do so). However, this is likely to include personal data. The Information Commissioner may argue that you should make the data anonymous, to the extent that you can without breaching the requirements of your auditors and HMRC, but in practice that is likely to be impossible. You may also want to keep other data for at least six years in case of legal action (the 'statute of limitations' generally allows you to sue and be sued up to six years from the event complained of), indeed your insurers may place an obligation like this on you. The breadth of these requirements means that, as a data controller, you need to ensure that your notification covers all the purposes for which you may need to retain data, and that you maintain a constant review of the data you hold to ensure that you delete any data that are no longer required.

This poses a special problem so far as backups are concerned: many companies will have a dusty cupboard containing backup tapes, possibly in an old format that the company no longer has the equipment available to read. These may contain data that are covered by the Act, and that accordingly should be kept accurate and deleted once no longer required. Many companies will take the view that as the Commissioner's primary role is to ensure that the data subjects are not harmed by the misuse of personal data, so long as the tapes are kept securely and the data on them is not merged with any live data without scrupulous checks, and any relevant guidance on the ICO website has been taken into account, the Commissioner is likely to conclude that the Data Protection principles are being adhered to, and will not seek to take enforcement action.

Processed in accordance with the data subject's rights

Personal data must not be processed:

- if the data controller has not complied with the data subject's rights of access to personal data;
- if the data subject has objected to processing on the grounds that to carry on with the processing would cause damage or distress;

- if the data subject has objected to direct marketing;
- if the data controller is in breach of the provisions of the Act that allow the data subject to object to automated decision-taking.

Secure

Personal data must be kept secure and protected from unauthorised access. This means that the data controller must not only take technical measures (like using password protected access), but also ensure that only suitable staff have access to it. The extent of the steps to be taken depends on the type of data and the likelihood of harm that may result (presumably to the data subject) from a security breach. What the appropriate technical measures are will change over time as technology and best practice change. For example, the Commissioner is likely to take the view that encryption should now be used wherever practical, and indeed has issued guidance to the effect that enforcement action is likely to be taken against organisations where laptops and other mobile devices containing personal data are stolen, and encryption has not been used.

You would be wise to put measures such as the following in place:

- Ensuring that all personal data is encrypted wherever practical, especially data on mobile devices such as laptops, memory sticks and smart phones.
- Limiting access to data through appropriate passwords etc.
- Limiting physical access to the disks and tapes on which the data is held.
- Vetting staff who have access to the data.
- Providing training in data security to staff who have access to the data.
- Keeping backups of data to ensure it can be restored in case of loss or error.
- Observing appropriate identification procedures to ensure that personal data are only disclosed to the appropriate people (e.g. giving the data subjects a password or pass phrase to verify their identity).
- Cross-checking the data to ensure accuracy (e.g. removing multiple entries, checking addresses against postcode databases, and analysing the data to throw out badly formed telephone numbers).
- Having procedures in place to ensure that data are erased once they are no longer required.
- Having a procedure to ensure regular updating of data (e.g. telephoning data subjects on a rolling cycle to check their data are being kept up to date).
- Reviewing on a regular basis all of the procedures in relation to the above to make sure they are still valid.

As part of the notification process, you are required to submit a brief statement of the steps you intend to take to comply with this principle. A good way to comply with both this requirement and the general obligation of this principle, is to perform a risk assessment relating to the data and to modify internal processes accordingly.

The Information Commissioner has stated that compliance with the International Standard 27001 provides a suitable benchmark for compliance. However, this is a very comprehensive standard and it is not necessary to be fully compliant with it in order to comply with this principle. More information can be obtained from the International Organization for Standardization.

'Proportionality' is a buzzword currently used a lot in the regulatory context: it simply means that the steps taken should be adequate but not excessive in relation to the likely harm that could be suffered arising from a breach. Clearly, an organisation holding health records would have to take significantly greater security measures than an organisation holding a mailing list of email addresses of people interested in gardening, for example.

Where you appoint a third party to undertake data processing for you (e.g. a payroll bureau), you must take steps to ensure that they comply with similar obligations in relation to data security, and you are required to have a written contract with them that imposes these obligations. Make sure you understand what practical measures the third party will take to safeguard information.

Again, showing that care has been taken in these matters is likely to count a lot if the ICO ever has cause to look into your organisation's data protection compliance.

Not transferred to countries without adequate protection

It is unlawful to pass personal data to any country that does not have adequate protection for data subjects. This is a contentious and difficult topic, but the major points are as follows.

- All EEA countries are deemed to have adequate protection. When new countries join the EU, it will become lawful to transmit data to those countries.

- The USA does not have adequate protection. However, the US Department of Commerce, in conjunction with the European Commission (EC), has set up a scheme called Safe Harbor (2000) that allows US businesses to sign up to a set of principles roughly equivalent to those in the Data Protection Act and that accordingly makes transfers of data to those companies legitimate. A full list of these companies can be found on the US Department of Commerce website.

- The EC periodically makes decisions that various territories do have adequate levels of protection and that data can be passed there freely. At the time of writing, only Argentina, Canada, Guernsey, Isle of Man, Jersey, Switzerland, Israel, Andorra and the Faroe Islands are deemed to have adequate levels of protection.

- Irrespective of whether the country in question has an adequate level of protection, the data subject can give consent to the transfer and the transfer may comply with certain other criteria (which can be found in Schedule 4 to the Act).

- The EU has produced model contracts that, in effect, impose obligations on recipients of personal data in countries outside the EU equivalent to those that exist in the EU. If an EU data controller enters into this model contract with a recipient outside the EU, then data transfer becomes legitimate. (There are separate model contracts for data controller to data controller transfers and data controller to data processor transfers).

- Transit of data through a country is not the same as transfer to a country. Internet traffic may pass through the USA, for example, en route from the United Kingdom to Germany but this does not amount to a transfer within the meaning of the Act. The best view is probably that if anything amounting to 'processing' goes on in a country, then there is a transfer to that country, but otherwise the data is just in transit and there is no breach of this principle.

RIGHTS OF DATA SUBJECTS

In brief, data subjects have the right to have their data processed only in accordance with the data protection principles set out above, and:

- to receive information about the identity of the person processing their data, the purposes of the processing and any other relevant details (including details of the source, or classes of source, of the data and the persons, or classes of persons, to whom such data may be disclosed);

- to receive a copy of the data that a data controller may hold on them;

- to object to automated decision-taking (the aim being to protect data subjects against processes such as automated credit-scoring, so data subjects can require that a human being is actively involved in the decision-making process);

- to prevent their details being used for direct marketing purposes;

- to prevent processing likely to cause damage or distress;

- to have inaccurate data corrected or erased;

- to receive compensation for breaches of the Act;

- to have the Commissioner consider a request for assessment where the data subject believes that the data controller may not be carrying out processing in accordance with the Act.

The right to receive information about the data processor

For processing to be fair, the data controller must provide information about who is processing the data and why they are processing it. They must also provide any other information that may in the circumstances be required to make the processing fair. This is why every company website should have a privacy policy setting out this information (almost any company website will involve an invitation to provide personal data to the company, even if it only consists of an email address for enquiries). The right to receive a copy of the data that the data controller holds is subject to a £10 maximum fee.

Complying with data subject access requests

You are obliged to provide a data subject with details of the data you hold on them. You should consider the following questions:

- Have they paid you a fee? You can set a fee for this, up to a maximum of £10.

- Is this their first request or have they requested before? If they have requested before, you are allowed to refuse a subsequent request before a 'reasonable interval' has elapsed (there is no guidance on what this means).

- Have they provided you with information about the data they are looking for? A request cannot be a fishing expedition through all of the data that you hold: you are entitled to be told what sort of data the subject is looking for, for example, mailing databases, accounts details, personnel records.

- Have they provided you with enough information so that you can be sure they are who they say they are (e.g. copy of driving licence and utility bill)?

- Is there any other exemption relating to the data or the application?

Once you are satisfied with the answers to those questions, you can proceed to collate the information, bearing in mind that:

- you must withhold or make anonymous information that identifies another data subject, unless you have that data subject's consent.

  For example, if an employee asks for details of complaints about them, releasing the complaints may identify the complainants, in which case the data cannot generally be disclosed without the complainant's consent. Simply removing the complainant's name may not be sufficient because the data subject may still be able to identify the complainant from the other contents of the complaint. In this case, you should decline the request, giving reasons. However, you can not use this as a blanket excuse to refuse disclosure because you are under a positive obligation to try to make the data available to the requesting data subject if you can.

  Make sure a copy of your reasoning is retained, in case you are required to justify your decision to the Commissioner or the Court. The question of disclosure is tricky and you should take expert advice in all but the most clear-cut cases.

- the time limit for compliance with the request is 40 days from the day you receive the request, the day you get the fee or the day you get the information containing details of the data subject's identity, whichever is the latest.

- the data provided to the data subject should be in a clear format that can be read by the human eye.

EXEMPTIONS

The Data Protection Act is a complex piece of legislation with many exemptions from its main rules depending on the circumstances. In the main, the exemptions are:

- from notification (as discussed in the section on notification, above);

- from providing information to the data subject about who you are and the reasons for processing their data (the 'Subject Information Provisions'); and

- from providing the data subject with copies of the information you hold about them (the 'Subject Access Provisions').

There is not scope in this book to go into the exemptions in any detail.

By way of example, there are general exemptions from the provisions of the Act in relation to national security, detection and prosecution of crime, giving and receiving legal advice, domestic purposes and journalism, literature and art.

More specific exemptions apply in certain circumstances, such as where disclosing the information would affect the value of a company's stock or where there are ongoing negotiations affecting the data subject (the aim being that a canny data subject should not be able to use the Data Protection Act to find out what pay award his employer is thinking of giving him). Establishing whether a particular exemption applies is far from straightforward, and although initial guidance can be found on the Information Commissioner's website, it is wise to take specialist advice before relying on any apparent exemption.

PENALTIES AND ENFORCEMENT

The Information Commissioner has the primary responsibility for enforcing the Act (or taking 'regulatory action', to use the appropriate ICO jargon). Since 6 April 2010, the Commissioner has had the power to fine organisations that breach data protection laws up to £500,000. Guidance on the ICO website states that a 'monetary penalty notice' may be handed out if a data controller has seriously contravened the data protection principles and the contravention was of a kind likely to cause substantial damage or substantial distress, but only where the contravention was either deliberate or the data controller knew or ought to have known that there was a risk that a contravention would occur, and failed to take reasonable steps to prevent it. At the time of writing, these powers have only recently come into force, so it is unclear how they will be used, but it seems likely that it will not be long before the Commissioner flexes these new muscles to impose a major fine on an organisation that commits a particularly flagrant (or well-publicised) breach. The guidance the Commissioner has released on the proposed use of fines makes it clear that an important part of their purpose is as a deterrent. Among the examples given in the guidance of the kinds of breach that are likely to be considered serious enough to warrant a fine are failures that result in the loss of unencrypted data (the 'laptop in the back of a taxi' type incident), or particularly sensitive data such as medical records.

The primary mechanism of enforcement, however, is likely to remain by means of an Enforcement Notice. When the Information Commissioner believes that a data controller is contravening the Act, he may issue an Enforcement Notice that sets out steps that the data controller must take to bring the processing within the law. Failure to comply with it is a criminal offence (and managers and directors of an infringing company will also be liable). There are some other criminal offences contained in the Act:

- Unlawful obtaining or disclosing of personal data.
- Selling or offering to sell unlawfully-obtained personal data.
- Enforced subject access. (This probably needs a little more explanation: it used to be a frequent practice for employers to require prospective employees to obtain a copy of their criminal record from the police prior to offering them employment. Clearly, the employer could not obtain this information directly but the employee could. It is now a criminal offence to require someone else to obtain personal data about themselves in connection with that person's work.)

There are also some administrative offences that make it a crime to interfere with the work of the Information Commissioner or the administration or enforcement of the Act. It is, as one might expect, a crime to fail to notify, to provide false statements to the Information Commissioner, to fail to notify him of any changes to a notification and to fail to cooperate with him in certain circumstances.

REFERENCES

European Commission (1995) *Directive 95/46/EC, Article 25(6)*.

European Commission Model Contracts available at http://ec.europa.eu/

Information Commissioner's website: www.ico.gov.uk

Specifically on what constitutes 'personal data', see
http://www.ico.gov.uk/upload/documents/library/data_protection/detailed_specialist_guides/what_is_data_for_the_purposes_of_the_dpa.pdf

and for enforcement and monetary penalties, see:
http://www.ico.gov.uk/upload/documents/library/data_protection/detailed_specialist_guides/data_protection_regulatory_action_policy.pdf

http://www.ico.gov.uk/upload/documents/library/data_protection/detailed_specialist_guides/ico_guidance_monetary_penalties.pdf

and on notification, see:
http://www.ico.gov.uk/what_we_cover/data_protection/notification.aspx

US Department of Commerce *Safe Harbor*:
http://www.export.gov/safeharbor/

8   DOING BUSINESS ONLINE

Jeremy Newton

The rapidly-changing world of electronic commerce continues to throw up new challenges for law-makers, for businesses, and for the lawyers who advise them. This chapter does not aim to discuss all the legal initiatives in depth, but it outlines the principal areas of legal compliance about which IT managers ought to know.

INTRODUCTION

The UK's first conference on internet law took place in 1995, when businesses were starting to get to grips with the legal issues of doing business electronically. A frequent comment at that point was that the internet was lawless: a kind of 'electronic frontier', where wrongdoers were protected both by the anonymity of cyberspace and the complexities of seeking legal remedies internationally. Early commentators took the view that the law would be hard-pushed to keep up with the development of ecommerce and the new challenges to which it gave rise.

Since then, electronic commerce has entered the mainstream of business, government and personal life to an extent that even the most ardent technophile could hardly have anticipated. In the UK, 71 per cent of retailers now use ecommerce and the internet as a channel to reach their customers, according to an Office of Fair Trading (OFT) press release in July 2010. The very term 'ecommerce' looks almost archaic: few people draw much of a distinction now between 'bricks' and 'clicks'.

Law-makers around the world have endeavoured strenuously to keep pace with the rapid developments in this field. In Europe, the broad legal and institutional framework for electronic commerce was largely in place by 2000. Ten years later, the massive growth of social networking websites, the commercial use of auction websites and technology, and the explosion of digital downloading are throwing up new challenges to conventional concepts of contract, copyright and privacy.

Against that background, this chapter will outline the following aspects of doing business electronically:

- The information to be made available to clients;
- The rules about forming contracts electronically (e.g. by email or via a website);
- The regulations about the client's rights of cancellation;
- The determination of the applicable law if the service provider and the client are based in different countries;

- The rules concerning marketing or other commercial communications sent electronically; and

- The implications of non-compliance with UK regulations.

TERMINOLOGY

Information society services: 'Any service normally provided for remuneration, at a distance, by means of electronic equipment for the processing... and storage of data, and at the individual request of a recipient of the service'. This encompasses (amongst other things) advertising and selling goods by email or on websites, as well as network access or hosting activities. The Electronic Commerce Directive (and the Regulations that implement it in the UK) deals generally with the provision of information society services.

Service provider: 'Any person who provides an information society service', for example a company that sells books over the internet.

Service recipients: 'Any person who, for professional ends or otherwise, uses an information society service, in particular for the purposes of seeking information or making it accessible'. This includes both individuals and corporate bodies. By contrast, a **consumer** is 'any natural person who is acting for purposes other than those of his trade, business or profession'. The significance of the distinction is that the law imposes more rigorous requirements on service providers in relation to their dealings with consumers than in relation to dealings with other businesses.

INFORMATION TO BE PROVIDED TO CLIENTS

The starting point for any discussion of the legal aspects of electronic commerce in Europe is the 2000 Electronic Commerce Directive, which originated in the European Commission and was implemented into UK law by the Electronic Commerce (EC Directive) Regulations 2002.

One of the key aims of the Electronic Commerce Directive was to promote trust and confidence in ecommerce. One of the main ways to achieve this is by ensuring greater transparency about the identity of any service provider.

The electronic environment can make it difficult for a client to tell exactly who he is contracting with and where they are established, so the Commission proposed that certain information requirements should be imposed on all ecommerce service providers in order to help promote trust in their identity. The Directive (and the UK Regulations) accordingly set out the information that a service provider must make available to service recipients.

Besides these general information requirements, however, the law imposes an additional set of requirements in relation to consumers entering into 'distance contracts'. These requirements arise mainly under the European Distance Selling Directive 1997 and have been incorporated into English law in the Consumer

Protection (Distance Selling) Regulations 2000. These Regulations are not directed exclusively at information society service providers; they apply equally to businesses selling goods or services to consumers by mail order, telephone or fax.

However, there is a significant area of overlap between the information requirements set out in the Electronic Commerce Regulations and those of the Distance Selling Regulations. For ease of reference, a consolidated checklist of these requirements is set out in the appendix at the end of this chapter. It should be stressed, though, that certain industries may be subject to additional legal requirements or codes of practice about the information that must be provided to clients.

Information requirements under the Electronic Commerce (EC Directive) Regulations 2002

Service providers must make the following information available in a form that is 'easily, directly and permanently accessible' (inclusion of this information on a website should be sufficient to meet this requirement):

- Name of the service provider;
- Geographic address at which the service provider is established;
- Contact details for the service provider (including email address) to enable direct and effective communication;
- Details of any trade or similar register in which the service provider is registered, together with the registration number;
- Details of any supervisory authority, where the provision of the service is subject to an authorisation scheme;
- Details of any professional body with which the service provider is registered and of how the applicable professional conduct rules may be accessed; and
- VAT registration number.

The Regulations also require that any statements as to prices must be 'clear and unambiguous' and, in particular, must indicate whether they are inclusive of tax and delivery costs. Additional information requirements apply where contracts are to be formed electronically.

Additional information requirements under the Consumer Protection (Distance Selling) Regulations 2000

Service providers must make the following information available in good time before the contract is made:

- The identity of the supplier and, where the contract requires payment in advance, the supplier's address;
- A description of the goods or services;
- The price of the goods or services (including all taxes);
- Delivery costs where appropriate;
- Arrangements for payment, delivery and performance;

- The existence of a right of cancellation;
- The costs of using the means of distance communication in question;
- The period for which the offer or price remains valid;
- Where appropriate, the minimum duration of the contract (in cases where the supply of goods or services is to be on a permanent or recurrent basis).

The information must be given in a clear and comprehensible manner, in a form appropriate to the means of distance communications used and with due regard to principles of good faith. The supplier must also inform the consumer if it proposes to provide substitute goods or services if those ordered are unavailable and, if so, that the cost of returning such substitutes will be met by the supplier if the consumer chooses to cancel the contract.

The Distance Selling Regulations go on to stipulate certain additional information that must be supplied either prior to the formation of the contract or, at the latest, by the time that either the goods are delivered or the services are performed. This information has to be provided 'in writing or in another durable medium which is available and accessible to the consumer'.

The general view is that an email containing this information should suffice because the consumer can then decide whether to store the information electronically or to print it. The additional information consists of:

- the identity of the supplier and, where the contract requires payment in advance, the supplier's address;
- a description of the goods or services;
- the price of the goods or services (including all taxes);
- delivery costs where appropriate;
- the arrangements for payment, delivery and performance;
- the existence of a right of cancellation and information about the relevant conditions, procedures and costs associated with cancellation;
- the geographical address of the supplier to which the consumer may address complaints;
- information about any after-sales services and guarantees.

It should be noted that failure to provide this additional information has implications for the enforceability of the contract because the duration of the client's right to cancel a distance contract depends primarily on the date on which this information is provided.

FORMING CONTRACTS ELECTRONICALLY

Legal structure of a binding contract
Under English law, the following elements must be present in order to create a legally binding contract:

- An **offer:** an expression of willingness to enter into a contract on certain terms, made with the intention that a contract will exist once the offer is accepted.

- An **acceptance:** the unqualified assent to the terms of an offer.

- **Consideration:** the element of value that each party gives the other under the contract (e.g. the provision of goods by one party in return for the payment of money by the other).

- An **intention** to create legally binding relations (which the law normally takes for granted in commercial contexts).

This analysis of the elements of offer and acceptance is important for any business that sells its goods or services electronically. The general rule is that a contract is formed when an offer has been accepted. But displaying products and prices in an electronic 'shop window' can amount to a unilateral offer that, if accepted, can create a legally binding obligation on the part of the supplier to fulfil an unlimited number of orders on those terms. There have been numerous illustrations of retailers being caught out by this principle such as the *Hoover Air Miles* debacle in the late 1990s. In the ecommerce space specifically, Argos was an early casualty in 1999, when it suffered some embarrassing adverse publicity after inadvertently advertising £299 television sets on its website at a price of just £2.99, with thousands of orders being placed before the error was noticed. (Argos managed to make a similar mistake a few years later, but many other companies, including Amazon, Kodak and PC World, have experienced similar situations.)

For this reason, it is important to ensure that offerings on a website are structured not as 'offers', but rather as 'invitations to treat'. In other words, the website does nothing more than invite offers from potential clients to purchase at the stated price, with the supplier then free to accept or reject the offer as it sees fit. The website should also state that no contract is formed unless and until the supplier has notified the client that it accepts the order. The risk can also be ameliorated by ensuring that the website terms and conditions include some suitable disclaimer wording, along the following lines:

> 'While we try and ensure that all the prices shown on our website are accurate, errors may occur. If we discover an error in the price of goods you have ordered we will inform you as soon as possible and give you the option of reconfirming your order at the correct price or cancelling it. If we are unable to contact you we will treat the order as cancelled. If you cancel and you have already paid for the goods, you will receive a full refund.'

Other legal formalities

The Electronic Commerce Directive requires all EU member states to ensure that their national law allows contracts to be concluded by electronic means and recognises the legal effectiveness of agreements formed in this way. (This was not really in doubt in the UK, but other member states had to get to grips with new and very different rules about the form of a contract in light of the Directive.)

There are some predictable exceptions to this general rule (e.g. contracts for the sale of land or those governed by family law), but the law is clear that the majority of commercial agreements can now be formed electronically and that electronic contracts should be upheld by the courts.

The Directive (and the UK Regulations) go on to stipulate the information to be provided by service providers where contracts are concluded in this way.

Besides the general information requirements set out above, if a contract is to be concluded by electronic means, the service provider must provide the following additional information in a clear, comprehensible and unambiguous manner before the order is placed by the service recipient:

- The technical steps required to form the contract (e.g. 'Click to confirm order'), so that the service recipient understands at exactly what point in the process he becomes legally committed to the contract.
- The technical means for identifying and correcting input errors prior to placing of the order.
- The languages offered for the conclusion of the contract.
- Any relevant codes of conduct to which the service provider subscribes and how these can be consulted electronically.
- Whether or not the contract will be 'filed' by the service provider (a legal concept that is primarily relevant to non-UK service providers and so is not dealt with further here) and, if so, how it can be accessed.

Orders placed through technological means must generally be acknowledged 'without undue delay' and by electronic means. (The requirements above do not apply, however, where contracts are concluded by the exchange of individual emails.) Any contractual terms and conditions provided by the service provider must also be made available in a manner that enables the service recipient to store and reproduce them.

PERFORMANCE AND CANCELLATION

As a further measure to protect consumers, the Distance Selling Directive required member states to introduce time limits for the performance of contracts by the supplier and to establish a right for the consumer to cancel the distance contract within specified time limits.

With regard to performance, the general rule is that the supplier must perform the contract within 30 days from the day following the date of the client's order (though the parties can agree otherwise). If the supplier cannot perform the contract within that period, it must inform the consumer and reimburse any sum paid, unless the contract provided for the supply of alternative goods or services.

With regard to cancellation, the Distance Selling Regulations contain detailed provisions describing how and when the cancellation right can be invoked and the arrangements for reimbursement and the return of any products supplied. A detailed discussion of these is beyond the scope of this chapter, but the major point to note is in relation to the timing of the cancellation period. The cancellation period begins on the date of the contract and ends on a date determined as follows:

- If the supplier has complied properly with all the 'additional information requirements', the cancellation period ends seven working days after the consumer receives the goods (or after the date of the contract for services).

- If the supplier has not complied with those requirements, but provides the additional information (in writing or another durable medium) within three months of the contract date, the cancellation period ends seven days after the consumer receives the information.

- If neither of the above applies, then the cancellation period ends three months and seven working days after the consumer receives the goods (or the contract for services is concluded).

There are a few predictable exceptions to this cancellation right (e.g. contracts for the supply of goods that are likely to deteriorate rapidly, contracts where the price of the goods is subject to financial fluctuations, contracts for audio or video recordings that have been unsealed, and contracts for newspapers or magazines), but most distance contracts with consumers do now carry this statutory cancellation right. Businesses selling their goods and services electronically must therefore ensure that their staff have a thorough understanding of the cancellation rules and time limits, in order to minimise the risk of legal complaints by dissatisfied clients.

JURISDICTION

Regardless of the legality of an electronic contract, doing business across national boundaries inevitably raises questions as to whose laws apply and in which country one party may sue another. For example, Yahoo! was ordered (by a French court) to block French users from viewing an online auction of Nazi memorabilia. The website in question was hosted in the USA (and Yahoo! is, of course, a US company), but the French court decided that it had jurisdiction to rule on the application of the French law prohibiting the display of Nazi symbols.

Operating as an information society service provider
The law relating to these issues is somewhat convoluted but, in the context of ecommerce, the main rules can be found in the Electronic Commerce Directive and in the UK Electronic Commerce Regulations, which regulate the principles applicable in what is called the 'coordinated field' (i.e. the set of requirements that relate to information society services or service providers, concerning the taking up and pursuit of the activity of an information society service, for example requirements relating to the process of forming a contract electronically).

Under the Regulations, service providers established in the UK, whether they are selling only into the UK or also overseas, must comply with any requirements within the coordinated field. UK enforcement authorities (like the Director-General of Fair Trading) are responsible for ensuring compliance by UK service providers but have no such responsibility with regard to service providers in other member states. By the same token, the equivalent legislation in other member states means that their national enforcement authorities can take action against businesses established in their respective countries in relation to the coordinated field, but not against UK businesses. This has become commonly known as the 'Country of Origin Principle' or 'Home State Regulation'.

It is important to understand the limits of this country of origin principle. It does not mean that a UK service provider is under no obligation to comply with non-UK laws. The coordinated field does not include, for example, requirements applicable to goods, so suppliers still have to be sensitive to differing national rules about quality, labelling and promotional arrangements.

The Regulations are also stated not to apply to matters such as data protection, competition law, gambling and taxation.

For companies looking to sell goods or services into non-UK markets, then, it remains as important as ever to understand the legal requirements of those overseas jurisdictions about the particular products on offer and the manner in which transactions are handled.

Consumer contracts

In terms of jurisdiction (i.e. which courts can hear a dispute), the Brussels Regulation that came into force in March 2002 provides that, in the event of a dispute based on a contract between an EU supplier and an EU consumer, the consumer will generally be able to go to his own courts to sue the supplier; or, to put it another way, the business 'plays away' in most cases. Any judgment given by the consumer's 'home' court would be enforceable through the courts in the supplier's jurisdiction. The other side of that coin is that a business that wants to sue a consumer also needs to do so in the consumer's own state.

(A few non-EU countries (Iceland, Lichtenstein, Norway and Switzerland) are also covered by the Regulation and Denmark, an EU member, opted out of the Regulation.)

A website is only caught by the Regulation if it is 'directing' its activities at the relevant states. There is little legal guidance on what that actually means, but a site is likely to be covered if it fulfils orders to consumers in a particular state or uses a particular state's language or currency for promoting its products.

The problem this poses for businesses is how to protect themselves against being sued in all the different territories. Businesses dealing in consumer products or services should include terms on the website clearly indicating their target markets and should ideally block orders from purchasers with a physical delivery address in other states.

Business-to-business contracts

Different rules apply in relation to business-to-business contracts, where the parties can generally exclude the operation of overseas laws and jurisdiction by clearly making the contract subject to the jurisdiction of the English courts.

MARKETING COMMUNICATIONS

The Electronic Commerce Directive (and the UK Electronic Commerce Regulations) set out strict rules as to how businesses go about marketing themselves electronically. These rules apply to a broad category of 'commercial communications' (practically any communication, in any form, designed to promote the goods, services or image of a business).

It is the responsibility of the service provider to ensure that any commercial communication provided by him in connection with an information society service:

- is clearly identifiable as a commercial communication;
- clearly identifies the person on whose behalf the commercial communication is made;
- clearly identifies as such any promotional offers or competitions, together with any related conditions.

The Regulations also set out special rules for unsolicited commercial communications sent by email (i.e. spam). These must be 'clearly and unambiguously identifiable as such as soon as they are received': the rationale being to give the recipient the opportunity to delete them immediately without troubling to open them.

The rules for dealing with spam are now contained mainly in the Privacy and Electronic Communications Regulations 2003. Under these Regulations, businesses must generally have the prior consent of the recipient before sending unsolicited commercial email to individual subscribers.

(Note that this requirement applies equally to text (SMS) messages as to email, which raises the question how a supplier can provide all the required information within the limit of 160 characters. At the time the Regulations were passed, the Department of Trade and Industry (DTI) guidance acknowledged this technological constraint, but concluded that the information requirements would be sufficiently met if the SMS message include the URL of a website where more information can be obtained.)

Companies should consult regularly and respect opt-out registers (e.g. the Email Preference Service) before sending unsolicited commercial communications.

CONSEQUENCES OF NON-COMPLIANCE

The consequences of non-compliance with the Electronic Commerce Regulations and the Distance Selling Regulations can be serious. The implications of non-compliance with the information requirements in the Distance Selling Regulations, in terms of a consumer's rights to cancel the contract, have been outlined above.

The consumer protection aspects of the Distance Selling Regulations and the Electronic Commerce Regulations are also enforceable by authorities such as the Office of Fair Trading or local trading standards offices, who can apply for an enforcement order (also known as a 'Stop Now Order') from the courts, requiring the service provider to cease any breach of the Regulations that harms the collective interest of consumers. Failure to comply with a Stop Now Order can ultimately result in a fine or imprisonment.

Leaving aside consumer protection specifically, the Electronic Commerce Regulations also provide:

- that the service provider's duties with regard to the information requirements and the provisions about commercial communications are enforceable by clients by means of an action for damages for breach of statutory duty;
- that failure to provide a copy of contract terms and conditions may give rise to the client seeking a court order requiring the service provider to comply; and
- that failure to provide the means for a client to identify and correct input errors at the time of placing an order results in the client having the unilateral right to rescind the contract.

OTHER CONSIDERATIONS

The law relating to ecommerce and doing business online continues to change, rapidly and dramatically. This chapter has discussed the rules that are likely to be relevant to businesses generally in their dealings with consumers, but has not endeavoured to address any of the issues specific to individual sectors (e.g. there are completely separate regulations on the distance marketing of financial services) or to businesses operating as intermediary service providers or ISPs (the Electronic Commerce Directive deals at length with the liabilities of ISPs in respect of content that they 'host' or 'cache' or for which they are otherwise a conduit). Nor has it touched on some of the more advanced considerations for the service provider, such as the use of electronic signatures.

However, there are numerous other sources of information for any company seeking to establish online operations:

- The Department for Business Innovation and Skills (BIS) provides guidance about distance selling and ecommerce, and its website includes links to the UK Regulations: see http://www.bis.gov.uk/files/file14635.pdf
- The Office of Fair Trading (OFT) website includes information for businesses about consumer protection, including a guide to distance selling: see http://www.oft.gov.uk/shared_oft/business_leaflets/general/oft698.pdf
- The Office of the Information Commissioner provides guidance about the collection and use of client data in the context of ecommerce operations, including a guide on the application of the rules concerning email and SMS marketing: see http://www.ico.gov.uk/for_organisations/privacy_and_electronic_communications_guide.aspx

APPENDIX: CONSOLIDATED INFORMATION REQUIREMENTS

Information to be provided by all service providers

- Name and geographic address;
- Contact details for the service provider (including email) to enable direct and effective communication;
- Details of any trade or similar register in which the service provider is registered, together with the registration number;
- Details of any supervisory authority, where the provision of the service is subject to an authorisation scheme;
- Details of any professional body with which the service provider is registered and of how the applicable professional conduct rules may be accessed;
- VAT registration number.

Note that all price indications must be 'clear and unambiguous' and must indicate whether they are inclusive of tax and delivery costs.

Additional pre-contract information to be provided to consumers

- Description of the goods or services;
- Arrangements for payment, delivery and performance;
- Existence of a right of cancellation;
- Costs (if any) of using the means of distance communication;
- Period for which the offer or price remains valid;
- Where appropriate, the minimum duration of the contract (in cases where the supply of goods or services is to be on a permanent or recurrent basis);
- Whether the supplier proposes to provide substitute goods or services (if those ordered are unavailable) and, if so, that the cost of returning such substitutes will be met by the supplier if the consumer chooses to cancel the contract.

Additional post-contract information to be provided to consumers

- The existence of a right of cancellation;
- Information about the relevant conditions, procedures and costs associated with cancellation;
- The geographical address of the supplier to which the consumer may address complaints;
- Information about any after-sales services and guarantees.

9 SETTING UP JOINT VENTURES

Andrew Katz

A joint venture is an increasingly popular way of doing business, especially in the high-tech arena. This chapter discusses the issues that you should consider when embarking upon a joint venture.

INTRODUCTION

A 'joint venture' is not a fixed legal term: it covers a multitude of different business structures, from straightforward channel-to-market arrangements (like agency and distribution) to collaborative partnerships between two or more parties, which may include the formation of a new business, complete with its own staff, premises, branding, products, supply chain etc.

What all joint ventures have in common is that each party believes it is offering something complementary to the other party (or parties). In combination, the joint venture is greater than the contributions of the individual parties.

Most joint ventures also have an element of sharing risk as well as sharing the reward (something that brings its own legal problems).

Perhaps the biggest mistake the joint venture parties can make is to concentrate on the mechanism of setting up the joint venture, without giving sufficient thought both to how the joint venture is to be run on a day-to-day basis and to how the parties are to exit from the arrangement. In terms of day-to-day management, the question is really one of managing expectations. Most joint venture documents give extensive thought to the amount of financial commitment that each partner will put into the project. Fewer, however, take time to think in terms of the non-financial input, particularly manpower. Even fewer joint venture documents adequately address the question of exit. Is one joint venture partner to be given an option to purchase the other? Is the entire joint venture to be sold as a going concern (and, if so, will it still require any input from the former partners)? The parties need to address those questions to maximise the success of a joint venture.

JOINT VENTURES AND IT PROJECTS

Perhaps the most compelling reason why joint ventures have been popular in the technology market is that they are perceived to be a quick way of getting a business up and running without a large cash commitment. Almost always, it is theoretically possible for a joint venture partner to buy in the skills it needs, if the cash is available. However, it may be more effective for a cash-strapped start-up to obtain that resource in exchange for a share in the rewards, rather than having to reach into its pocket and fund it. Much of the resource required may have a low marginal cost to the supplier, when provided to the joint venture, but would be much more expensive to purchase on the open market.

CASE STUDY

New.com wishes to offer a transaction-based service on the internet. Rather than purchasing both the computer hardware and the software it requires on the open market, it sees a joint venture relationship with the supplier of the software and with an internet hosting company as a low-risk and low-cost means of bootstrapping the resources needed to run the project.

The software company's cost is little more than running off a copy of its software on CD and the internet service provider can (at least initially) provide some disk space and bandwidth for the project that may not have been used in any event. They are supplying resources at low marginal cost to themselves, in circumstances where they would probably not have made a cash sale to New.com in any event. For them, there is little initial risk, investment or effort, coupled with large potential gains if the project takes off.

Care has to be taken in managing the expectations of New.com and the other partners. For example, can the joint venture expect the same level of support and attentiveness from the software company as its fee-paying clients? Will New.com become resentful of the other two partners when the venture becomes successful and it realises that its profits would have been much greater if it had bought the software and hosting for cash on the open market?

Occasionally, a joint venture is the only way forward in a relationship where a party has unique assets (e.g. intellectual property such as patents or software) that it is unwilling to transfer or license directly to the other party. That partner may feel more comfortable where the licence is granted to a third party over which it has some control, rather than on arms' length terms.

Frequently, the sales staff of the joint venture partners can be used to cross-sell each other's products, thus giving bigger market penetration and the benefit that the names of the joint venture partners themselves will add credibility to the joint venture project.

ESTABLISHING A JOINT VENTURE

Non-disclosure agreements
Potential joint venture partners will necessarily spend some time finding out about each others' businesses and plans before committing to final documentation. This will frequently involve the parties disclosing sensitive information and,

before any of this information is disclosed, all parties should have entered into a non-disclosure agreement (NDA). Disclosures may involve patentable inventions, so failure to enter into an effective NDA could affect the validity of any later applications for patents. As well as covering secrecy, an NDA can cover areas such as non-poaching of staff during and after the negotiations and ownership of intellectual property created during negotiations. The parties' lawyers can advise on the terms of a suitable NDA.

Heads of agreement

The heads of agreement (or heads of terms) document sets out the commercial terms on which the joint venture will operate, in less legalistic terms than the full documentation, but nevertheless covering all the commercial bases of the deal. The key here is to negotiate the heads quickly, so that the parties do not end up negotiating the same points twice. The heads are not typically legally binding (in lawyers' jargon they should be 'subject to contract' and the lawyers should ensure that they contain wording that expresses this properly).

Even so, in practice it can be difficult for a party to change its mind on a point once it has been enshrined in the heads. A few points follow on from this:

- Establish what is legally binding and what is not as soon as possible. It is possible for parties to create a contract by exchange of letters alone. To avoid this happening, ensure that all correspondence involving joint venture negotiations is marked 'subject to contract', until the final documentation is ready to be signed.

- Do not start operating the joint venture until you have final, signed documentation. If you do so, you could be deemed to have entered into a contract with your joint venture partner on terms that only a court case will be able to unravel.

- Establish who is going to pay the professional advisers' costs, whether or not the joint venture goes ahead.

Many joint venture negotiations end up nowhere, but that is likely to be a lot better than a failed joint venture for all parties, in terms of cost, loss of management time and market perception. The heads of agreement document allows the parties to reach a red or green light as quickly as possible before too much money and management time have been wasted.

Managing expectations: the business plan

For a successful joint venture, the extent and nature of the involvement of each party needs to be explicitly agreed and recorded as soon as possible. A software supplier in a joint venture with a hardware supplier may assume that its products are going to be sold by a hardware supplier's sales staff and that the products will be co-branded, but unless this is explicitly stated at the outset, the hardware supplier may turn out to have different expectations. To argue 'we will both make more money that way' is never quite as simple as it seems and the perceptions of the partners must coincide. The documentation setting up the joint venture must address these issues explicitly.

The business plan is a critical document in articulating the joint aims and aspirations of the parties. A plan for regular review and updating of the business plan is vital in that disagreements arising out of the business plan can be dealt with before they grow into larger operational issues. Unstated assumptions tend to lead to disputes and a comprehensive business plan can usually weed out erroneous assumptions ('What do you mean you've put in a £2000 monthly licence fee for the supply of your software? You're supplying it for free, aren't you?').

Day-to-day management
The partners need to consider how the joint venture will run on a day-to-day basis. It may seem to be micromanagement to think about things like the design of the letterheads or who will sign off stationery expenses, but it is at this level where real disagreements can surface (as anyone who has ever sat in a board meeting or partners' meeting can testify).

Transpose your own experiences onto the joint venture: think about the processes you are familiar with in your own business and use them as a basis for setting up the business processes in the joint venture. If you have an operations handbook for your own business, use that as a starting point and try to develop a similar handbook for the joint venture. If you do this in conjunction with the other partners then you should end up with a workable model for day-to-day management that has flushed out potential disagreement. This will not be a simple or straightforward process, but working together on the handbook and the business plan will give each partner an invaluable feel for the style and culture of the joint venture.

As an aside, do not fall into the trap of believing that, because you have invested significant time and cost in investigating and negotiating a joint venture, you are obliged to enter into it. If, as part of the process of working together on setting it up, you become sure that you and the other partners cannot work together, walk away.

Ownership of intellectual property
Joint ventures frequently involve the development of intellectual property (IP). The parties may collaborate to develop new software, for example based on the software of one of the parties or combining the hardware of one party with the software of another. Generally, the IP will belong to the joint venture, but the parties need to address whether the partners are allowed access to it for their own purposes and, if so, on what terms and what happens to the IP in the joint venture exit arrangements.

Commonly, the joint venture will grant a royalty-free licence on the IP to the partners. If the joint venture folds, rather than have a squabble over who gets the IP, a sensible route is to put in place a mechanism whereby the IP can be exploited by each of the partners as if each partner owned it. Any subsequent developments belong solely to the partners who made them (this is known in the software business as 'forking'). The mechanism for achieving this can be a little complicated, but it is often the fairest way to proceed.

Exit arrangements
Joint ventures rarely last for ever and the partners should have a view as to how the joint venture is to end. Is the business secure enough to be sold on the open market? Can one party buy out the other? For example, if a channel-to-market

joint venture establishes a bridgehead into a new jurisdiction, the supplying party is increasingly likely to want to purchase the joint venture to bring it into the group structure, in which case there should be an explicit mechanism for this to happen at an appropriate price.

This is part of the management of expectations: are the partners expecting a capital gain on exit within a defined period or a flow of profits from the venture? The exit aspirations of the venture need to be articulated because a venture in which one partner is keen on maximising short-term profits and the other demands constant reinvestment with a view to growing the joint venture for eventual trade-sale is heading for disaster. Joint ventures in which the partners are at loggerheads are likely to decline and fail very quickly, both because they are unlikely to have management teams that are sufficiently independent (or have the inclination) to steer the venture away from trouble, and because the partners are likely to be providing non-cash benefits to the venture that can easily be withdrawn in the event a dispute arises.

If the exit aspirations involve a sale of the joint venture company (or if there are plans for raising external finance), then the joint venture company has to be groomed for an inevitable due diligence process, and the partners' involvement in the joint venture company may have to be placed on a more arms' length basis than was probably the case when the joint venture was established.

The joint venture may be so intertwined with the business of one or more of the partners that it cannot effectively stand alone; in those circumstances the venture has to be viewed as an income-only rather than a capital growth proposition and an orderly wind-down needs to be planned for when the joint venture comes to an end.

STRUCTURE OF A JOINT VENTURE

Having decided on the aims of the joint venture, the partners need to settle on the most appropriate structure. At its simplest, the joint venture may consist of cooperative channel-to-market arrangements. A simple channel-to-market joint venture is characterised by a fairly straightforward distribution or agency arrangement, possibly with some additional items bolted on. For example, there is likely to be a trade mark licence that permits the agent/distributor to use the principal/supplier's trade marks. The principal/supplier may also provide additional resource, in terms of, for example, office space, software, consultancy or administration.

Distribution and agency agreements
What lawyers call a 'distribution agreement' is probably better known as a reseller agreement. The supplier sells the goods to the distributor; the distributor becomes the owner of the goods and pays the supplier for them.

The distributor then sells the goods on to its client. In this case, there are two separate sales involved: the supplier to the distributor and the distributor to the client.

In contrast, an agency relationship involves an agent appointed by the principal to find clients. The agent may then pass details of the client back to the principal who can conclude the deal or the agent can be granted power to sign on the principal's behalf and conclude the deal for the principal. In each case, the agreement will set out precise limits of the power involved.

A distributor makes his money by selling at a higher price than that at which he purchases. An agent makes his money by receiving a commission on the sales that he makes. Where goods are being sold, the relationship is pretty straightforward. For services (including software), the distinction is more unclear. Legal theory lags somewhat behind what happens in practice and, although there is a billion-dollar industry in reselling shrink-wrapped software, lawyers are still pretty much at loggerheads as to what happens as a matter of legal theory. When dealing with services, the lawyers drafting the documents defining the relationship must take extra care because there are some important legal distinctions between the two models (in terms of liability, regulation and termination).

Both agency and distribution models can form the basis of a simple joint venture relationship, frequently where the supplier (or principal) wishes to use the distributor (or agent) to break into a new market.

Licensing and royalty deals

Licensing deals are very common in IT and are another form of a simple channel-to-market joint venture arrangement. Where a channel-to-market deal involves licensing it usually either echoes a reseller model (the owner sells software to the reseller who then sells it to the client, taking a cut in the process) or a royalty model (the owner permits the reseller to duplicate and sell copies of the software, remitting to the owner a percentage of its revenues as royalties). The former route tends to be used for shrink-wrapped software and the latter for Original Equipment Manufacturer (OEM) or component software.

'Bolt on' terms

Whenever any of these forms of channel-to-market arrangements is employed, there may well be additional duties and obligations placed on each party that deepen the relationship and make it more of a joint venture.

On the part of the owner, additional obligations are likely to be:

- provision of training;
- provision of marketing support;
- permission to use the owner's names/logos;
- provision of front-line or second-line support to the reseller or its clients;
- provision of updates to the software;
- financial support for marketing;
- protection of its intellectual property for the benefit of the reseller.

On the part of the reseller, typical obligations are likely to be:

- sales targets;
- staffing requirements;
- provision of front-line support to clients;
- localisation of products to local markets;
- provision of marketing information back to the owner and/or other resellers;
- protection of the owner's intellectual property.

Financially, the parties may be tempted to structure the deal so that they set up a new accounting ledger for the venture (without setting up a new company or other legal entity) into which they invest certain sums and then split the profits in a certain ratio. This has the danger that the relationship legally forms a partnership, with some unfortunate consequences.

Distribution and agency need not involve the creation of a new legal entity. Other forms of joint venture usually do. For this reason, and also for reasons of increased flexibility, more transparent exit arrangements and ease of introduction of new players, a large number of joint ventures involve the establishment of a new legal entity to undertake the joint venture activity.

WHEN IS A PARTNERSHIP NOT A PARTNERSHIP?

Lawyers tend to be much more precise about the way in which they use various terms than businesses do. For example, 'partnership' has a very strictly defined meaning at law, whereas many companies will refer to their 'partners' in a much looser sense. This can lead to problems.

In summary, where the parties are sharing risk as well as reward, there is always a danger that they will be regarded as 'partners' in the eyes of the law (even if the contract between them states that they are not). This has some undesirable consequences, one of which is that each partner becomes liable to the other for any losses of the partnership (and can bind the other in contracts). Another is that they become intertwined with each other for tax purposes (they may be required to file a separate partnership tax return, for example). A partnership agreement is the classic way of dealing with these issues.

Partnership agreements

In England and Wales, partnerships are governed by the Partnership Act 1890 (despite its age, this is still the current legislation). A huge number of businesses, including almost all solicitors and a very large number of accountants and other professional practices, are run under partnership agreements. A partnership under the Act consists of a number of partners (individuals or companies) who have come together for a common business aim (with a view to making a profit). The liability of the partners is unlimited, meaning that if the partnership incurs losses, each partner is individually liable for, potentially, all of those losses. Partners agree the proportions in which they share any profits of the venture and also the proportions in which any losses are to be borne. Any business relationship having these characteristics is a partnership (whether the partners like it or not). The burden of unlimited liability is often enough to frighten off partners from using this structure. It is possible, however, to have a complex structure where each of the partners will form a limited company that becomes a partner. This way, the partners can benefit from the limited liability afforded by using a limited company.

Partnerships do not have to publish their accounts.

Limited partnerships

There is another structure called a 'limited partnership', which is basically the same as a partnership, but with some sleeping partners who are not allowed to get involved in the business of the partnership and are allowed to limit their liability. The active partners still retain unlimited liability.

Limited partnerships have to be registered at Companies House. They are rare: do not confuse them with limited liability partnerships (LLPs), which are a totally different animal with a confusingly similar name.

LEGAL PERSONS

Limited companies, limited liability partnerships and European economic interest groupings are examples of 'Legal Persons', meaning that they have a legal existence independently of their directors or members. They can enter into contracts in their own name, they can sue and be sued, they can commit criminal offences. In fact, in the eyes of the law, they can do almost anything that a natural person (generally described as an 'individual' by lawyers) can do. Of course, they always need the intervention of an individual as an agent (such as a director) to make that legal relationship, but when acting in a company's name, a director is not also acting as an individual. If a director signs a contract on behalf of the company, it is the company that is liable, not the director. This is in contrast to partnerships, which (in English Law, but not in Scottish Law) have no separate legal personality. A partner signing a contract on behalf of the partnership is always personally liable for the contract, as are the other partners.

If all the directors and shareholders of a company die in a plane crash, the company continues to exist. If any partner in a partnership dies, the partnership ceases to exist, unless the remaining partners agree otherwise.

Limited liability partnerships

A limited liability partnership (LLP) is in effect a hybrid of a partnership and a limited company. It is a concept relatively new to English Law. Like a limited company, it is a legal person and its existence is independent of its partners (called members). The members are insulated from the debts and liabilities of the partnership in much the same way as shareholders are in a limited company.

LLPs offer interesting possibilities for tax planning (they are 'transparent' for tax purposes, meaning they are not taxable themselves, but are taxed through their members). Members can be other corporate bodies (e.g. limited companies or other LLPs, as well as individuals). In exchange for receiving limited liability status, LLPs, like limited companies, have to publish certain information, such as their accounts, at Companies House.

LLPs are likely to continue to grow in popularity as vehicles for joint ventures. One potential drawback is the need to set out what the parties each receive from the LLP by way of profits.

Limited companies

Limited companies are legal persons that consist of shareholders, who own the company, and directors, who undertake its day-to-day management.

Shareholders have no right to get involved in the day-to-day running of the company, a right which is entrusted to the directors. The shareholders' control of a company is ultimately enshrined in their power to remove and appoint directors. There is (usually) nothing stopping a director from also being a shareholder of the company. Normally, the shareholders' liability to the company is limited, in that a shareholder cannot be held liable for the debt or other liabilities of the company. A director is liable for any defaults as a director but, as a shareholder, the liability is (almost always) limited. Of course, a shareholder may lose the value of any shares held if the company folds.

Limited liability is very attractive to companies that want to join forces in an untried area. The parties form a company in which they each hold shares to carry out the venture. If the venture folds and the company fails, the parent companies will (in most normal circumstances) be insulated from any losses in the joint venture company (although parties dealing with the venture will be aware of this and may try to protect their interests by entering into a parent company guarantee).

Lawyers are very familiar with the limited company as a vehicle for joint ventures and will automatically think of it as an appropriate structure. The checklist set out in the appendix at the end of this chapter assumes that a limited company is the appropriate vehicle, although the issues will also translate to the other entities.

Other structures

The structures described above all arise under English Law (the law of England and Wales). Other jurisdictions have more or less comparable structures. When the joint venture crosses jurisdictions, always consider which jurisdiction is appropriate for forming the joint venture vehicle. For example, Limited Liability Corporations in the USA (especially the Delaware LLC) offer flexibility of structure and scope for tax planning.

A European economic interest grouping (EEIG) is a creation of the EU. It is broadly similar to a partnership in that an EEIG has partners (at least two of which must be from different member states in the EU), who have joint and several liability and whose liability is unlimited. Unlike a partnership, the EEIG is a legal person. Like a partnership, it is transparent for tax. As an organisation designed to be non-profit making (although profits are not prohibited), it is perhaps more suited to joint ventures aimed at research and development rather than to profit-making channel-to-market joint ventures. To put EEIGs into perspective, there are currently around 200 of them registered in the UK.

There are other UK structures, such as companies limited by guarantee, unlimited companies, friendly, industrial and provident societies, and companies incorporated by Royal Charter. They may all to a greater or lesser extent be involved in joint venture activity, but their uses are very specialised and are not covered here.

THE OPERATING AGREEMENT

All joint ventures should have some sort of operating agreement that sets out the main facets of the relationship. What should be covered is dealt with in greater depth in the checklist in the appendix to this chapter.

The names and, to a certain extent, the structure of the various documents comprising the operating agreements will vary depending on the type of joint venture. For example, where a joint venture is formed using a limited company as

Table 9.1 Factors to consider when forming an entity

	Informal channel-to-market structure	Partnership	Limited company	Limited liability partnership (LLP)
Taxation	Uncertain	Transparent (but must file partnership return)	Taxed as an entity in own right	Transparent (but must file partnership return)
Third-party liability assumed by partners	Unlimited, especially if the venture is deemed to be partnership	Partners are jointly and severally liable	Partners normally protected by limited liability	Partners normally protected by limited liability
Complexity	Simple	Reasonably simple	Moderate to complex	Moderate to complex

(Continued)

Table 9.1 *(Continued)*

	Informal channel-to-market structure	Partnership	Limited company	Limited liability partnership (LLP)
Certainty	Good, unless venture deemed to be a partnership	Good	Good	Fairly good (this structure is still relatively new)
International recognition	Good	Moderate	Good	Good (but new)
Ease of exit	Difficult to unbundle	Moderate (can sell business and/or underlying assets, but partners may retain some liabilities)	Good (can sell shares and/or underlying business)	Good (can sell partnership interests or underlying business)
Finances made public	No	No	Yes	Yes
Identity of partners made public	No (except in certain cases related to competition law)	Yes	Yes	Yes
Separate audit requirement	No	Not generally	Yes (above thresholds)	Yes (above thresholds)

the vehicle, the core documents will be the articles of association of the company coupled with a shareholders' agreement. There may be separate licence agreements (for the provision of intellectual property to the joint venture), management agreements (for the provision of specific management services by the joint venture partners) and property licences or leases (if one or more of the joint venture partners is providing space for the joint venture at their premises). For a partnership, the core document will be the partnership agreement. However, whatever structure is finally adopted, the fundamental issues that need to be adopted in the agreements are largely the same.

COMPETITION LAW

Whenever businesses start to collaborate, there may be a suspicion that they are no longer competing with each other, and, as a result, any form of joint venture may fall foul of competition law.

Competition law is very complex, and this book has space for no more than the briefest summary. Within the UK, competition law is enshrined, in the main, in the Competition Act 1998 and the Enterprise Act 2002. Within the context of the EU, competition law is based on Articles 81 and 82 of the Treaty of Rome (now Articles 101 and 102 of the Treaty of Lisbon). European and UK law are to a large extent harmonised, in that the 1998 Act was based on the European legislation and there is a strong interrelationship between the two.

UK competition law is concerned with activity that tends to restrict or distort competition within the UK, and European competition law is concerned with activity tending to restrict competition between European member states. International joint ventures may also be subject to the competition law (sometimes called 'anti-trust' law) of other jurisdictions (notably the USA).

Competition law is based on the premise that competition between businesses is a good thing and that if businesses get together to act in concert (such as forming a cartel), they not only decrease competition by effectively substituting one composite business where there were previously two, but the more powerful composite business can dictate terms to the market.

On the other hand, it also recognises that when small and medium businesses get together, they can combine to provide a more competitive force in the marketplace by competing with the larger players in that market.

Competition law is therefore aimed at prohibiting activity that has an anti-competitive effect (such as businesses with large market shares combining to dominate the market), while encouraging activity that (broadly) allows smaller businesses to combine forces to compete with the bigger players.

This means that there is activity that is (almost) always absolutely prohibited by competition law (such as price fixing) and activity that is prohibited unless it is deemed sufficiently low level not to affect the market.

Low-level activity can be determined by:

- a judgment call that what the parties are doing does not distort or restrict competition and is therefore legal (something that is almost impossible to prove and that is therefore fraught with danger);
- being below certain prescribed thresholds of activity in terms of the market share of the businesses concerned (called *de minimis*);
- being expressly permitted by the competition legislation because there are specific rules in that market sector (block exemptions);
- the competition authorities examining the arrangement and declaring it permissible.

An anti-competitive arrangement is void. A third party adversely affected by such arrangement can sue the partners for damages and there may be penal sanctions (i.e. fines).

Joint ventures, because of their nature, will almost always raise competition law questions, and it is critical to have the arrangements scrutinised at an early stage so that these questions can be addressed. The worst-case scenario is where two direct competitors, each with a large market share, form a joint venture. At the other end of the spectrum, two small businesses working in different fields or at different levels of the supply chain (e.g. a software developer and a value-added reseller) are unlikely to face many general competition law issues. Price fixing is probably the biggest danger area for smaller businesses and this can arise indirectly as well as directly:

- Partners dictate resale prices to the joint venture;
- Partners provide a price list to the joint venture from which the joint venture may not deviate;
- Partners set the joint venture's prices at a fixed margin over the suppliers' prices.

Specific advice should always be taken in this complex area.

APPENDIX: CHECKLIST FOR A JOINT VENTURE OPERATING AGREEMENT

This checklist sets out the main points that should be addressed irrespective of which business structure is adopted.

- Are the scope and nature of the joint venture clearly defined?
- What assets, resources (services and people) and finance will the joint venture need, both initially and over time? Which are to be provided by the partners and which from third parties?
- Are the partners providing trade mark licences or other IP to the joint venture?
- Are the partners trading with the joint venture (e.g. agency, distribution, licensing)? Are transfer pricing issues relevant?
- Are there any legal hurdles to overcome from the partners' perspective (e.g. is consent required from an investor to take shares in a joint venture)?
- Where is the joint venture to be physically located? Are the partners to provide premises (and associated services)? If so, on what terms?
- What computer hardware and software will the joint venture need?
- Where is it coming from and who will support it? Will additional licences be needed or can the software be operated on a bureau or application service provider basis from the partners? Will the systems have to interoperate with the partners' systems?
- Who are to be the professional advisers and suppliers (lawyers, auditors, tax advisers, insurers etc.) to the joint venture?

- Does the joint venture need to be registered for VAT?
- Who handles the day-to-day personnel, management, payroll etc. issues?
- Does the joint venture have appropriate Data Protection Act notification and can personal data be legitimately transferred between the partners and the joint venture?
- Are there any sector-specific regulatory issues?
- Are there any restrictions on the partners competing with each other or the joint venture? Have competition law aspects been considered?
- Do you need provisions preventing partners from poaching staff from the joint venture or each other?
- What is the nature and structure of the joint venture vehicle? What capital/income contributions are the partners to make?
- Should there be any restrictions on the sale of the partners' interest in the joint venture vehicle (e.g. shareholdings) to third parties or businesses within the partners' group?
- Who are the partners' representatives on the management team (e.g. appointed directors)?
- How are meetings of the partners (e.g. shareholders' meetings) and joint venture management (e.g. directors' meetings) to be convened and run? What decisions can be made at these meetings?
- What powers should be granted to the management team (e.g. are they allowed to raise bank borrowings without reference to the partners)?
- What is the procedure for introducing new partners or allowing existing partners to leave?
- What is the policy for accounting/distributing profits (e.g. a dividend policy)?
- What value (if any) is attributed to intangibles contributed by the joint venture partners?
- Is there a fixed or minimum term for the joint venture?
- What happens if there is a deadlock in decision-making between the partners?
- How does the management team get paid (if at all)? Are they entitled to expenses?
- Can a defaulting partner be forced to sell its interest? If so, at what price? How is that price calculated?
- What constitutes a default of the agreement? Breach of the main operating agreement? Breach of an ancillary agreement (e.g. a supply agreement)? Insolvency?
- What governing law is to cover the agreements (e.g. English)? Whose courts have jurisdiction? Is there a mechanism for dealing with disputes by escalation, arbitration or mediation?

Reproduced by permission of Moorcrofts LLP, www.moorcrofts.com

10   CLOUD COMPUTING

Stuart Smith

WHAT IS CLOUD COMPUTING?

> Cloud computing is best described as 'a model for enabling convenient, on-demand network access to a shared pool of configurable computing resources [...] that can be rapidly provisioned and released with minimal management effort or service provider interaction'.
>
> (National Institute of Standards and Technology (NIST), www.nist.gov/itl/cloud/index.cfm)

It consists of three different types of service provision. In each case the services are hosted remotely and accessed over a network (usually the internet) through a customer's web browser, rather than being installed locally on a customer's computer. Firstly, SaaS (software as a service) refers to the provision of software applications in the cloud. Secondly, PaaS (platform as a service) refers to the provision of services that enable customers to deploy, in the cloud, applications created using programming languages and tools supported by the supplier. Thirdly, IaaS (infrastructure as a service) refers to services providing computer processing power, storage space and network capacity, which enable customers to run arbitrary software (including operating systems and applications), in the cloud. These three elements are together referred to as the cloud computing 'stack'. This chapter concentrates on the issues surrounding the provision of SaaS.

The supply of IT services in the cloud has been enabled both by the evolution of sophisticated data centres and widespread access to improved bandwidth. These technical advances mean that services may be hosted on machines across a wide range of locations but, from the customer's perspective, they simply originate in the 'cloud'.

The cloud model enables customers to access, from any computer connected to the internet (whether a desktop PC or a mobile device), a multitude of IT services rather than being limited to using locally installed software and being dependent on the storage capacity of their local computer network.

This model of IT service provision is one that is growing exponentially. It is estimated that one third of all revenue generated in the software market today relates to the delivery of cloud computing services, and that the value of the UK cloud computing market could reach around £10.5 billion in 2014, up from £6 billion in 2010.

THE SERVICES IN THE CLOUD

The multitude of IT services available in the cloud include familiar web-based email services such as Windows® Live Hotmail® (Microsoft®), Yahoo!® Mail, Gmail® (Google), and the search engine facilities Google, Bing™ (Microsoft®), Yahoo!® and AltaVista®. They also include the social networking services of Facebook, Twitter, Friends Reunited, Bebo, Flickr®, YouTube, MySpace and LinkedIn®, which provide chat, instant messaging and file sharing services. But there are a growing number of other services available. Two examples from different ends of the spectrum are Zynga®, which provides online gaming services, and Wikileaks, which publishes and comments on leaked documents alleging government and corporate misconduct. These services are often provided free of charge to the user.

There are also a range of paid-for business-orientated IT services. These are provided by suppliers including Google, Microsoft®, Amazon, Salesforce.com® and Tempora. They offer a suite of services to assist with business management. Google offers Google Docs for word processing, Business Gmail for emails, Google Calendar for diary management and Google Sites for website management, and it even offers different editions of its applications for different sectors (education, governmental and non-for profit). Microsoft® offers Windows® Azure that allows users to build and host applications on Micorsoft® servers (PaaS).

Amazon Web Services (AWS) offers its Elastic Compute Cloud (Amazon EC2), enabling customers to rent space on Amazon's own computers from which they can run their own applications. Tempora provides a time recording and profitability analysis system for creative agencies and professional service firms and Salesforce.com® provides customer relationship management solutions.

THE EVOLUTION OF CLOUD COMPUTING

Long before the term cloud computing was coined, software suppliers were providing services to their customers from remote servers via internet-enabled computers. This was called Application Service Provision (ASP) and was the original platform of IT service delivery to emerge from the convergence of computing and communications in the mid-1990s. However, the ASP model ultimately was an experiment that failed. Firstly, it involved more complicated initial installation and configuration (at the customer end) than is involved with today's on-demand cloud services. Secondly, it originated as a means of providing software on a one-to-one basis rather than on the one-to-many (multi-tenant) basis of cloud computing, where one supplier has many customers. Consequently, ASP lacked the huge advantage that cloud computing enjoys, of being very scalable.

The emergence of software as a service (SaaS) in around 2001 signified the beginning of software delivery based on multi-tenant architecture involving network-based access to software managed from a central location and removing the need for customers to install patches or upgrades.

The term SaaS is useful because it highlights the principal difference between the internet-based model of software provision and the more orthodox licence and installation-based model. The latter involves a customer being granted a licence to use a software package, while the former involves the provision of a web-based service under a contract for services. There are considerable differences between a software licence and a contract for services. The important clauses in a cloud computing contract for services are dealt with later in this chapter.

CLOUD FORMATIONS

The cloud environment is subdivided into public, private, hybrid and community clouds.

- **Public clouds** are those in which services are available to the public at large over the internet in the manner already described in this chapter.

- A **private cloud** is essentially a private network used by one customer for whom data security and privacy is usually the primary concern. The downside of this type of cloud is that the customer will have to bear the significant cost of setting up and then maintaining the network alone.

- **Hybrid cloud** environments are often used where a customer has requirements for a mix of dedicated server and cloud hosting, for example if some of the data that is being stored is of a very sensitive nature. In such circumstances the organisation may choose to store some data on its dedicated server and less sensitive data in the cloud. Another common reason for using hybrid clouds is where an organisation needs more processing power than is available in-house and obtains the extra requirement in the cloud. This is referred to as 'cloud bursting'. Additionally, hybrid cloud environments are often found in situations where a customer is moving from an entirely private to an entirely public cloud setup.

- **Community clouds** usually exist where a limited number of customers with similar IT requirements share an infrastructure provided by a single supplier. The costs of the services are spread between the customers so this model is better, from an economic point of view, than a single tenant arrangement. Although the cost savings are likely to be greater in a public cloud environment, community cloud users generally benefit from greater security and privacy, which may be important for policy reasons.

SILVER LININGS AND THUNDER CLOUDS

The main benefits and drawbacks of cloud computing are as follows.

Advantages
Access to resources
The greatest advantage of cloud computing is the access it provides to the processing power of multiple remote computers. This enables customers to take advantage of greater computation speed and larger storage capacity than most organisations can provide on their premises and at a fraction of the cost.

Mobility
Customers can access the services from almost any location in the world because the services are web-based (and because of the advent of mobile devices). This can enable employees to access important business tools while they are on the move. For example, the employee can fill in a Tempora online timesheet whilst on a train, providing the rest of the business with access to that data in real time.

Easily scalable
Both the monthly subscription and 'pay as you use' charging models make it easy for the amount of service being provided to be increased or decreased. Should a customer want to increase the number of 'seats' included in its subscription to Tempora or the amount of megabytes of storage space rented from AWS, this can be done easily. The supplier simply provides access to additional users or increases the storage space available in exchange for higher monthly payments by the customer. The scalability of the cloud computing model makes it especially attractive to growing organisations with varying levels of demand for computer resources (e.g. where an organisation's website receives higher volumes of visitors at certain times of year).

Data security and storage capacity
Data security is of particular importance as lapses in procedure can cause severe financial and reputational damage. For the majority of organisations, the data security and data storage capacity offered by data centres is far superior to that which can be afforded in-house. This is because they specialise in the secure storage of data.

Cost savings
Most business-orientated cloud computing services are paid for and the payment model is usually a rental arrangement based on monthly subscription charges (per user or 'seat') or a 'pay as you use' system. This means that there is no large up front payment as there would be with the purchase of a licence in the orthodox software licence model. Although there may be an initial setup or configuration fee, this is usually very low by comparison.

The monthly subscription charges will also usually include support and maintenance fees, which would be significantly higher in the orthodox software licence model. Also, customers do not need to invest in secure servers because hosting is provided by third-party data centres and is included in the subscription charge.

The 'pay as you use' system is of particular benefit to an organisation with peaks and troughs in its demand for computing resources. It is cheaper than paying for exclusive use of enough resources to meet peak demand when it is not required, as is the case where all computation is carried out by an organisation in-house.

Additionally, cloud services reduce the need for an organisation to maintain in-house expertise in their own technological infrastructure, which reduces IT costs.

Finally, cloud computing services do not represent a capital expenditure, so customers lose less if they switch suppliers.

Maintenance and support

The supplier will usually offer ongoing support services. However, remote hosting of the services makes the process of maintaining and supporting the services less intrusive for the customer. The supplier can handle backups, updates and upgrades automatically and remotely without visiting a customer's site. This will generally mean that maintenance and support can be carried out more quickly. In addition, customers are able to piggy-back on their suppliers' upgrades in computing resources and are not locked into using infrastructure purchased at great cost 10 years previously.

Environmentally friendly

It has been suggested that data centres are a 'green' alternative to in-house computing and this is a hotly debated topic. This is because servers in very large data centres typically run at around 80 per cent capacity, while an in-house server might run at five per cent capacity, to allow for peaks in resource demand; and a server running at five per cent capacity uses only slightly less energy per hour than one running at 80 per cent, while doing 16 times less computation. Nevertheless, it is probable that the existence of cheap and more easily accessible cloud computing architectures has increased the overall demand for computation, outstripping the energy-efficiency gains that have been made in data centres. One option is to choose a supplier that uses a data centre that makes use of solar technology or wind cooling, or a data centre that is based in an area where local electricity comes from a renewable energy resource.

Free trials

Some suppliers offer the opportunity to trial their product for a period without charge. This is made easier by the supplier's ability to terminate access at the end of the period and provides them with the opportunity to 'hook' the customer. This business model is sometimes referred to as a 'freemium'.

Disadvantages
Internet reliability

Clearly where IT services are provided over the internet, lack of internet access or slow connections will hinder access to those services inaccessible. Where those services are business critical this can be a major problem. However, as internet access improves, this should be a diminishing concern. Also, it should be remembered that there is no guarantee of uninterrupted service even with locally hosted software applications or data storage, which can be rendered inoperable by defects or bugs.

Dependence on the supplier

With cloud computing the customer is dependent on the supplier for day-to-day access to the IT services rather than just for support and maintenance. If the supplier is in financial trouble, is reliant on an unstable subcontractor or is involved in litigation, its ability to provide the services may be affected. These issues could leave the customer without access to business critical systems.

However, dependence on a supplier is a common concept for most organisations and the usual risk assessment can be carried out to mitigate that risk. Due diligence checks on the supplier may disclose whether it is, for example, in financial trouble and references can be sought from existing or past customers to establish whether the supplier has a history of reliability. The customer can always seek to include certain measures in the contract to provide protection from the risks mentioned, as is set out later in this chapter. Ultimately, if in too much doubt, the customer may need to choose an alternative supplier.

As part of supplier selection, the customer should consider what steps will be required to switch suppliers if this proves necessary. For example, what termination notice periods apply, how the customer's data will be retrieved from the supplier-controlled servers (including in what format) and what level of migration assistance is available from the supplier. Furthermore, it is prudent to establish what level of interruption to operations would be caused by switching suppliers; in other words, identifying how long it would take to get up and running with an alternative supplier.

Some cloud computing suppliers also provide IT services in the orthodox licence model. Where this is the case, it may be possible to agree that failure of the cloud computing service would trigger an orthodox licence of the software to be hosted on the premises by the customer.

Finally, there are also data protection and security concerns associated with cloud computing and these are discussed in more depth below.

DATA PROTECTION AND SECURITY

The servers used by suppliers of cloud computing services to host their customers' data can be located anywhere in the world. Where the customers' data includes personal data, and that data is hosted by the supplier on a third-party server, it can be difficult for even the third party or the supplier to know exactly where that data is stored. Customer data may even be spread over a network across different territories. This raises concerns for the customer because European Union legislation places responsibility for ensuring compliance with data protection laws on the customer (data controller), even where the supplier (data processor) or its third-party hosting provider is in possession of that data.

As a result, when a European-based organisation uses cloud computing services, it is liable for any failure by the supplier to process (store) that customer data in accordance with EU data protection legislation. Such a breach could occur, for example, if the supplier (with or without its knowledge) were to process data in a country outside the EEA (EU countries plus Norway, Iceland and Liechtenstein), where the hosting provider is not signed up to the Safe Harbor Principles, not subject to an exemption or where that data has not been transferred under a contract stipulating compliance with EU data protection rules.

If there is any question over whether a supplier's procedures comply with the EU data protection legislation, clarification can be sought from the Information Commissioner.

As a data controller, the customer is required by the data protection legislation to carry out due diligence before it appoints a supplier to process customer data. This due diligence should establish that the supplier adopts procedures that comply with data protection requirements. Furthermore, the customer is under an obligation to continue to monitor the supplier's procedures to ensure that they remain compliant.

It is also necessary for customers to notify individuals where their personal data may be transferred to third parties, outside the EEA, in order that such processing is fair and lawful.

The customer's obligations also extend to protecting personal data from unlawful processing including accidental loss or destruction and unauthorised alteration or disclosure. As a result, it is important that customers are notified by their supplier of any security breach involving their data.

Permanent data loss should not be a problem from huge data centres like those of Google, Amazon, IBM® and Microsoft®. These and other data hosting providers, with the latest security technology and backup systems, are in reality less likely to lose data than an individual is likely to lose a laptop or flash memory stick. However, cloud computing customers should still keep backup copies of their data where possible.

IMPORTANT CLAUSES IN A CLOUD COMPUTING CONTRACT FOR SERVICES

The agreement between supplier and customer is essentially a normal contract for services but with particular emphasis on the areas set out below. Although the contract will normally be on the supplier's standard terms, click-wrapped and difficult to negotiate, the customer may wish to insist on amendments in respect of those issues below that are of most concern or, where this is not possible, to find an alternative supplier.

Service rental
The supplier should grant the customer a non-exclusive right for either a certain number of authorised users to access its service, or for the customer to use a certain amount of computation resource (e.g. data storage). In exchange, where a per-seat model is used, the customer should be prohibited from allowing more users than a subscription permits to access the service, and should be obliged (as far as is reasonable) to prevent unauthorised access to the services by a third-party organisation.

The supplier should be required to provide a clear statement or specification of the services to be provided.

Customer obligations

The customer will be required to make payment in accordance with the supplier's normal payment terms and payment method. The customer should also be required to provide all necessary cooperation to the supplier in performing the service. It is important for the supplier that it is not responsible for service failure where the customer does not adhere to the supplier's maintenance specifications (e.g. regarding the customer's internal networks or communication links). Additionally, the customer should be required to use the service in accordance with the supplier's instructions.

Supplier obligations

The supplier should warrant to perform the service with reasonable care and skill and to use commercially reasonable endeavours to correct any non-performance promptly. The supplier should also warrant that the service will fit its specification and that the supplier maintains public liability and professional indemnity insurance (which should cover data loss).

The supplier is unlikely to give a warranty that the service will be uninterrupted, error free or will meet the customer's requirements. This is because suppliers are usually relying on third-party hosting providers who operate on low margins and will themselves, give few, if any, warranties to the supplier.

Data processing, protection and security

It is of importance to the supplier that it establishes in the contract for services that it will be the data processor and that the customer will be the data controller in relation to all customer data.

It should also be set out in the contract that the customer owns all data received by the supplier in the course of providing the services as well as any output data generated by the supplier for the customer. The customer should seek certainty over how its data would be retrieved on termination of the contract.

The supplier will want to ensure that in the event of any loss or damage of customer data, the sole remedy available to the customer will be the supplier's commercially reasonable endeavours to restore that data from its latest backup copy (maintained in accordance with the specified backup policy).

The customer should seek the supplier's agreement to comply with a specified data protection and security policy, which mirrors the obligations of a data processor under the Data Protection Act. The customer may even seek an indemnity from the supplier in case of any breach of the Act, but this may be difficult to obtain. If any data protection or security breach does occur the supplier should be required to provide the customer with details of that breach immediately.

The supplier will also insist that the customer ensures it is entitled to transfer any personal data to the supplier (including that data subjects have given any necessary consent). Furthermore, the supplier should obtain the customer's agreement in order to transfer and store customer data outside the EEA.

For customers that do not wish their data to be transferred outside the EEA, there are some suppliers that will promise to keep their data within that geographic area. However, as already mentioned, there is some question over how a supplier can make this guarantee in respect of the data it processes, and the customer (as data controller) should remember that it has ultimate responsibility for its own data.

It is worth noting that a further economic model for cloud computing services involves the supplier generating revenue from secondary uses of the customer's data (e.g. the sale of that data for marketing purposes). As a result, the customer should ensure it is aware of, and happy with, the purposes for which the supplier may use its data.

Indemnities
The customer should expect to indemnify the supplier against any loss it suffers in connection with the customer's use of the services and the supplier should grant an indemnity to the customer in respect of any intellectual property rights claim that is made against the customer regarding its use of the service.

Limitation of liability
The supplier will seek a liability cap, and this is likely to reflect the value of the contract and should insist on the customer accepting sole responsibility for results obtained from the use of the service. Furthermore, the supplier will exclude liability for any loss of profits suffered by the customer or any loss or corruption of data. The supplier will also exclude liability for delays or loss resulting from the transfer of data over communications networks.

Customers should always aim to avoid a situation where the supplier's liability is severely limited, especially in relation to business critical services, because the customer may be left without an effective remedy in the case of a serious service breakdown.

CONCLUSION

Cloud computing usage will increase rapidly in the future. With the internet becoming more reliable and offering users more flexible and agile technologies, the concerns over internet connectivity, data security and protection are likely to be outweighed. As a result, organisations will increasingly be able to take advantage of the benefits offered by this unstoppable trend in IT service provision. The cloud is not going to be blown away.

11   OPEN SOURCE SOFTWARE

Andrew Katz

INTRODUCTION

Google, Amazon and Facebook all run on open source software, as does the French tax system. Transport for London's Oyster® Card system relies heavily on open source components. The mobile phone operating systems, Android and Symbian, are both open source software. Many consumer products, including cars, TVs and DVD players, rely on open source software. Governments around the world are increasingly asking suppliers to tender using open source components. Open source is now mainstream, and customers are increasingly seeking open source solutions (and suppliers are increasingly providing them). Acquiring and using open source software in your business does present some specific legal issues. They are, in the main, easily manageable, but IT managers should be familiar with the issues.

WHAT IS OPEN SOURCE?

Software source code is equivalent to its blueprint. A programmer writes source code, and then uses software tools (compilers and linkers) to generate the object code from the source. The object code is what the computer runs.

Traditional (proprietary) software is supplied solely as object code. For example, a retail box of Microsoft® Office purchased from PC World includes a DVD that contains the object code of Word, Excel® and so on, but none of the source code, which is a closely guarded Microsoft secret. The source code is not needed to run the software, but it is (in practice) needed to correct bugs or change the program.

With access to the source code, users can change the software (including changing its functionality, as well as fixing bugs) and examine how it works. (In practice, a relatively small proportion of users has either the desire or the ability to do so, but the very availability of the source code has consequences discussed below.)

Open source software, by contrast, allows users access to the source code, but source code access is far from the whole story. Open source software also guarantees the user certain freedoms. As well as access to the source, the user must legally be able to adapt the software for any purpose, correct bugs, run the software, and also be able (although not necessarily required) to pass the software, including any changes to it, on to any third parties, under a licence that allows similar changes and freedoms, and without making a charge.

126

An organisation, the Open Source Initiative (OSI), has codified these characteristics, and they can be found here: www.opensource.org/docs/osd

Another (older) organisation, the Free Software Foundation (FSF) (www.fsf.org) exists to promote 'free software'. There are philosophical differences between the organisations (in a nutshell, the FSF believes non-free software is immoral; the OSI believes open source is a better way of developing software, but doesn't take a moral stance).

In practice, the definitions of open source and free software are very similar and, although they can generate lively debate, the differences rarely cause a problem from a legal or business point of view.

The Free Software Foundation's four freedoms are:

- The freedom to run the program, for any purpose (freedom 0).

- The freedom to study how the program works, and change it to make it do what you wish (freedom 1). Access to the source code is a precondition for this.

- The freedom to redistribute copies so you can help your neighbour (freedom 2).

- The freedom to distribute copies of your modified versions to others (freedom 3). By doing this you can give the whole community a chance to benefit from your changes. Access to the source code is a precondition for this.

(GNU, www.gnu.org/philosophy/free-sw.html)

The word 'free' in 'free software' relates to 'freedom', as in the freedoms above, and not necessarily free as in zero-price: think 'free speech' rather than 'free beer'. (As it happens, free software is frequently zero-price as well, but this is not an essential feature of the concept.) The terms 'FOSS' (Free and Open Source Software) and 'FLOSS' (Free, Libre and Open Source Software) are also occasionally used in order to avoid alignment with either the open source or free software camps.

These freedoms (whether FSF or OSI) are guaranteed through the legal mechanism of licensing.

Computer software is protected by copyright (see Chapter 4). Open source software is no different from proprietary software in this regard. Use of software (with the possible exception of public domain works, see below) without a licence is an infringement of copyright, and open source licences, in common with proprietary software licences, grant certain permissions to use the software so that the use is no longer a breach of copyright. In the case of free and open source software, those permissions are much broader than the permissions granted by proprietary software licences.

Table 11.1 compares typical open source licences with typical proprietary software licences.

Table 11.1 Comparison of open source and proprietary software licences

	Free/open source licence	Proprietary software licence
Payment required for exercise of licence rights	No	Yes (usually)
Software can be used for any purpose	Yes (note: cannot be restricted to non-commercial use, for example)	Licences frequently prohibit use for certain purposes (e.g. creating a competing product, use in safety-critical circumstances, use for outsourcing to another business), or restrict use to specific activities (e.g. to academic use only)
Access to source code	Yes	No (although possibly through an escrow arrangement, or a shared source licence)
Reverse engineering/decompiling	Permitted (although decompiling is not necessary, as the source code is available)	Normally not permitted (to the extent that prohibition is permitted by law)
Assignment	Permitted without restriction	Restricted to the extent permitted by law
Sub-licensing	May be restricted, because sub-licensing is not normally necessary	Usually prohibited
Number of users	No restriction	Usually restricted (although may be a site licence, or an enterprise-wide licence)

(Continued)

Table 11.1 *(Continued)*

	Free/open source licence	Proprietary software licence
Territory/location	Usually worldwide (although, with some licences, may be restricted to certain jurisdictions if there are patent concerns)	Usually limited to specific territories. May be limited to a specific location, or even licensed for use only on a specific CPU
Right to copy to take backups	Unrestricted	May be restricted to the extent permitted by law (perhaps to a certain number of copies)
Perpetual	Yes (may be subject to termination for breach)	May be term restricted, or automatically renewable. Will be subject to termination for breach
Contractual licence	Not usually (i.e. the licence granted may be conditional, but does not place any contractual obligations on the licensee)	Yes (i.e. places contractual obligations, such as the obligation to pay licence fees, on the licensee)

Open source software authors choose to release their code under one or more open source/free software licences. The choice of licence will depend on whether:

- the software is dependent on other open source software released under a particular licence;
- the software is intended to be part of, or be used in conjunction with, a project that traditionally uses a particular licence;
- the author wants to restrict the code from being incorporated in a non-free project;
- there are software patent concerns;
- the author wants to maximise the number of potential licensees;
- the author wishes to use a particular licence with which he feels the intended licensees are familiar;

- there are specific issues that the author wishes addressed (e.g. whether the software can be amended and used as part of a software as a service offering, without the source code being made available).

Sometimes, the open source software is issued under more than one licence simultaneously (dual licensing), and the licensee can choose which of the dual licences to adopt. This issue is explored later.

Note also that free and open source software licences may not restrict the licensee from making commercial use of the software, or for charging for services supplied in connection with it. Much open source software is written by commercial businesses, and is used by commercial businesses, so it is important not to confuse free and open source software with 'trialware' or 'freeware'. When referring to software that is not free or open source software, the preferred terms are 'non-free' or 'proprietary', but not 'commercial'.

THE PUBLIC DOMAIN

Under English law, software, as a literary work, can only enter the public domain (i.e. be released from copyright) once the copyright term attaching to it has expired. Since the term of protection of literary works is so long (author's life plus 70 years), and computers are such a recent invention, no software in the UK has yet entered the public domain, nor will it do so for a long time. Software authors occasionally attempt to donate code to the public domain. Whereas this may work in other jurisdictions (notably in the USA), it does not, technically, in the UK. However, such an attempted grant is most likely to be interpreted as a permissive licence (which would, in practice, be a free or open source licence).

OPEN SOURCE AND COMMUNITIES

The open source licensing model, together with free software development tools (in both senses of the word 'free') and the existence of the internet to facilitate communication, have led to the emergence of communities of developers and users around certain software projects. This phenomenon (contrasted with the proprietary development model) was explored by Eric S. Raymond in his influential paper *The Cathedral and the Bazaar* (available as a free download from http://catb.org/esr/writings/homesteading/).

Theoretically, the open source model works like this: when a programmer writes a piece of code to solve a specific problem, he or she makes it publicly available so that other programmers with a similar problem can find the code and adopt it. They in turn adapt it to their needs, correcting bugs and adding features. As they do this, they feed the changes back to the project (which is typically hosted at a website like sourceforge.net). The internet (usually through a website or mailing list) enables the contributors to discuss with each other the requirements of the software, what the bugs are, which features need adding and in what priority and so on.

The relationship has been described as one of pure meritocracy: the only criterion for code's inclusion into the project is whether it is effective and of suitably high quality. Naturally, those submitting the most and highest quality code become more respected in the project discussions, and greater weight is given to their contribution in any debate. All the contributors are also aware of the possibility of 'forking', which means that anyone within the project community (or even outside it) can take all of the code and use it as the basis of their own competing project. In practice, this rarely happens (and if it does happen, it is unlikely that both branches of the fork will thrive).

This development model sounds utopian, but has in fact been shown, time and again, to work effectively. The classic example is the development of Linux itself (more diplomatically, and accurately, called GNU/Linux), which was started by Finnish student Linus Torvalds as a project to develop an operating system kernel (see Glyn Moody's book *Rebel Code, Linux and the Open Source Revolution* for the complete story). It has led to the complete Linux operating system that now competes head-to-head with Microsoft's suite of operating systems amongst others, and is used to power Amazon, Google, Facebook and over 91 per cent of the world's 500 most powerful supercomputers, as well as devices like satnavs and mobile phones.

This model contrasts with the traditional software development methodology that suggests a hierarchical top-down approach, whereby requirements are determined and increasingly abstracted until they reach the level of code. This approach to engineering is in turn reflected in the management model, with the coders working under line managers, working under project managers and so on.

Unfortunately, as effective as the open source model has been, in many cases, it is by no means universal, and gives the misleading impression that open source code is largely written by loosely knit groups of students and hackers who do it for the love of coding and the kudos, but without payment. There are, equally, many open source projects that have been closely controlled by, or developed by, commercial organisations, and the programmers working on those projects are paid a wage for the job, and are just as likely to work in a sleek modern office as they are in their bedroom. For example, Oracle®'s Open Office (which it acquired through its acquisition of Sun Microsystems) was a Sun development project. Firefox was originally spun out of Netscape in a similar way, and MySQL (now also acquired by Oracle through the Sun acquisition) was developed by commercial programmers.

Corporates such as IBM®, which are heavily involved in open source, have modified their management model so that the projects more closely approximate the classic open source development model, both because it has been shown to work, but also because it is more likely to attract external contributors. It also assists in attracting good programmers, because as well as getting paid, programmers (or at least, good ones) prefer the meritocratic environment of an open source project to traditional management hierarchy.

From a purely legal perspective, the open source development model raises a number of legal questions, mainly surrounding liability and code ownership. We deal with these issues later in the chapter, but first, we need to put open source code in a commercial context.

OPEN SOURCE SOFTWARE BUSINESSES

Companies like IBM spend a lot of money on programmers and other contributors (such as testers and documentation authors) working on open source projects. The open source code they write will become available to their competitors. Why is this of benefit to them?

From a purely financial point of view, the first point to note is that licence fees typically make up a relatively small proportion of the costs of a software project. A (proprietary) software project consists of a number of elements, such as needs requirement, development specification, integration planning, integration, custom programming, configuration, user interface design, staff training, change management, data migration and validation, testing, documentation creation, compliance checking, and ongoing maintenance, hosting, connectivity costs and support. All of those elements have to be paid for, in addition to any licence fees.

Those same elements will also exist in an equivalent open source project, the only exception being that licence fees will not be payable. For a large project, the initial licence fees may amount to 20 per cent of the project, so the supplier will still generate 80 per cent of the revenue of the proprietary provider (and will not have to pass back any licence fees to upstream licensors).

So the financial 'downside' is not as great as may first appear. In addition to that, from the engineering perspective, there are positive advantages to the open source model. The first is that active participation in (or establishment of) an open source community is likely to lead to greater participation by other people from outside the company, which generates a virtuous circle of increasing quality and functionality in the code, and an increased market share. It also gives the corporate that is actively involved a greater say in the future development path of the software, which will be an advantage when selling the ancillary services to customers (customers being more likely to buy support services from a company that is actively involved in the development project in the first place). The community also creates a pool of potential high-quality and pre-screened recruits.

The second is that the community model essentially allows a company to participate in shared research and development with other companies without any formal collaboration agreement being put in place. This works as follows: where a piece of software is providing what is really a commodity service, it becomes difficult to differentiate it from similar pieces of software supplied by other providers. This commoditisation has arguably happened in relation to web servers and relational databases for example, so there is little point in a company developing a web server from scratch (with all of the developer effort that entails) when there is little likelihood of being able to effectively differentiate it from similar programs in the marketplace. It makes more sense for the company to become part of an existing open source project (like Apache), to apply a relatively small amount of development effort (and take advantage of the development effort applied by others), and to deploy its programming resource in areas where it can differentiate (and therefore charge a premium), like providing customisations for clients, or even providing proprietary extensions to the underlying code (although this latter option, called 'open core', is criticised for being anathema to free software, and, to a slightly lesser extent, open source).

As a rule of thumb, companies that generate a large proportion of revenue from services are more likely to be in favour of open source than those that generate revenue mainly through software licence fees.

RUNNING OPEN SOURCE IN YOUR BUSINESS

For the customer, open source looks very attractive. The upfront costs are likely to be less than for a proprietary system with equivalent functionality, because there are no licence fees. More importantly, there are no ongoing licence compliance costs, because there is no restriction on the number of seats on which the software can be installed, so there is no need to audit usage; and there will be fewer issues with corporate transactions: for example, a restructuring will not require consent to assign the licences. (This is all true for licences, at any rate, though it may not be true for associated support contracts. However, open source companies' support contracts do, by and large, try to mirror the ethos of the underlying licences, and tend to be less restrictive than those of proprietary software companies.)

Open source software by its nature tends to be modular, and to adhere to standards. This is mainly because there is rarely any advantage in an open source project working outside the standards system, whereas proprietary software companies have a vested interest in trying to lock customers in. An advantage for the customer is that it is relatively easy to remove one open source component and replace it with another adhering to the same standards.

The quality of open source software itself is, arguably, as variable as proprietary software. Where software is written by companies like IBM, customers will take some assurance from the expectation that IBM will apply the same high-quality standards to its open source offerings as it does to its proprietary products; and they may be more cautious about software written by a more loosely knit developer community. However, it is by no means the case that community-built software is any worse quality than proprietary code, and indeed there are good reasons to assume the opposite:

- A coder working for a proprietary company is aware that his or her code is unlikely to be open to third-party scrutiny. Elegance and programming finesse are less important than whether the software works (at least on the first test run). By contrast, coders working on open source projects are painfully aware that their work is laid bare to their peers (who have a reputation for being highly critical).

- The generation of quality code will assist a programmer in advancement through the project hierarchy, gaining kudos among peers, and even helping as an employment CV.

- Some proprietary software contains logic bombs to impair the software's functionality if triggered, to force users to pay maintenance or licence fees. Open source code is extremely unlikely to contain any such logic bombs or other 'malware' like viruses. The source code is freely available and published, so anyone seeking to disrupt an open source project in this way would be very quickly found out and ostracised, and removing the offending code would be a trivial job for a competent programmer.

- Open source code is unlikely to contain any arbitrary hard-coded limitations. Proprietary software frequently contains such hard-coded limits (e.g. the maximum size of a mailbox a mail server can handle, or the maximum size of a disk that a formatting program can format using a specific file system). These limits are frequently included to encourage the user to pay for an upgrade for a higher specified version, but are pointless in open source, because, firstly, the higher specified version would itself be open source, and, secondly, the limitations can easily be removed by programmers with access to the source code.

From a legal point of view the warranties of performance and compliance with specification that apply to an open source contract should in theory be no different from those that would apply to proprietary contract. However, this does need to be considered in context (see below). There are some special considerations relating to intellectual property that we consider later.

Note that if you are purely consuming open source software (and do not intend to distribute it yourself), the legal issues are relatively straightforward. If, on the other hand, you are using open source software in products that you distribute to others (usually your customers, but it could include self-employed subcontractors, or even, in certain circumstances, group companies), then you are, in effect, a software company, and the legal situation is more complex. We touch on this issue in places, but a detailed analysis of open source software as it applies to software companies is beyond the scope of this chapter.

OPEN SOURCE AND LICENSING

Like proprietary software, open source software is protected by the law of copyright, and can only be lawfully used with the licence of the copyright owner. There are hundreds of different forms of open source licence that the owner might use as the basis of offering the software to the public (and unwise owners sometimes attempt to write their own licences as well), but a vast majority of projects are available under the top 10 licences. The licences vary in their length and what they are trying to achieve, from the incredibly short: 'You can do whatever you like with this software', to the GNU General Public License version 3, which, as well as being a software licence, has also been described as a call to arms and a manifesto.

Open source software licences can be divided into two broad camps: academic and copyleft.

Academic licences tend to be short and grant very broad freedoms, including the freedom to incorporate the code into just about any other project, including a proprietary project.

Copyleft licences are more restrictive, and use the mechanism of copyright to limit the extent to which the code can be incorporated into other projects, especially proprietary ones. It is the copyleft licences that cause most concern from a legal point of view.

As an IT manager, the question of open source licensing will increasingly arise in relation to any development project.

Academic licences

Two academic licences are MIT (Massachusetts Institute of Technology) and BSD (Berkeley Software Distribution, named after the University of California at Berkeley): hence the name 'academic'. The Academic Free License is also important. The text of these licences can be found by clicking their names at www.opensource.org/licenses/alphabetical

Compliance with academic licences is straightforward. It usually requires accompanying the software (usually in its documentation) with a liability disclaimer and copyright notice. It does not require the grant of access to the source code (which is why academic code can be incorporated into proprietary software).

There are more complex academic licences that also contain patent clauses (such as Apache – see below).

From an IT manager's perspective, since a business other than a software company is unlikely to be licensing the software it uses out to third parties, there is little to be concerned about from a copyright perspective as regards software licensed under an academic licence. However, as the terms of the academic licences do not require the supplier to provide the customer with source code, IT managers should ensure that any contract they sign includes some alternative means of getting hold of the source code should this be required in the future. (If it is a standard well-known package, like the FreeBSD operating system, the source code should reliably be available from elsewhere.)

Copyleft licences

Copyleft licences, paradoxically, are intended to guarantee freedom by imposing restrictions. They usually require that if copyleft code is modified and distributed, that the distribution takes place under the same licence, and that that the source code is available to the recipient. The idea is that once software has been released as free software, it cannot then pass into proprietary software. The trick was most famously employed by Richard Stallman, founder of the Free Software Foundation, in the GNU General Public License (GPL), which has now reached version 3. Version 3 is gaining ground, but version 2, released in 1991, is still the most commonly applied open source licence (it governs the Linux kernel, for example). They are known as GPL3 and GPL2 respectively, and their text can be found at www.gnu.org/licenses/licenses.html. The term 'copyleft' was popularised by Richard Stallman to apply to licences of this type (although he did not originate it).

This chapter is not the place for a detailed discussion of licence terms. However, the intention is that if a program is distributed under the GPL, and that program is then modified or parts of it are used in another program, then that other program itself can only be distributed under the GPL. From a legal perspective (and there is some debate about this), if a derivative work of a GPL work is created, it may only be distributed under the same version of the

GPL (unless the version of the GPL attached to the program explicitly says that any later version may apply). English law, unlike US law, has no formal definition of 'derivative work', and there has been much debate over the extent to which one program (released under the GPL) has to be incorporated into another so as to require that the latter program can only be released under the GPL. This is the derivation of the so-called 'viral' or 'cancerous' nature of the GPL (or, if you are less polemical, its 'reciprocal' nature, also sometimes referred to as 'share alike'). The GPL (like most open source licences) has no jurisdiction clause, so its interpretation will vary according to the local law of the jurisdiction in which it is tested. This can vary significantly.

There are a number of licences that contain copyleft provisions to a greater or lesser extent. Some of them, like the various versions of GPL, and the Open Software Licence, are called 'strong copyleft'. This is because the copyleft provisions apply irrespective of whether (a) the changes are made to the original file, or (b) whether they are incorporated in any way into another project. 'Weak copyleft' licences, like the Mozilla Public License, only apply the copyleft rule in relation to specific files: if parts of the work are extracted and used in different files, the copyleft obligation no longer applies.

Unfortunately, copyleft licences (and especially strong copyleft licences) are rarely compatible with each other. In other words, code released under a specific copyleft licence (e.g. GPL2) cannot be combined into the same project as copyleft code under another licence (e.g. Open Software Licence). This is because each licence will require that the resulting project, if distributed, is released under that licence, and only that licence, to the exclusion of the other licence.

One practical effect of licence incompatibility is that it reduces the ability to combine open source projects that may, technically, be highly complementary (it is also one reason why some open source projects are released under a number of different open source licences: see Dual licensing models below).

(By contrast, academic licences do not insist that the code released under them is distributed under the same licence, so there is no problem with taking BSD code, for example, and incorporating it into a GPL project, which would then have to be released under the GPL.)

Licence compatibility is a major issue for software companies, but customers need to be aware of it as well. Tools such as Black Duck and Palamida can be used to scan code, determine which licences apply to it, and assist in determining whether compatibilities exist.

From a legal perspective, if code is distributed that is derived from material released under incompatible licences, then the distributor will be in breach of copyright in respect of at least one of the licences.

Dual licensing models

If a copyright owner chooses to release software under any non-exclusive licence (all open source licences are non-exclusive), there is nothing preventing the same software from being simultaneously released under any number of other non-exclusive licences. This ability is exploited by some companies (such as Oracle, in relation to both MySQL and the mobile edition of Java). Thus a user may choose to use MySQL under the GPL, or, if it wishes to create an amended version of the MySQL code and distribute it, it has two options: either to release the source code to the amended version, as required by the GPL, or to pay Oracle a fee, and take a proprietary licence of the code that permits the release of amended object code, without being required also to release the corresponding source.

Sometimes, software is made available under different open source licences simultaneously. This can be to assist with licence compatibility (see above), or simply as a convenience to customers, who may be more familiar with the terms of one licence than another, and so perceive that there will be fewer legal headaches in agreeing to the licence terms that they already know.

SOFTWARE DEVELOPMENT IN CONTEXT

Software development projects increasingly involve integrating, configuring and, occasionally, modifying components from different sources, as opposed to writing code from scratch. Although commercial software libraries are widely available, there is a vast quantity of open source components available from repositories such as sourceforge.net, Koders.com, CodePlex and Google Code. The effect of this is that all coders are aware of the availability of these open source repositories of code, and will be keen to use them where possible to save time and effort. This means that almost all software development projects are likely to be open source projects, at least in part (and regardless of whether the employer intends it or not). Hence the advisability of an open source policy (see below).

CONTRACTING OPEN SOURCE PROJECTS

Contracts and the open source methodology

As a customer, negotiating an open source project is little different from negotiating a proprietary software project. The provisions relating to ancillary services surrounding the core development work (such as integration, training, migration and support) will, from a legal perspective, be the same.

There is, however, an important practical difference in terms of the way that the project may be carried out, which arises from the open source development methodology, and that is that the whole project may be less rigid and structured, and that the requirements document is vaguer. Under a traditional software development methodology, taking a top-down approach, a great deal of effort is employed defining the needs, requirements and specifications, and that is then tightly circumscribed, before any coding commences. Any changes from specification will be subject to a rigid change control procedure, and will be subject to additional cost. In contrast, although this approach is sometimes taken in relation to open source software, it is frequently the case that the first stage of a project is to rough out specifications, then generate a prototype, which is refined through constant involvement with the client until, eventually, the project has reached a stage where both parties are happy with it.

There are advantages and disadvantages to this approach: the obvious disadvantage, to a lawyer, is the lack of certainty. If there was no initial specification, and the project fails to fulfil the clients' requirements, how can the client demonstrate to a judge that the supplier has failed? This equally causes issues for the supplier if it is looking for payment from an unsatisfied client.

The advantage to both parties is that, if they can establish an effective working partnership, the project can progress in a freer and less formal manner, with quick decision making and constant refinement of the prototype, until a release version of the product is completed.

The contract itself may well be significantly shorter where the open source methodology is employed. Lawyers are limited to the extent that they can manage risks in this more collaborative approach to development, and there is no substitute for doing adequate due diligence on the supplier. This will typically involve taking detailed references from previous customers, and asking them pertinent questions about the development process. If possible, the customer should test the supplier by engaging them on a relatively small, non-business critical project before moving to more significant work. Crucially, the parties will need to ensure that sufficient customer staff time is allocated to working with the supplier, that the customer's staff have sufficient authority to make decisions, and that they are sufficiently aware of the business needs to be fulfilled by the project.

Identifying licensing requirements
Internal use
If, as a customer, you are using the software for internal purposes only, then there are, in practice, unlikely to be any licensing issues.

If the software contains elements that are licensed under the GPL, you will be entitled to receive the source code. However, this does not mean that the source code is automatically made available to the public, so if you perceive proprietary advantages in maintaining the privacy of the source code that has been developed for you, then you have no obligation to release the source code to any third party (unless you decide that you are going to distribute the software further).

Note that if the supplier is technically in breach of the GPL itself, this will not mean that the customer is in breach, because the customer does not derive title to GPL code through the supplier: when you obtain GPL code, which is owned by a number of parties, you receive parallel licences from each of the owners, not a single licence from your immediate supplier. GPL wording explicitly confirms this point.

You need also to consider whether you are willing that the code created for you can be reused by third parties (potentially your competitors). This is an issue that will also arise in proprietary software contracts, but is a little more subtle in the context of open source code. If it is necessary to retain a restriction on reuse of the code, then the safest mechanism is for the contract to engage the supplier as an agent to develop code on the customer's behalf and, as a customer, insist of a copy of the source code. This is a common, but an arguably unnecessary, process as the GPL permits private transfer of the source code without it being made available to the public. It may be possible to negotiate restrictive covenants that prevent the supplier from developing a similar application for a competitor, but detailed advice should be obtained from legal counsel.

If the software is to be accessed by the public through the internet (e.g. as software as a service), there are special concerns if any of the code is released under certain licences, such as the Affero GPL or the Open Software Licence, which require that anyone accessing the software over a network is also entitled to access the source code. In this case, the customer should insist that the supplier not use any software licensed under the specific licences where this is an issue.

External use
Particularly careful attention is needed if you plan to make the software available outside your own organisation, for example by distributing it to third parties (such as customers or agents), and especially if any software is going to be embedded in devices supplied to the public like mobile phones or MP3 players. If there is any question that the source code should not be released to the public, the customer will need explicit verification that the licences of software used by the supplier are compatible with this aim. External distribution of free software is a complex issue beyond the scope of this chapter.

Summary
The supplier needs to be aware not only of the technical requirements for the software, but specifically what the customer intends to do with the software in terms of onward distribution, or access by third parties through the internet, to ensure that licence requirements are fulfilled.

As well as ensuring that these requirements are dealt with in the contract, they should also be verified by undertaking proper due diligence.

Warranties and indemnities
The considerations relating to warranties and indemnities for an open source project are broadly similar to those of any other software project. Two points to bear in mind:

- Warranties and indemnities are of no value if the entity giving them does not have sufficient financial strength; and

- Warranties and indemnities are not an adequate substitute for due diligence on the underlying subject matter.

If the customer is being offered very broad intellectual property warranties and indemnities, then it is wise to check that, if there is any question of the suppliers' ability to meet them, they are covered by insurance. Insurers are increasingly making insurance available to cover open source related risks, but this is still (at the time of writing) relatively unusual.

Warranties of performance and compliance with specification will mirror those from an equivalent proprietary software project and are not covered in this chapter. Note that they will frequently exclude issues caused by the underlying operating system and other such components as a provider of a Windows®-based

system will be unlikely to give a performance warranty covering Windows®
issues. The provider of a Linux-based system will not give a warranty covering
Linux.

Warranties and indemnities relating to intellectual property may well be more
complex than those contained in proprietary software contracts, reflecting the
difference in software methodology. In particular, the supplier may be prepared
only to warrant the code it has supplied itself, but not any third-party code it
has incorporated, in which case the customer will have to assess whether it is
prepared to take the risk itself in third-party code. However, even if it is agreed
that the customer will take the risk of third-party code infringement, then the
supplier should warrant that it has taken reasonable care in selecting the code,
bearing in mind the licences under which the customer has asked to receive it,
and that it is not aware of anything that would conflict with those licences.

More information about warranties and indemnities in the context of open source
can be found in the risk grid published by the Free Software Foundation Europe
and is available at www.ifosslr.org/ifosslr/article/view/10.

A mature customer may well have its own open source policies and procedures,
and require that the supplier adhere to those policies and procedures when
providing code for the customer. They will typically include documenting the
provenance of code (see below).

OPEN SOURCE SOFTWARE AND DUE DILIGENCE

Due diligence is relevant to open source both when contracting an open source
project (see above), and in the context of M&A transactions.

An in-depth analysis is beyond the scope of this chapter, but the aim of a due
diligence process is to ensure that (a) the target company has the right to use the
code in question, and (b) the target has the right to enforce violations of the rights
attached to the code by third parties. The second is almost invariably significantly
less important than the first, and should be borne in mind as part of a risk-based
due diligence exercise.

The existence of good open source policies and procedures will give a great deal
of comfort. The policies and procedures themselves will be considered below, but
documentation that demonstrates knowledge of open source issues, and active
engagement with the compliance process, is critical. The process should encom-
pass everyone involved in code creation, from coders through to management.

In practice, it will rarely be possible to document the precise provenance of every
piece of code (especially in GPL code, like the Linux kernel, where the individual
authors will retain their own ownership). There will always be a residual risk of
possible infringement. (The transparency of open source code tends to highlight
this risk over proprietary code, but it is, of course, equally possible that proprietary code contains infringing components.)

(The only case of any note on proprietary code finding its way into open source code was launched by SCO against IBM and other companies, starting in March 2003. The cases were finally dismissed in 2010, in favour of the defendants. What is notable is that SCO never particularised its infringement claims (which commentators overwhelmingly agreed were baseless), because, had it done so, the Linux community would immediately have started writing non-infringing portions of all code alleged to have been infringed.)

Given the availability of code from sourceforge.net et al, it is entirely likely that coders working to a tight deadline for proprietary companies will be tempted to use open source code, even if it is only available under an incompatible licence. As noted above, there are tools from companies like Black Duck, and also open source offerings like FOSSology and the Binary Analysis Tool, which will undertake a scan of code (whether source code or object code), and assist in identifying what components it contains, and under what licences. These tools can be a useful aid to due diligence. The aim is not to eliminate risk, but to assess it, and by amending procedures, code, contracts and outsourcing to insurance, render it manageable and within the parameters the business's management is prepared to accept.

OPEN SOURCE POLICIES AND PROCEDURES

A policy like 'no open source' is unlikely to be acceptable: coders under a deadline, and knowing there is a quality open source solution to their specific problem available, are likely to ignore it. This is exactly how open source turns up in proprietary software projects without the knowledge of the supplier or customer.

Accordingly, a more enlightened approach to open source code that involves setting out the goals of a specific project, in terms of acceptable in- and out-licences, the provenance of code, and the documentation and records that need to be kept to demonstrate this, is likely to deliver business benefits in terms of decreasing risk, decreasing programming effort, and increasing coder satisfaction.

OPEN SOURCE SOFTWARE: EMPLOYEES AND CONTRACTORS

The copyright in employees' work done during the course of their employment will automatically belong to their employer. Independent contractors' work will not. However, questions of code ownership may well arise, and it is sensible, in the case of employment contracts, and critical, in the case of contracts for independent contractors, explicitly to set out the terms on which copyright works generated are transferred to the employer.

A subtle issue that arises in relation to open source code is that employment contracts may contain terms that explicitly restrict the freedoms that open source licences may try to guarantee, for example in terms of restrictive covenants and confidentiality. Technically, if these restrictions conflict with the licence terms of software used by the employer, the employer may find itself in breach of the relevant licence.

A further point is that an enlightened employer may well request the employee to be actively involved in the community of the software he or she is working on at work. It is possible (even likely) that some of this work will take place outside the scope of employment. Employees' contracts therefore need to grant them the freedom to do this, as well as ensuring that their terms do not conflict with the terms of software licences.

Many projects request that contributors sign a contributor agreement. The terms of these vary dramatically, but it is important that the contributor agreement is considered carefully, both from an employment perspective, and also to ensure that the employer is not giving away rights unnecessarily (e.g. a very broad patent licence), or granting unacceptable indemnities.

OPEN SOURCE SOFTWARE AND PATENTS

Patents raise a special problem for open source projects. Most open source bodies oppose software patents, although companies like IBM (which are patent holders as well as having a significant open source business) are understandably keener to support patents within the context of open source.

A patent that impinges on open source software will also impinge on proprietary software that does the same job in a sufficiently similar way. On the one hand, the very availability of the source code means that it may be easier for a patent owner to tell whether a piece of open source code infringes the patent than would be the case for an equivalent piece of proprietary code (where the underlying mechanism is obscured). On the other hand, the open source community is likely to respond to a patent threat by quickly replacing the relevant code with non-infringing code (where such replacement is possible), Thus, patented algorithms, like those for the creation of MP3 files, have prompted the development of free codecs, such as Ogg Vorbis, which does a similar job without patent encumbrance.

Patent pools, such as the Open Invention Network (OIN), have arisen. Their aim is to acquire patents, funded by their members, and grant licences to those patents to anyone who uses the patents in a particular context (in the case of the OIN, it is the Linux system). Anyone using the Linux system (member or not) automatically receives a licence from the OIN under their patents. The intent is that the OIN will acquire patents for the benefit of the whole Linux community.

From a contracting perspective, open source software licences will frequently contain patent licences (which grant downstream recipients the benefit of any patent rights that the licensor has, either for a specific use, or for all uses). These licences, while beneficial if you are a downstream recipient, can cause unwanted patent leakage for any patent holder releasing code under these licences, and this is a particular issue for patent holders releasing open source code (and may influence their list of acceptable licences).

ASSOCIATED LICENCES

Outside software, there are other licences that have 'open' characteristics to them. For documentation, the GNU Free Documentation Licence, and certain variants of the Creative Commons suite of licences are available. Creative Commons licences are also suitable for other content such as music, photographs, videos and films (but are not themselves suitable for computer software). There have been efforts to apply open source licences in other contexts, such as databases and hardware, but developments in these areas are not as advanced or as fully understood as those relating to software.

FURTHER INFORMATION

Free software foundation: www.fsf.org

Open Source Initiative: www.opensource.org

Free Software Foundation Europe: www.fsfe.org

If you want to get a feeling for what Linux can do, download and burn a 'live CD' that will load a temporary instance of Linux onto your computer (even if it's running Windows®), together with a suite of open source software to try. Even though I have never come across a situation where a live CD has caused any damage to the underlying Windows installation, as with any trial software, it's wise to try it on a non-critical computer that, if it does contain any important data, has been backed up first. Likewise, you can download any number of open source programs (for Linux, Windows, Apple OS/X, or even other more obscure operating systems) from a number of locations (the same warning about using a non-critical computer and backing up applies). To try a Linux distribution, visit www.ubuntu.org

Other open source software (for a variety of operating systems, and not just Linux) can be found here:

www.sourceforge.net

code.google.com/hosting/

www.codeplex.com

www.koders.com

Further relevant information can be found here:

www.openinventionnetwork.com

www.creativecommons.org

www.ifosslr.org

12 WEEE REGULATIONS

Andy Lucas

If your company uses or sells electrical or electronic equipment, then you need to know about the Waste Electrical and Electronic Equipment (WEEE) Regulations 2006, which were created in an effort to reduce the environmental impact of equipment disposal. If you are the user of the equipment, the Regulations may help you dispose of it more cheaply. If you are the producer, you need to understand what your obligations are under the Regulations, to avoid fines levied by the Environment Agency and to keep your customers happy. It's a red-tape bonanza, and there is no escaping it.

INTRODUCTION

The Waste Electrical and Electronic Equipment Regulations ('the Regulations') allocate responsibility for the environmental impact of the disposal of electrical and electronic equipment (EEE or 'equipment') between various players in the supply chain. The Regulations most impact producers, but also affect distributors, importers, households and businesses. They have created a cottage industry around the collection and recycling of EEE.

The Regulations create obligations in relation to both new equipment that producers make (at its end of life), and to waste equipment that is superseded when the new equipment is put on the market. It is important to know the type of equipment and the dates involved because this can change who bears the burden under the Regulations. There are also obligations relating to new equipment at its start of life, such as marking it and providing information on the environmental impact.

There is no need under the Regulations to get your hands dirty actually handling waste equipment, but the Regulations do set the default position for who is financially responsible. Businesses should be aware of the costs, especially when negotiating new contracts and procurements.

THE PLAYERS

The Regulations are full of counter-intuitive labels for the various parties: voluntary schemes with no choice, compulsory schemes with a choice, producers who don't produce, and commercial consumers, let alone the new national bodies created and three letter acronyms used. It is important to keep the right definitions in mind because they are not always obvious.

Environment Agency, Scottish Environmental Protection Agency and Northern Ireland Environment Agency

The Regulations are enforced by the Environmental Agency (EA) in England and Wales, the Scottish Environment Protection Agency (SEPA) in Scotland and the Northern Ireland Environment Agency (NIEA) in Northern Ireland. These agencies also coordinate liaison groups with industry, produce further guidance and updates, and are a useful resource to answer specific queries. The EA website is www.environment-agency.gov.uk and is a good first port of call for further information.

Producers

A 'producer' is anyone who, whatever the selling technique used (including distance communication) manufactures and sells equipment under its own brand, sells someone else's equipment under its brand, or imports or exports equipment on a professional basis into an EU country.

Distributors

A 'distributor' is anyone who provides equipment on a commercial basis to the party who is going to use it. This encompasses equipment hire and leasing companies, wholesalers and distance sellers. (Note that a business can be both a producer and a distributor at the same time, for example by manufacturing equipment and selling it directly to people who will use it. If so, you must comply with both the producer and the distributor obligations.)

Consumers

Members of private households have certain rights but no obligations under the Regulations. These rights also extend to small operations that, because of their nature and size, are similar to private households.

Approved Authorised Treatment Facilities and Approved Exporters

Collected waste equipment must be treated in the UK, or exported to be treated. Approved Authorised Treatment Facilities (AATFs) and Approved Exporters (AEs) are the approved bodies that do this, either by parties providing waste equipment directly to them, or by collecting it themselves from a designated collection facility site and then processing it. The AATF or AE then issues evidence that it has taken on the waste equipment and that it is being handled in line with the Regulations.

Distributor Take-back Scheme/Valpak

The Distributor Take-back Scheme (DTS) is run by the private firm Valpak. Distributors can satisfy their main obligations by joining Valpak's scheme, who then authorise, organise and fund Designated Collection Facilities (see below).

Designated Collection Facilities

Designated Collection Facilities (DCFs) are a national network of collection facilities, run either independently or by Local Authorities. To be a DCF, a collection facility must satisfy a Code of Practice that includes accepting household WEEE for free and passing on all WEEE to a producer compliance scheme. In exchange for these restrictions, the DCF is entitled to free clearance of WEEE by the Producer Compliance Scheme.

Producer Compliance Scheme

Producers must join a Producer Compliance Scheme (PCS) through which they discharge some of their obligations. The PCS arranges the treatment and recycling of the equivalent waste (for household) or the specific waste (for non-household) equipment to satisfy the obligations of its collective membership. Each producer must join a PCS for each compliance period (though a producer can join one PCS for household waste equipment and one for non-household waste equipment). Each PCS is an accredited private entity that can set its own fee structure and membership criteria: for example, only large or small producers, or certain categories of waste equipment. Producers are also allowed to set up their own private PCS of which they are the only member.

Vehicle Certification Agency

The Vehicle Certification Agency (VCA) is an agency of the Department for Transport and enforces distributor obligations and producer obligations relating to marking equipment with the 'crossed out wheeled bin symbol'.

WHAT IS EEE AND WHAT DO THE REGULATIONS COVER?

It is clearly important to understand exactly what 'electrical and electronic equipment' means for the purposes of the Regulations. The starting point is that EEE is any equipment that is dependent on electric currents or electromagnetic fields in order to work properly, or equipment that generates, transfers or measures such currents and fields.

Not all EEE is within the scope of the Regulations, though. The Regulations only apply to equipment that falls within one of 10 broad categories, such as 'large household appliances', 'small household appliances' and 'IT and telecoms equipment' (see Figure 12.1 for the full list). Illustrative lists of what comes within those categories are provided in schedule 2 of the Regulations.

There are also exemptions that should be taken into account. For example, equipment that does not need electricity for its primary function, and equipment whose main power source is not electricity, are exempt from the Regulations.

There are also geographical limitations on the equipment covered by the Regulations. The Regulations only apply to EEE that is put on the market in the UK. 'Placing on the market' is the initial action of making a product available for the first time in that market, with a view to distribution or use in that area. This takes place as the product is transferred from the manufacturing stage, with the intention of distribution or use on the market. The notion of putting on the market relates to each individual unit, and not the type of product, or the product line as a whole.

Why is this relevant? Unfortunately, this kind of non-obvious distinction can completely change the nature of the obligations under the Regulations. As an illustration, consider the case of a leasing company that leases out photography equipment in the UK. That company's obligations will depend entirely on where the equipment was originally 'placed on the market'.

Figure 12.1 WEEE categories

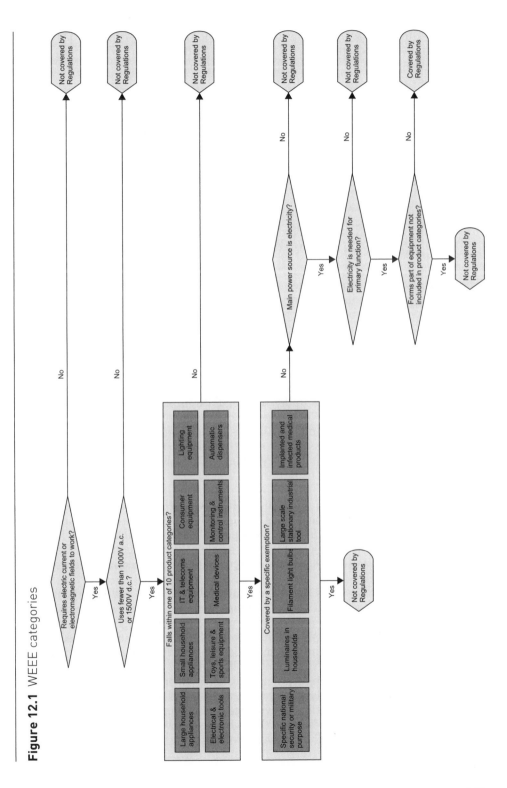

- If the equipment was purchased in New York, the leasing company is the importer of the equipment, and would be regarded as the 'producer' of the equipment, with responsibility for the cost of handling when it becomes waste.

- If the equipment was purchased in Paris, the leasing company would bear the costs in the UK, but should be able to recover those costs under French law from the French producer (any single unit has a 'producer' for each member state it has been put on the market in).

- If the equipment was purchased in London, the leasing company would not be regarded as the producer.

Similarly, someone who refurbishes and sells old televisions is the producer if they bought them in Sofia, but not if they bought them in London, and not if the television was ever sold in the UK in the past, no matter what countries it has since passed through.

There are also separate categories of EEE that require separate reporting: any display equipment, cooling appliances containing refrigerants and gas discharge lamps should be separately dealt with and considered.

From here on, for simplicity the terms 'EEE' and 'equipment' will refer just to items that the Regulations place obligations on.

Household and non-household equipment

For equipment that is covered under the Regulations, a further key distinction is whether it is 'household' or 'non-household' equipment. The obligations and scheme setup for producers and distributors differ greatly based on this question. The requirements for businesses that sell to private households (or businesses similar to private households) are very different from those for business that sell to non-households.

An interesting issue lies within this distinction: while the Regulations refer to equipment used in private households (or equivalent to private households), which is a question of fact, it is not always possible at the point of sale to know how equipment will be used, and it is not feasible at end of life to track the history of each item's use, so equipment needs to be categorised in some way.

The Department for Business Innovation and Skills (BIS) has set out guideline criteria that indicate when an item of equipment relates to non-households. For example, one indicator that a particular item is 'non-household' is that there is a signed contract that assigns end-of-life responsibilities and ensures that equipment will not be disposed of through municipal waste streams. Another indicator relates to the features of the equipment itself: equipment that requires specialised training, licences, special configuration, a professional environment, or is unsafe for the public or particularly large or heavy, will generally not be household equipment. Alternatively, statistical evidence that equipment does not end up in municipal waste streams can be used (BIS stresses, however, that common sense should also be applied, as well as these guidelines.)

KEY OBLIGATIONS ON IT BUSINESSES

The Regulations will affect businesses in different ways depending on the type of products sold, how they are sold and to whom they are sold. The basic breakdowns are producers versus distributors, and household equipment versus non-household equipment. Business managers should know both their obligations as producers and distributors, as well as their rights as users of non-household equipment.

Producers

As noted above, you are likely to be regarded as a 'producer' for the purposes of the Regulations if you are selling the equipment under your brand or importing/exporting it. The main producer obligations are as follows:

- Producers must join a PCS. The PCS will collect and recycle the right amount of equipment to satisfy the regulatory requirements of all its members. To do so, they require information about the amount of equipment the producer sells, along with the category it falls in and whether it is for household or non-household use.

PCSs are free to charge as they want for their services, which include registration, administration, collection, treatment, recovery and recycling of waste equipment. They also collect and pass on the Environment Agency registration fee (which varies from £30 to £445, based on the size of the business). Basic prices usually relate to business turnover and tonnes of waste equipment recycled, because this affects the proportion of waste in that category that must be handled. Like any business, PCSs compete to offer a complete package including additional services such as web-based monitoring, audits of WEEE compliance and Europe-wide solutions.

It is well worth shopping around and speaking to various PCS schemes to see which would be most appropriate for your business. The Environment Agency lists all the approved PCSs on their website (as of 2011, 36 schemes in England, Wales and Scotland). The three most used schemes (WEEECare, Valpak and B2B Compliance) are used by over 40 per cent of signed up producers. By 15 November of each year, producers should be signed up for a PCS for the next calendar year (or two PCSs: one for household equipment and one for non-household). Producers that only start producing after this deadline have a 28-day window to arrange membership.

For household equipment, the PCS covers the cost of collecting, treating, recovering and disposing of a volume of waste equipment in proportion to their clients' UK market share for that category. For non-household equipment, the PCS covers the cost of collecting, treating, recovering and disposing of the actual waste equipment that the producer sold on or after 13 August 2005, when it becomes waste. (If the producer sells equipment that replaces pre-13 August 2005 equipment, then they have to also handle the pre-13 August 2005 waste equipment that their new product is replacing.)

Alternative arrangements can be made for both household and non-household equipment, but these are the default positions.

- Producers must add the 'crossed out wheeled bin' logo to their equipment, along with their producer identifier mark and producer registration number. This must be added in a visible, legible and indelible form to each piece of equipment. Details are available in BS 50419. The black bar beneath the logo represents that the product was first put on the UK market after 13 August 2005.

- Within one year of placing a new type of equipment on the market, producers must make available information concerning its reuse and environmentally sound treatment. This includes the materials and components, and the location of any dangerous substances used.

- Producers are also given a producer registration number by their PCS, which they must provide to distributors. This allows accurate equipment reporting generally, but is particularly important for non-household equipment where the distributor will pass this number on to the user. For non-household equipment, all the recycling obligations lie with the producer, and none with the distributor. The user, equipped with a producer registration number can therefore identify and contact directly the original producer.

Distributors

The Regulations create different obligations for distributors of household and non-household equipment. Only distributors of household equipment have waste handling obligations. Distributors of non-household equipment must pass information between the producer and user (such as telling the user who the registered producer is, and telling the producer details of non-household sales for their own reporting), but have no obligations in the actual handling of waste.

Distributors of household equipment also have a role as the information link between the producers and the users of the equipment. This involves providing information about the environmental impact of waste equipment, the benefits of recycling, and the arrangements available to them for free disposal of their waste equipment.

Distributors also have 'take-back' obligations when they sell household equipment. These can be discharged in one of three ways:

- The distributor can provide a free service to take back, on broadly a 'like for like' basis, equipment they sell. The obligation exists where the waste equipment is of an equivalent type and has fulfilled the same function as the new equipment. Government guidance gives examples such as taking back a cassette player for an MP3 player, or a VCR for a DVD player. Distributors may offer additional services, such as collection from the user's home, but this does not itself satisfy their obligations, and any costs should cover just the collection and handling.

- The distributor can join the national Distributor Take-back Scheme (DTS). This scheme funds collection facilities that consumers can take their waste equipment to. Unlike joining a PCS, there is no market in the DTS, there is just one operator called Valpak. The membership fee for the DTS is banded by equipment sales value during the period 1 October 2008 to 30 September 2009. A new joiner with sales value of under £100,000 would pay £200 to cover membership up to December 2012. Distributors with an equipment sales value over £1.5 million during the period pay a membership fee based on the actual numbers of different types of equipment they sold. For example, each fridge or freezer sold between 1 October 2008 and 30 September 2009 attracts a membership fee of 16 pence, and each television a fee of 6.16 pence. There are various tiers and levels of membership for the 'phase 2' period that covers up to December 2012, the specifics of which are available on the Valpak website.

- The distributor can also provide an alternative free take-back service that is accessible to the customer. This applies most usually for distance sellers such as internet retailers. A pre-paid return envelope for example would satisfy this.

Once the distributor has received household waste equipment, they are obligated to handle it in a way that optimises the reuse and recycling of the equipment. There are generally two options for this: either to pass it on to a PCS who must take it for free (though can charge to collect it) or to arrange themselves for it to go to an AATF. If a waste management licence is needed for this transport and the distributor does not have one, then they should use a registered waste carrier.

Distributors also have record keeping obligations. These do not relate to individual sales, but to the number of returned units they receive and the number of units they pass on to PCSs. Distributors should keep these records for four years.

KEY COMMERCIAL ISSUES

The burden of the cost of processing non-household equipment is very different from that of household equipment. For non-household equipment, the position is set out in the flowchart shown in Figure 12.1.

Cost burden
A key point to note is, in the default position, the double disposal required where equipment is produced that replaces pre-13 August 2005 equipment. The producer must bear the financial cost of handling both the equipment being replaced (at the time of sale), and the cost of handling the equipment he has produced (at its end of life). PCS membership will cover this, but it is producers that fund the PCSs.

Even with non-household equipment put on the market on or after 13 August 2005, the default position passes the financial burden of its end-of-life handling to the producer (via their PCS). It is accordingly critical that producers are aware of their obligations, and factor in the costs of PCS membership and other waste equipment handling at the time of negotiations. If no alternative arrangement is made, these costs should be included in the producer's financial models and this burden made clear to the other side in negotiations.

On the other hand, purchasers of non-household equipment may well be best served staying quiet on waste equipment arrangements. If nothing else is arranged, then the producer of any new equipment purchased (or their PCS) will bear the costs of handling it when it becomes waste.

This is the case whether or not they are aware of this obligation, and so some producers might offer prices that do not factor in these hidden costs. Of course, negotiations should always be conducted with the bigger picture in mind, and the risk that this stealth might harm commercial relations or fetter future partnership opportunities should be considered.

In practice, these subtle legislative distinctions are normally overridden by alternative contractual arrangements. This does not make them irrelevant though: they represent the default, and if you make a concession from them you should be looking for something back in return.

Collection v. disposal

The legislation is not clear exactly what the 'collection' of waste equipment entails. While the legislation refers to a producer's obligation to finance collection, government guidance says this can be satisfied by providing an appropriate system, such as collection points. There is clearly scope for ambiguity, and there can be a huge difference in cost. Take for example the cost of 'collecting' the network cabling installed in an office building, versus the cost of collecting it once it has been placed in a skip outside. Each party should consider its expectations at the negotiation stage to prevent disputes later down the line.

FURTHER INFORMATION

Department of Business, Innovation and Skills: www.bis.gov.uk/weee

Valpak: www.valpak.co.uk/dts

Environment Agency: www.environment-agency.gov.uk/business/topics/waste/32084.aspx

13 FREEDOM OF INFORMATION

Victoria Hordern

Any private computer company doing business with the public sector must recognise the influence of the Freedom of Information Act 2000. Freedom of information is about the public's right to know how public money is spent and how public sector decisions are made. This chapter aims to give the reader a working knowledge of the rules under the law, what exemptions exist to withhold information and how a private computer company should prepare for a request for disclosure of its commercial or sensitive information.

INTRODUCTION

The introduction of the Freedom of Information Act 2000 (FOIA or the Act) was part of the newly elected Labour Government's drive in 1997 to shake up the British constitutional system. All public authorities are required to provide people who exercise their rights under the Act ('requestors') with information that the public authority holds regardless of where it came from or who owns it. The changes were part of moving from a 'need to know' to 'right to know' culture. In practice, the right to environmental information has been around for a lot longer (where a requestor asks for disclosure of environmental information the Environmental Information Regulations 2004 apply rather than FOIA). Furthermore it is likely that the reach of the Act will be extended so that the access to information regime will become even more important.

As a consequence, all private companies dealing with the public sector need to consider carefully the information they provide to public authorities. The advent of Public Private Partnerships (PPP) and Private Finance Initiatives (PFI) in the 1990s has led considerably more private companies to provide services both to and on behalf of local and central government. When contracting on this basis, private companies inevitably provide considerable amounts of information to a public authority about their business proposal. Disclosure of this information under FOIA can present a commercial risk to private companies and put them at a disadvantage with competitors. Furthermore, the FOIA itself does not provide a private company with any sanctions to stop disclosure. Consequently a private company is relatively powerless when facing a disclosure by a public authority of its confidential information and is forced to rely on contractual or common law remedies. On a practical level, private companies need to focus on maintaining a good working relationship with the public authority and encouraging the public authority to involve them when a request relates to information about the company. From a legal perspective, the private company should ensure that there is a clear FOIA clause in any contract or non-disclosure agreement.

Of course there is nothing to stop a private company making a FOIA request itself to a public authority in order to understand certain issues within the public authority or to obtain information about competitors held by the public authority. However, be aware that making requests in your own name could influence the public authority's attitude towards you!

TRANSPARENCY AGENDA

The incoming 2010 Coalition Government has set out plans to open up government data that includes the commitment to publish online all new central government IT contracts with a value of more than £10,000. Central government in this context includes agents and agencies of central government, all non-departmental public bodies, the National Health Service (NHS) and trading funds. Guidance produced by the Office of Government Commerce (OGC) indicates that redactions from IT contracts may be made by a public authority before publication in line with available exemptions under the FOIA. Otherwise, the contract should be published in full. In this context, suppliers should be given the opportunity to identify which pieces of information they regard as exempt under FOIA and why. However, a public authority is not obliged to withhold information by relying on exemptions cited by the supplier. The Transparency Agenda marks a shift towards proactive publication, and suppliers of IT services to the public sector should therefore assume in most instances that information contained in the contract they sign will be published.

PUBLIC AUTHORITIES

One of the first questions to consider when thinking about FOIA is to check to see whether the organisation you are dealing with is a public authority under FOIA. Sometimes this can be straightforward since you can check on the organisation's website to see whether they indicate what their status is under FOIA, but it may not always be clear. Most public authorities are listed by name under Schedule 1 Part I of the Act. However, there are other rules that catch organisations that are not listed but may be publicly owned companies or otherwise designated by the Secretary of State as a public authority. In reality, in the last few years, the Secretary of State has proposed designating very few new organisations as public authorities: the Association of Chief Police Officers and the Universities and Colleges Application Services are recent examples. At the time of writing there is no one comprehensive list of public authorities that are caught by FOIA.

A PUBLIC AUTHORITY'S OBLIGATIONS

As well as providing a publication scheme (which is typically accessible through the public authority's website and sets out what information is routinely made available), a public authority must comply with two obligations under FOIA in response to a request for information. It must:

- confirm or deny whether it holds the information; and
- make such information available.

The public authority is required to respond to the requestor within 20 working days of receiving a request either providing the information requested or setting out the specific exemptions and an explanation as to why such information cannot be disclosed. When exemptions require an examination of what is called the public interest test (defined below), the public authority may take a further 20 working days (i.e. 40 working days in total) to consider the public interest arguments if it so requires. However, the public authority must still respond after the initial 20 working days to notify the requestor of the exemption it seeks to rely on and that it needs longer time to consider the public interest test. A public authority cannot indefinitely delay responding fully to a request.

In certain cases the request may not be formulated clearly, may be too general or ask for access to a lot of information. The public authority cannot simply refuse a request on those grounds. It is under a duty to provide advice and assistance to requestors, which may require seeking clarification from the requestor as to the actual information they are seeking, helping the requestor focus their request and providing information that it is able to locate within a specific period of time. However, there are limits to the amount of effort the public authority is required to expend in order to determine whether it holds information (discussed below).

PROVIDING INFORMATION TO THE PUBLIC AUTHORITY

Where private company information is subject to disclosure
Since the Act catches all information held by a public authority, this will include all information supplied to a public authority by a private company in the context of discussions, contract negotiations and contract delivery. This means that the tender document prepared by the private company setting out its business proposal and references from previous customers will be caught. Likewise, at contract negotiation stage, the technical specification, service level agreement, IT and security policies, methodologies and algorithms that underline the particular solution (once provided to the public authority) are caught together with the payment schedule that sets out the unit costs for particular products and services that the private company will provide to the public authority. Given that FOIA will apply to all information held by a public authority you should consider whether you need to provide to the public authority any information beyond that which is strictly necessary to include in the contract as part of documenting the legal agreement between the parties.

Where the private company is required contractually to help a public authority locate the information that is requested under FOIA
Where a private company provides a service on behalf of a public authority, the company must recognise that the information it holds on behalf of the public authority is subject to FOIA. This rule ensures that public authorities cannot avoid the effects of FOIA by procuring private companies to hold information for them. In most contracts, the public authority will seek to impose an

obligation on the private company to assist the public authority in complying with any FOIA request (or indeed request under the Data Protection Act 1998) to disclose information. When faced with this obligation, the company should consider how it would go about locating and providing the information. For instance, will the IT system be designed to run searches that will be able to easily locate information? Additionally, the company should consider whether it wishes to provide this assistance as part of the overall services to the public authority or whether it wishes to seek a reimbursement of its costs for this exercise. It is better for discussions on this point to occur at contract negotiation stage rather than at the time that a public authority is pressing the company for assistance so that the public authority can comply with the 20 working day limit.

THE REQUEST PROCESS

It is important to bear in mind that there is no requirement on the public author-ity under the FOIA to involve the private company when the private company's information is requested. A timeline of a request is set out below.

Request received by the public authority

Once a request is received, the public authority must assess its scope and decide whether it understands what information is being sought. The public authority must treat the request as applicant-blind and motive-blind so it cannot make a decision not to disclose information to a particular requestor because it suspects their motive. The only exceptions to this rule are where the request is vexatious or compliance would exceed the appropriate limit (see below).

The public authority must then consider whether it holds the information in question and should seek to locate it within its records and files.

Once the information has been located, the public authority should consider whether the information should be disclosed or whether it can rely on an exemp-tion to withhold the information. Even if an exemption is available, the public authority is not required to rely on it. It is at this stage that a public authority should seek to involve a third party, such as a private company, if the information in issue relates to that third party.

Once the public authority has reached a decision about whether to withhold all or part of the information or whether to disclose all, it will respond to the requestor. Some public authorities maintain a disclosure log on their website with access to all the responses they have sent to requests.

After the response is sent to the requestor, it will only go further if the requestor seeks an internal review of the public authority's decision.

If the requestor disputes the public authority's decision, the public authority must conduct an internal review that must be carried out by a suitably senior and independent person within the public authority.

The internal review must take place relatively quickly and the requestor be provided with the results of the review.

Appeal to the Information Commissioner's Office

If the requestor remains unsatisfied with the way that their request has been handled, they can then take the matter to the Information Commissioner's Office (ICO). The ICO hears all appeals from a FOIA request at an initial stage but private companies cannot directly present their arguments to the ICO. In the early days of FOIA, the ICO was faced with a huge backlog of appeals from FOIA requests that meant that the process took months or even years. More recently, the ICO has improved the efficiency of the appeals process although it can still take some time.

The ICO considers the complaint from the requestor, contacts the public authority to ask for the relevant information that is the subject of the request for it to assess and then makes a decision, which is published on the ICO website. The decision sets out whether the public authority was correct to rely on an exemption to withhold information or whether the ICO considers the public authority was wrong and should now disclose the information.

Appeal to the Information Tribunals

Either the requestor or the public authority can challenge the ICO's decision by appealing to the relevant Tribunal. New rules that came into force in 2010 mean that appeals from the ICO's decision are either heard at First-tier Tribunal (Information Rights) level or at Upper Tribunal level.

If the matter is significantly serious the appeal goes to the Upper Tribunal (e.g. appeals against national security certificates are automatically sent to the Upper Tribunal). Otherwise most matters are dealt with by the First-tier Tribunal. It is at the Tribunal stage that third parties (such as private companies) can be joined to the proceedings in order to represent their interests before the Tribunal. For instance, T-mobile joined as a third party when an appeal was brought by Ofcom against an ICO decision that required disclosure of information that impacted on the mobile phone industry.

The Tribunal considers the arguments and comes to a decision, which is published on the Tribunal's website. Further appeals to the appropriate court are only permitted if there is a dispute on a point of law.

WITHHOLDING INFORMATION

It is important that private companies are aware of the circumstances in which a public authority can withhold information under an exemption. FOIA provides two types of exemption: absolute and qualified exemptions. Absolute exemptions do not require any consideration of the public interest test. However, all qualified exemptions require the public authority not only to consider whether the information is exempt but also to determine whether in all the circumstances of the case the public interest in maintaining the exemption outweighs the public interest in disclosure (the public interest test). Since the default position under FOIA is that the public interest always favours disclosure, in order to rely on a qualified exemption, the arguments in favour of maintaining the exemption (i.e. withholding the information) must always outweigh the arguments in favour of disclosure.

The public authority must consider public interest arguments both in favour of disclosure (e.g. holding public authorities accountable for the spending of public money, helping the public understand decisions taken etc.), and in favour of withholding (e.g. timing of the request may be critical, the public authority's ability to procure services from the private sector would be damaged etc.). It is important to note that what is 'of interest to the public' is not the same thing as what the public interest test recognises as 'in the interests of the public'. Furthermore, the public interest test is concerned with the public as a whole not with the interests of the individual requestor.

For the purposes of private sector companies engaging with the public sector, the most common exemptions that the public authority will consider in order to withhold information are set out in Tables 13.1 and 13.2.

The rules also allow public authorities to refuse to respond to requests where the request is designed to disrupt the working practices of the public authority. A public authority can refuse to answer a request that is vexatious or repeated as defined in guidance from the ICO and Tribunal decisions. Furthermore, a public authority need not respond to a request where the actual time spent determining whether the information is held, locating, retrieving and extracting the information would exceed certain time frames: 24 hours for central government and 18 hours for all other public authorities. The rule is known as the

Table 13.1 FOIA absolute exemptions

Section	Exemption
40	Personal information: where disclosure of information by the public authority would contravene its obligations to comply with any of the data protection principles under the Data Protection Act 1998.
41	Information provided in confidence: where disclosure of information by the public authority would give rise to an actionable breach of confidence action by a third party.
44	Prohibition on disclosure: where disclosure is prohibited by or under any enactment, is incompatible with any Community obligation or would constitute or be punishable as a contempt of court.

Table 13.2 FOIA qualified exemptions

Section	Exemption
22	Information intended for future publication.
36	Information where disclosure would inhibit the free and frank provision of advice or exchange of views.
42	Information protected by legal professional privilege.
43(1)	Trade secrets: where the information is a trade secret.
43(2)	Information the disclosure of which would prejudice commercial interests.

appropriate limit or cost limit and is set down in regulations. It also provides that the public authority can charge a requestor in certain circumstances, but it does not set out any mechanism for private companies to be reimbursed for any time spent assisting a public authority to comply with a request.

IMPACT OF FOIA ON PRIVATE COMPANIES

Private companies now have to operate on the basis that any information they provide to a public authority could be disclosed in the future. Such disclosures may take place regardless of the confidentiality clauses in any contract between the public authority and the private sector company since a statutory obligation to disclose outweighs any contractual obligation on the public authority. In other words, the public authority may have to disclose confidential information under FOIA even if this disclosure would put it in breach of contract. This may give rise to commercial, reputational and privacy risks for the private company.

Commercial

Much of the information that a private company provides to a public authority will relate to business practices or commercial matters within the private company. There are a number of exemptions that may be relevant here and we set out below brief background on two exemptions in particular: confidential information (s. 41) and commercial prejudice (s. 43 (2)).

The test in relation to confidential information requires a number of different elements. Firstly, the information must have been obtained from another party (i.e. not the public authority). Secondly, the information must be confidential. Thirdly, the information must have been imparted in circumstances importing an obligation of confidence (i.e. the receiving party should have been reasonably aware that the information must be held in confidence). Fourthly, the disclosure of the information must be to the detriment of the party providing the information to the public authority. Fifthly, there must be no public interest defence to the disclosure and, lastly, any action for breach of confidence should, on a balance of probabilities, succeed.

The test in relation to commercial prejudice is whether, at the date of the request, disclosure of the information would be likely to damage a party's commercial interests (whether the public authority, computer company or another party). Therefore, if consulted by the public authority about a FOIA request, or in identifying information that may fall within this description for inclusion in a schedule to the contract listing confidential and commercially sensitive information, the company needs to be able to clearly distinguish between information that is not really commercially sensitive and information that is. In support, the company should provide arguments about the damage the release of such information will actually cause the company (i.e. disclosing unit prices would allow competitors to undercut the company's position). Furthermore, to the extent that the company can assist the public authority in considering the public interest factors (since s. 43 (2) is a qualified exemption), the company should provide the public authority with arguments that the public authority can then consider when deciding whether it can rely on an exemption. The Office of Government Commerce Civil Procurement Policy and Guidance provides a useful starting point for thinking about when this exemption might apply to specific information.

Reputational

It goes without saying that disclosure of information under FOIA can have a serious effect on the reputation of numerous actors: the public authority as well as third parties involved.

Privacy

Depending on the information that is disclosed, there can be risks to individuals' privacy if information about their public or private role is disclosed.

DEALING WITH FOIA

Private companies should follow these steps:

- Prepare for company information to be put into the public domain particularly in light of the Transparency Agenda.

- Devise a PR strategy for dealing with this eventuality.

- Think carefully about the information provided to public authorities and in what context. Public authorities will not necessarily know how sensitive the information is to the company unless they are told. A public authority could be entitled to consider that information provided voluntarily, without any warning to a public authority about its sensitivity, could be disclosed under FOIA.

- When entering into contracts, ensure that there is a robust FOIA clause that requires the public authority to notify and consult the company when it receives a request that affects company information.

- If the company is providing a service to a public authority that involves the company collecting information on behalf of the public authority, bear in mind that the company will be holding information on its behalf and, therefore, such information is subject to FOIA. As a result, the public authority may require the company to help with compliance with its responsibilities under FOIA by searching for and locating this information. This activity may impact on the company's resources depending on how many requests of this nature are received. The company should consider at contract negotiation stage whether it is prepared to absorb these resource costs or whether it proposes to charge the public authority for this assistance.

- When entering into a contract with a public authority, seek to identify early on the information that is confidential or commercially sensitive to the company and identify this information in a schedule to the contract explaining why the exemption should apply and providing any public interest arguments. This is particularly important due to the new Transparency Agenda, which requires the proactive publication of IT contracts. Although this is not a guarantee that this information will not be disclosed it does provide a clear indication of the views of the parties at the time the contract was signed.

- Seek to be involved in helping the public authority assess the relevant exemptions when information is requested. However, do not try to control the public authority's FOIA process and be realistic about the information the company wishes to withhold. A blanket exemption for the whole contract is not going to be persuasive. Furthermore, a public authority is not obliged to take account of the company's arguments and can still disclose regardless of what the company says.

- The ultimate remedy available to a private company if a public authority is due to disclose information that the company considers is exempt from disclosure is to seek an injunction to prevent disclosure. In reality, hardly any companies have gone down this route and the company will need to have been informed in advance that a disclosure is due in order to seek an injunction preventing disclosure.

PROCUREMENT

When bidding for substantial public sector IT projects, the tender process is run according to UK procurement rules. Under procurement rules, public authorities are required to disclose certain information at particular points in the procurement timetable. For instance, once a contract award decision has been made, the public authority must provide all those expressing an interest in tendering for the work (besides the successful tenderer) with information such as the award criteria and weightings, the score that the particular recipient obtained against those award criteria and weightings, and the score that the winning tenderer obtained. On the basis that this information is intended for future publication, once the award has been made, a public authority may well consider applying the exemption under s. 22 (along with any other available exemptions) if it receives a request for disclosure of this information before it has been published to the interested parties. However, to rely on this exemption, the public authority must be able to demonstrate that it is reasonable in all the circumstances that the information should be withheld from disclosure until the date intended for publication. Additionally, since s. 22 is a qualified exemption, the public interest test applies.

DRAFTING A CLAUSE

The following lists some issues that a private company should consider when negotiating a contract or non-disclosure agreement with a public authority:

- Is the public authority required to publish the contract as part of the Transparency Agenda?

- Is there an opportunity to provide a schedule setting out the information you consider to be confidential or commercially sensitive?

- Will the public authority notify you if it receives a FOIA request that relates to information you disclose to the public authority in connection with the contract?

- If the public authority agrees to notify you, will it do so immediately or use reasonable endeavours to do so or within a specified time period?

- Is there any obligation on the public authority to consult with you when a FOIA request relates to information you disclose to the public authority in connection with the contract?

- Is the public authority under any contractual obligation to take your arguments into account when applying exemptions?

- If you will hold information on behalf of the public authority under the contract, under what circumstances can the public authority require you to search for and provide information in response to a FOIA request?

- Will the cost of the resources you apply to searching and providing information be paid for by the public authority or will you absorb these costs?

- To what extent are you required to search for information?

- Within what time limits are you required to provide this information?

FURTHER INFORMATION

Information Commissioner's Office: www.ico.org.uk

Information Tribunal: www.informationtribunal.gov.uk

Ministry of Justice and FOIA: www.justice.gov.uk/about/freedom-of-information.htm

Ministry of Justice Section 45 Code of Practice: www.justice.gov.uk/guidance/docs/foi-section45-code-of-practice.pdf

OGC Civil Procurement and Policy Guidance (v2): www.ogc.gov.uk/documents/OGC_FOI_and_Civil_Procurement_guidance.pdf

OGC Transparency: www.ogc.gov.uk/policy_and_standards_framework_transparency.asp

14   RESOLVING DISPUTES

Sara Ellacott

This chapter considers the most commonly used methods of dispute resolution, their advantages and disadvantages, together with a consideration of the relevant procedures associated with each method. Mediation is discussed after litigation and arbitration, but you should note that it has gained popularity in the UK with the courts, government agencies and the private sector.

INTRODUCTION

Taking time to consider how to deal with potential disputes at the very outset of a complex technology project can sometimes be regarded as defeatist; the parties are keen to work together and do not want to dwell on the potential difficulties they may face. The reality, however, is that during the life cycle of the majority of technology projects a variety of disputes will happen for a wide variety of reasons:

- business requirements change;
- delays mount up;
- complex terms give rise to various interpretations.

Despite the best intentions of the parties, careful planning and excellent working practices, problems can and do still arise. Time is therefore well spent considering the various methods of dispute resolution available, before the need to use them actually arises in practice.

OVERVIEW OF DISPUTE RESOLUTION METHODS

There is a wide range of potential dispute resolution methods available, the most common of which are:

- negotiation;
- escalation to senior management;
- expert determination;
- litigation;
- arbitration;

- competition bodies (e.g. OFT, European Commission);
- mediation.

There is no 'one size fits all' method of dispute resolution, so your choice will ultimately depend on what you require out of the dispute resolution process, for example:

- Do you require damages/compensation for a particular breach of contract or misrepresentation?
- Is obtaining interim injunctive relief a necessity?
- Is an ongoing relationship important?
- Is it important to maintain confidentiality as to the issues in dispute and the resulting settlement (if any)?

Depending on your needs, the different methods of dispute resolution will be more or less suitable.

KEY FACTORS IN DISPUTE RESOLUTION

When deciding on any dispute resolution method, there are a number of common factors that should always be taken into account. These include:

- **Impartiality** – is the adjudicator impartial and seen to be impartial?
- **Expertise** – has the adjudicator the correct level of expertise to deal with the issues in dispute?
- **Speed** – how long will it take the adjudicator to reach a decision?
- **Cost** – how expensive will the process be?
- **Certainty** – will the decision be binding and can it be appealed?
- **Confidentiality** – will the decision/settlement be confidential?
- **Motivation** – who, if anyone, has a vested interest in the dispute and its resolution?
- **The business relationship** – can the relationship continue after the dispute is resolved?
- **Ease of enforcement** – can the decision be enforced domestically and/or abroad?

Each method of dispute resolution has its advantages and disadvantages, and we will consider each method against these key factors before addressing the relevant procedures associated with it.

SPECIFIC DISPUTE RESOLUTION METHODS

Negotiation

Direct commercial negotiation between the parties is one of the most popular and successful ways of resolving disputes. Table 14.1 shows how negotiation relates to the key factors.

Table 14.1 Negotiation

Impartiality	Not relevant (the parties are negotiating for their own benefit).
Expertise	Not particularly advantageous or relevant (although the people involved with the technology project will have first-hand knowledge of the issues in dispute and how they can be resolved).
Speed	Good: negotiations can be undertaken as quickly as the parties require (although it is up to the parties to ensure that they do not drag on indefinitely, without any actual formal resolution of the dispute).
Cost	Good: the costs incurred will primarily be those of the parties involved in the negotiations (additional costs may be incurred if the parties use internal or external legal advisors).
Certainty	Not good: the parties will come to a settlement only if they choose to do so.
Confidentiality	Good: such negotiations can be conducted on a 'without prejudice' and confidential basis. This encourages openness between the parties and ensures that the negotiations cannot be used in formal evidence if they break down and the parties end up using another form of dispute resolution. This is important, as the parties may be prepared to make concessions in their negotiating positions for the sake of reaching a compromise, which they would not be prepared to concede if they were litigating the dispute.
Motivation	Good: such negotiations usually involve those most heavily involved with the project on a day-to-day basis (the project manager, the IT director, the account manager, the commercial team etc.). These parties are most closely aligned with the project and therefore have a vested interest in resolving issues.

(Continued)

Table 14.1 *(Continued)*

Business relationship	Good: such negotiations often allow for a positive ongoing working relationship (in some cases, it can be stronger than the one that existed before the dispute). This is particularly important for those in technology projects, which often last for a number of years.
Enforcement	Not good: any settlement can only be enforced by one party suing the other for breach of contract (i.e. breach of the settlement terms). This can be time-consuming and expensive.

Escalation to senior management

Some technology contracts require that the parties try and resolve disputes through senior management before resorting to external methods.

The advantages and disadvantages of this method are generally very similar to those of negotiation, but there is a particular 'plus' when it comes to motivation. Sometimes those at the 'coalface' of a large-scale technology project can become too emotionally involved to resolve a dispute: they allow their personal prejudices to prevent them seeing the advantages of a commercial resolution. Escalation to senior management can cut through such prejudices, and so allow for the 'bigger picture' to be considered and a commercial resolution found.

Expert determination

Expert determination is now a very popular method of dispute resolution in the construction industry, and it is also well suited to the settlement of technology disputes (although its take-up in the IT sector has not been as widespread as many people had previously envisaged).

It is a procedure by which an independent third-party expert makes a decision on the dispute. The expert does not act as a judge or as an arbitrator. Table 14.2 shows how expert determination relates to the key factors.

Table 14.2 Expert determination

Impartiality	Good: the parties have to agree on an expert so they will only agree to someone they both believe to be impartial.
Expertise	Good: the parties will choose an individual who is an expert in the technology or project type (e.g. CRM, ERP) in dispute.

(Continued)

Table 14.2 *(Continued)*

Speed	Good: the process can be set up as quickly as the parties can agree (subject to the expert's availability).
Cost	Good: in contrast to both litigation and arbitration, the process is relatively inexpensive.
Certainty	Good: the result is contractually binding and thus difficult to appeal. This often brings finality to the dispute. The law on expert determination is, however, not conclusive and is still developing. Moreover, there are no arrangements or laws that allow for the enforcement of an expert's decision abroad.
Confidentiality	Good: the procedure is confidential, and this is clearly beneficial to a technology supplier, which would not want its customer base to become aware of any particular problems with its technology offering.
Motivation	Not a particularly relevant or overriding factor.
Business relationship	Good: expert determination may help to preserve a business relationship because it is slightly less adversarial than litigation or arbitration.
Enforcement	Good: failure to adhere to a decision will be a breach of contract. An expert's determination can thus be enforced by obtaining summary judgment and using general enforcement methods.

The procedure adopted for expert determination depends on the terms of the parties' contract (although they may decide to put a dispute to expert determination by later agreement). The 'terms of reference' set out how the expert is required to act and should include clear definitions of:

- the issues under dispute;
- the material the expert is expected to review;
- what the expert is allowed to consider (matters may arise from investigations that the parties to the dispute feel the expert is not equipped to deal with);
- the procedure and timescale to be followed;
- the nature of the submissions each party is allowed to make;
- what type of hearing is required;
- how the final decision is to be delivered (i.e. orally or in writing).

The expert is usually appointed from a recognised body. The parties may appoint a panel of experts rather than an individual; each person having been selected to provide a different type of expertise and perspective.

The parties may agree grounds upon which a decision may be challenged.

If there is no express agreement, then common law inserts the following grounds as reason for appeal:

- Fraud by the expert;
- Failure by the expert to treat the two parties fairly or equally;
- A 'material departure' from the instructions by the expert (any departure from the instructions that is more than trivial will be a 'material departure' irrespective of the consequences);
- A 'manifest error' by the expert (i.e. a blunder or omission capable of affecting the determination). It must have a significant consequential effect on the outcome of the determination; a minor mistake will not render the decision invalid, unless the parties have agreed that it will in their terms of reference;
- An error in an accountant's certificate that details the adjustment in value of a purchase price when that price is being determined by the expert.

Litigation
Litigation is the traditional method of resolving contractual disputes. The landscape of civil litigation changed with the introduction of the Civil Procedure Rules 1998 (CPR). The CPR continues to place an emphasis on the front-loading of legal costs, by the parties having to properly set out their claims at an early stage in the proceedings. Table 14.3 shows how litigation relates to the key factors.

Table 14.3 Litigation

Impartiality	Good: judges are impartial.
Expertise	Good: the technical expertise of judges has improved a lot in recent years, particularly those in the Technology and Construction Court (TCC). Judges can also appoint experts to advise them on technical issues.
Speed	Still not good: the courts are concerned with giving a decision (based on law) that is fair and objective. The speed of the decision-making process can therefore be secondary to obtaining a correct adjudication and the matter may go to appeal. However, the CPR allows for the courts to manage cases strictly and this has helped to reduce the timescales of litigation.

(Continued)

Table 14.3 *(Continued)*

	It is now possible to bring an action to trial within a year of the proceedings being commenced, particularly if the court orders a speedy trial (this is certainly no slower than most arbitrations). Large and complex IT cases can and do, however, still take a number of years to reach conclusion (the recent *BSkyB* v. *HP/EDS* case being a prime example).
	It is possible to make an application for urgent injunctive relief. This can often bring a matter to a very swift resolution; the party against whom the injunction is granted often looks for a commercial resolution at that time.
Cost	Still not good: particularly if complex areas of IT law or technical matters have to be considered and expert evidence is required. The winning party does, however, generally have the ability to claim back a proportion of its costs from the losing party, which helps to reduce the financial burden.
Certainty	Good: litigation in the UK, and in most other jurisdictions, is governed by the rules of the relevant courts. The rules do allow for some flexibility but they are not as flexible as other forms of dispute resolution. Litigation has the advantage of finality (although the appeal process can lengthen the final outcome) and results in a binding judgment.
Confidentiality	Not good: most court papers and hearings are open to the public (the press can be admitted to the court room).
Motivation	Not a relevant or overriding factor.
Business relationship	Not good: as an adversarial process, litigation encourages tenacious contests, often bitterly fought by the parties.
Enforcement	Good: the binding judgment in a domestic technology dispute is enforceable through the courts. The position is less clear when one looks at international technology disputes: if the defendant is based outside the jurisdiction of the court and has no assets within that jurisdiction, the judgment may have little effect.

The procedure for litigation is:

1. The party who believes its rights have been infringed (the 'claimant') sends a 'letter before action' to the infringing party (the 'defendant'). It is essential that the letter before action sets out the claim in sufficient detail to enable the defendant to fully understand the case against it. Thus the claimant

generally must undertake a significant amount of preparation before sending this letter. When dealing with IT issues, this preparation can be particularly detailed and time-consuming. Failure to send such a detailed letter can have costs implications at the end of the case.

2. The defendant will usually respond in writing to the claimant's letter before action. At this stage, the parties may also attempt to negotiate a settlement on a 'without prejudice' basis (or explore alternative dispute resolution methods, particularly if required to do so by a contract between them, or the courts).

3. If the parties are unable to reach settlement, the claimant may elect to issue legal proceedings in the appropriate court (most likely the Technology and Construction Court (TCC)). The claimant must serve upon the defendant a 'claim form' (a formal court form containing brief details of the claim) and 'particulars of claim' (a more detailed document setting out the claim and the remedies sought).

4. The defendant must acknowledge service of the claim and may at that stage elect to admit the claim, or defend all or part of it. If intending to defend the claim, then the defendant must file with the court a 'defence' (a response to the claim, including the reasons why the defendant is not liable). A defendant who also has a claim against the claimant may file a 'counterclaim' (a document similar to the claimant's particulars of claim). If the defendant fails to acknowledge service of the claim or file a defence, the claimant may apply to the court for judgment in default of a defence.

5. The court allocates the claim to the appropriate 'track' (small claims, fast-track or multi-track), depending upon the value and complexity of the claim. Technology disputes are dealt with by way of multi-track. Each party completes an allocation questionnaire providing details about the dispute, to assist the court with allocation.

6. The claimant may also choose to serve a 'reply' to the defendant's defence and a 'defence to counterclaim' if appropriate. (If the claimant fails to defend a counterclaim, the defendant may apply for judgment in default.) Unless there are exceptional circumstances, the claimant's reply and defence to the counterclaim brings an end to the process by which the parties set out their legal positions in writing. The remainder of the litigation process focuses upon the collection and exchange of each party's evidence.

7. The court sets the timetable (or directions) for the further steps in the proceedings, including disclosure and inspection of the parties' documentary evidence, exchange of witness statements and expert reports, dates for any interim hearings (e.g. the trial of a preliminary issue or a pre-trial review). The court is guided by information provided by the parties in their allocation questionnaires, which may include each party's preferred directions. The court may also order that the parties attend a hearing, known as a case management conference, to discuss directions. It is a particular feature of the CPR that the courts now take a very 'hands on' approach toward case management. It is fairly common for the directions to include a short stay of proceedings for the parties to attempt to reach settlement by alternative dispute resolution methods, such as mediation.

Following completion of the steps set out in the timetable for directions, the matter will go to trial. Trial may take the form of a single hearing, or the court has the option of trying a key preliminary issue on its own, on the basis that if this is decided in a certain party's favour it may end proceedings (or encourage an out-of-court settlement) and save the cost of a full hearing. After hearing the parties' cases at trial, the court gives its judgment and may grant leave to appeal.

There may also be a separate hearing to determine how legal costs are to be divided between the parties (generally the losing party pays the winner's costs, although the courts have a wide discretion to order costs on the most appropriate basis). If a party fails to comply with any order of the court, it may be necessary for the other party to go back to court to seek a further order for enforcement.

Arbitration

Arbitration is seen as the traditional alternative to litigation. It is a private and binding adjudicative process and was conceived as a way of providing a solution for commercial disputes in a practical and cost-effective way. Table 14.4 shows how arbitration relates to the key factors.

Table 14.4 Arbitration

Impartiality	Good: the parties choose the arbitrator, so it can be assumed that they are happy with the impartiality of the individual. In an international arbitration, it is common to have a tribunal of three arbitrators, with the chairman being neutral and each party appointing an arbitrator, who may well be of their nationality.
Expertise	Good: the appointed arbitrator will possess particular commercial or technical expertise. If necessary, more than one arbitrator (one technical, one legal, for example) can be appointed.
Speed	Good: arbitration offers some opportunities for innovation and for devising an appropriate cost-effective procedure for a particular dispute. The speed of domestic technology arbitrations may well rest on the development of such procedures. (There are also opportunities for doing this in international technology arbitration, but the costs of such arbitrations are generally substantial.)
Cost	Not good: a large-scale technology arbitration is likely to be at least as expensive as litigation, if not more so. Arbitration is only cheaper if it disposes of a dispute more quickly and efficiently than court proceedings. Whether this is so depends on the cooperation of the parties to achieve that end and the strength of the arbitral panel. Since the arbitrator's engagement is a matter of contract, dates that are fixed will be kept by the tribunal.

(Continued)

Table 14.4 *(Continued)*

	However, if the parties allow their disputes to spill over into the procedural conduct of the arbitration, this may well nullify such cost benefits.
Certainty	Good: there is very little difference between litigation and arbitration in this respect. However, one of the main differences between the two procedures is that an arbitrator may not have to decide according to law. This does not mean that an arbitrator should disregard the rules of law altogether, but the parties can authorise the arbitrator to decide not strictly in accordance with the law (e.g. in order to prioritise commercial fairness over strict legal entitlement).
Confidentiality	Good: only the parties to the dispute may attend the arbitration hearing, and all documents prepared by both parties for the purpose of the arbitration are confidential and protected from disclosure in any subsequent proceedings. Although not true in all jurisdictions, non-statutory arbitration in the UK is private. This is a clear advantage because many arbitrations involve an investigation of material that is considered to be commercially sensitive, whether financially or because of the technology under consideration.
Motivation	Not a relevant or overriding factor.
Business relationship	Not good: like litigation, arbitration is an adversarial process involving procedures that can be tenaciously utilised by lawyers. The outcome is often a breakdown in relationships.
Enforcement	Good: The Convention On The Recognition And Enforcement Of Foreign Arbitral Awards 1958 (known as the 'New York Convention') provides for the awards from arbitration to be upheld internationally. The Convention has attracted near universal adherence (144 countries have signed up to it). Enforcement under the New York Convention is not always easy but it undoubtedly gives an arbitral award greater international effectiveness than a court judgment.

The framework for arbitration is governed by statute. Contracts often contain clauses that refer any dispute to arbitration. If such a clause exists, the parties must adhere to it rather than issuing proceedings in the courts.

The parties to the contract select the arbitrator together on the basis of expertise in the field from which the dispute stems or on which the contract is based.

The arbitrator's conduct is governed by the ordinary rules of natural justice, evidence, and the civil burden of proof (the case must be proven 'on the balance of probabilities'). The parties are, however, at liberty to dispense with the ordinary rules of evidence and allow the arbitrator to carry out a more inquisitorial role.

If there is no governing arbitration clause, the parties may opt to engage in arbitration by agreement. In this instance, the parties meet and agree the terms of the arbitration agreement after the dispute has arisen. As is the case when an arbitration clause in a contract is being drafted, the parties are at liberty to determine the timescale, applicable law, procedure, and venue of the arbitration as well as the arbitrator they wish to use. In effect, the parties tailor the personnel, procedure and hearings to their particular needs.

During the arbitration proceedings, the arbitrator gives directions and may hold hearings in much the same way as a judge would in litigation proceedings. The arbitrator does this in accordance with the rules adopted by the parties, be they of their own invention or adopted from a particular institution's prescribed rules. The arbitrator may have to decide on the rules of the arbitration if the parties are unable to agree. The parties are able to refer issues to the courts if the arbitrator is guilty of any misconduct. The courts may also determine points of law and support the arbitrator by making various orders.

The arbitrator will hold a final hearing at which he or she will make an award to one of the parties. There is no requirement for the arbitrator to give reasons for the award he or she makes. However, if one of the parties asks for reasons and he or she refuses to give them, then the court (on application from the party concerned) may order him or her to do so. The award made is legally enforceable against the other party, but a party is allowed to appeal to the court against an award on a point of law.

Mediation

Mediation involves the appointment of an independent, qualified mediator (or mediators) to assist the parties in reaching an agreed settlement. A mediator does not usually have an adjudicative role in the proceedings, nor is it the mediator's role (unless expressly asked to do so by the parties to the mediation) to pass judgment, or to give an opinion on the merits of the parties' individual cases. Rather, the mediator's role is to facilitate the resolution of the dispute in question.

The use of mediation in the technology industry has continued to increase, particularly as parties to a dispute now face increasing pressure from the courts to resolve their differences through alternative dispute resolution methods rather than court proceedings. The CPR states that the court must further the overriding objective by actively managing cases, including 'encouraging the parties to use an alternative dispute resolution procedure if the court considers that appropriate and facilitating the use of such procedure', and there has been a corresponding increase in court-ordered mediations.

Moreover, the government is encouraging the use of mediation in the public sector. Under the Lord Chancellor's Pledge, alternative dispute resolution methods should be considered and used in all suitable cases wherever the parties accept it. This covers government departments and agencies.

If a party in a technology dispute refuses an invitation to mediate, without a legitimate reason for such a refusal, it may risk being criticised by the courts should the dispute result in legal proceedings. That party could also face cost penalties regardless of the outcome of such legal proceedings, should a court consider a refusal to mediate to constitute unreasonable conduct.

Table 14.5 shows how mediation relates to the key factors.

Table 14.5 Mediation

Impartiality	Good: the parties choose a mediator, so they will be able to select a person who they regard as possessing impartiality.
Expertise	Not relevant: the mediator's expertise does not necessarily need to be legal or technical; it is more important that the mediator is well-trained and able to facilitate an open and constructive discussion. If necessary, the parties could appoint an additional, more technical, mediator.
Speed	Good: mediation ends when the parties reach a settlement, or when a party or mediator decides to terminate the process. Commonly, mediation does not last more than a day (much less time than arbitration or court proceedings). The time spent preparing for a mediation is also much less than the time spent preparing for litigation or arbitration.
Cost	Good: the costs are a fraction of those that would be incurred were legal proceedings to be initiated. Moreover, the significant costs orders and damages awards that may be awarded in court proceedings can be avoided.
Certainty	Moderate: if successful, mediation results in the resolution by an agreement of the parties. It may not be a 'correct' legal decision, but resolution will in general be 'fair' because it will be consented to by both parties.
Confidentiality	Good: mediation is a strictly confidential process. All representations made during this process (whether written or oral) are also 'without prejudice' and therefore any documentation produced for the purposes of the mediation and admissions made during it cannot, in most cases, be relied upon as evidence by the parties in court proceedings should the mediation prove unsuccessful.
Motivation	Good: parties who agree to mediate are usually committed to reaching a commercially acceptable resolution, particularly if an ongoing business relationship is a possibility.

(Continued)

Table 14.5 *(Continued)*

Business relationship	Good: the mediation process is significantly closer to business negotiations than to adversarial courtroom procedures, so business relationships can better be preserved.
Enforcement	Not good: the process of mediation is non-binding and the parties cannot be forced to settle their dispute unless a consensus to do so is reached. If a settlement is agreed, it only becomes binding upon the parties once the terms have been recorded in a settlement agreement and the agreement is executed by all parties concerned. If a party refuses to carry out the terms of settlement, it is necessary to commence an action on the settlement agreement, to obtain judgment and then to seek execution of the judgment. Experience, however, suggests that parties who have mediated a settlement of their dispute tend to carry out voluntarily the terms of settlement and that a formal enforcement procedure is rarely necessary.

The parties are expected to agree upon a choice of mediator. The choice of mediator will invariably be determined by the nature of the dispute, and the mediator may be a lawyer, an accountant or a technical expert. In the IT industry, a legally qualified mediator with knowledge of the industry, or possibly a technically-qualified expert, would be preferable. A venue for the mediation also needs to be agreed upon. This is usually a venue independent of the parties.

The process usually follows this format:

1. The parties prepare written case summaries that are exchanged with each other and provided to the mediator in advance of the mediation. This allows the mediator to understand the issues in dispute and the parties' respective positions. The case summaries should highlight any facts and issues that have been agreed by the parties as well as those that remain in dispute. These summaries are usually supported by an agreed bundle of relevant documentation to which the parties can refer in their summaries. This is usually made up of contracts, correspondence, notes of meetings, relevant technical papers etc. The mediation takes place shortly after the exchange of case summaries and copy documentation.

2. The mediation commences with a joint session attended by all the parties (and their legal representatives) and the mediator, at which the parties are invited to give a short presentation of their positions in relation to the dispute.

3. The parties retire to separate rooms and a series of what are termed 'caucus' sessions commence. The sessions involve the mediator visiting each of the parties to discuss and explore their respective legal positions. The mediator will use these caucus sessions to establish if there is any middle ground between the parties that may form the basis of a negotiated settlement.

4. The mediator may call the parties back for further open sessions to discuss any progress that has been made or issues that have been raised.

5. If the parties are successful in establishing a commercial resolution to the dispute the mediator will expect them to sign up to written terms of settlement prior to the close of the mediation. Most mediation organisations insist upon the parties having personnel with the appropriate authority to settle the dispute. Mediators are particularly keen on any agreement reached being drawn up and signed by the parties on the day of the mediation because this avoids the parties subsequently disputing the terms of any agreement reached.

CONCLUSION

There is no 'right answer' when choosing a dispute resolution process. Each dispute resolution method has advantages and disadvantages that will play a part in the decision-making process.

The courts, and the increasing range of arbitration bodies, continue to take action to improve their offerings as dispute resolution providers. Mediation also continues to gain popularity in the UK as a commercial and cost-effective way of resolving disputes. A refusal to consider the available dispute resolution methods could have heavy cost implications, and they are accordingly worth addressing properly during the contract negotiation phase of a technology project, as well as in the early stages of any actual dispute.

INDEX

academic licences 134
acceptance testing
　definition xv
　procedure 12, 17
　software development
　　contracts 9
　systems procurement
　　contracts 17
access, staff usage policy 36
agency agreements, joint ventures
　108
alternative dispute resolution
　(ADR)
　definition xv
　in contract 2
application service provider (ASP)
　xv, 65, 118
Approved Authorised Treatment
　Facilities (AATFs) 145
Approved Exporters 145
arbitration
　agreement in contract 2
　as dispute resolution method 172
asset register 71
asset transfer 72

backup of data
　cloud computing 123, 124
　data protection issues 86
　specimen policy 38
benchmarking 70
boilerplate terms 2
business process outsourcing (BPO)
　xv, 65
business-to-business contracts 99

cancellation rights, under Distance
　Selling Regulations 97–98
change control
　clause in contract 17–18
　definition xv
Civil Procedure Rules 1998 (CPR)
　definition xv
　dispute resolution 169, 171
　mediation 172
cloud computing
　advantages 119–121
　backup requirements 123, 124
　contract for services 123–125
　　customer obligations 123–124
　　data protection issues 124–125
　　indemnities 125
　　limitation of liability 125

service rental 123
　supplier obligations 124
costs 120
data protection issues 122–123,
　124–125
definition 117
disadvantages 121–122
due diligence 121–122, 123
environmental issues 121
evolution 118–119
free trials 121
generally 117
internet reliability and 121
maintenance and support 121
mobility 120
resource access 119
sale of data 125
scalability 120
security 120, 124–125
services 118
storage 120
supplier dependence 121–122
types of cloud 119
Code of Advertising Practice 84
community clouds 119
Community designs 54
Competition Act 1998 114
competition law
　definition xv
　joint ventures and 114–115
Computer Misuse Act 1990 32
computer usage policies
　action plan 33
　backup of data 38
　breaches 38
　confidentiality 37
　data protection 38
　drawing up 32
　generally 33
　hacking 32
　misuse 38
　password protection 38
　record keeping 37
　security of data 37
　specimen 39
confidential information, protection
　of 51–52
confidentiality
　business emails 37
　consultancy services contracts 5
　FOIA and 159
　IT contracts 11
consequential loss, liability for 23

consultancy services
　confidentiality 5
　contracts for 5
　copyright 5
　deliverables 5
　insurance 5
　key personnel 5
　payment arrangements 4
　termination rights 5
consumer 93
consumer contracts 99
Consumer Protection (Distance
　Selling) Regulations 2000
　cancellation rights 97–98
　information requirements 95
　non-compliance 101
contra proferentem rule 23
contracts
　boilerplate terms 2
　business-to-business 99
　cloud computing services 123–125
　confidentiality 11
　consultancy services 5
　consumer 99
　deliverables 5
　entire agreement clause 2
　FOIA clause 162
　force majeure clause xvi, 2
　form 1
　formation 97
　function 13
　governing law and jurisdiction
　　clause 2
　hardware maintenance 6
　hardware purchase 6
　implied terms 13–14
　legal structure 95–96
　letters of intent 3
　main points 12
　open source software 140
　pre-contract correspondence 11
　selection of lawyer 2
　service level agreements (SLAs)
　　11
　software development 11
　software licences 7
　software maintenance 8
　suppliers
　　assessing suitability 3
　　proposed terms 3,15
　support duration 11–12
　training requirements 12
contributor agreements 142

cookies
  definition xv
  regulation of use 84–85
copyleft licences 134–136
copyright
  consultancy services contracts
    5,19
  creation of 50
  databases 50
  definition xv, 40, 49
  developed software 9, 19, 56, 127
  duration 50
  Internet and 49
  linking, infringement caused by 49
  manuals 50
  moral rights and 50
  open source software 127, 134
  registration 50
  software 42, 50
  websites 45, 50
country of origin principle 99
Creative Commons licences 143
cyber-squatting 46

data controller xvi
data protection
  backup tapes 85
  cloud computing 122–123,
    124–125
  computer usage policies 38
  consent to processing 81–82
  data obtained from third party 81
  data subject rights
    see data subjects
  due diligence and 79
  enforcement 91
  exemption from requirements
    89–90
    notification 77, 90
    subject access provisions 90
    subject information provisions
      90
  fines for breach 74, 90
  list brokers, information from
    80–81
  manual data 76
  marketing, opting out 85
  notification with Information
    Commissioner
    changes 79
    exemptions 77, 90
    parties liable 77
    procedure 79
    renewal 79
    templates 79
  personal data
    definition xvii, 76
    security 79
      International Standard 87
      procedures 87
      proportionality 87
    transfer to other countries
      87–88, 122, 124–125
  principles
    accuracy 83
    adequate, relevant and not
      excessive 82
    fair and lawful processing
      80–81, 123
    not kept longer than necessary
      85
    not transferred to countries
      without adequate protection
      87–88, 122, 124–125

    processed in accordance with
      data subject's rights 85–86
    processing for limited
      purposes 81
    security 87
  processing
    by third parties 87
    consent to 82
    definition 80
    fair and lawful 80–81, 123
    in accordance with subjects
      rights 85–86
    limited purposes 81
    without consent 81
    scope 76
  security of personal data 79
    International Standard 87
    procedures 87
    proportionality 87
  sensitive personal data
    consent to processing 82
    definition xviii, 76
    terminology 74
Data Protection Act 1998
  criminal offences within 91
  Enforcement Notices 90
  exemptions
    notifications 76–77, 90
    subject access provisions 90
    subject information provisions
      90
  fines for breach 74, 90
  marketing, right to opt out 85
  notifications
    exemption from requirements
      77, 90
    personal data under 87
    procedure 79
  principles of data protection 80
  scope 76
  sensitive personal data under
    76, 82
  terminology 74
data subjects
  access requests
    complying with 89
    definition xvi
    exemptions 90
    time limit 89
  consent to processing 80
  definition xvi
  information provisions
    complying with 80
    exemptions 90
  marketing, opting out 85
  provision of details to 80
  rights 75, 88
    access requests 89
    information on processor
      88, 90
    marketing 85
    processing in accordance
      with 85–86
database right
  definition xvi, 40
  generally 44, 50–51
  linking, infringement caused by
    49
databases
  copyright 49–50
  intellectual property rights and
    45
  licences to use 44
  protecting own rights 45

decompilation of software 43
deliverables, consultancy services
  contracts 4
Department for Business
  Innovation and Skills (BIS),
  non-household equipment 148
description, implied term 13–14
design rights 40
  Community designs 54
  definition xvi
  UK design right 53–54
  UK registered designs 53
Designated Collection Facilities
  (DCF) 145
Direct Marketing Association 84
direct marketing, data subjects'
  right to opt out 85
Disability Discrimination Act 1995
  35
disclaimers, on business emails
  32–33
disks, staff usage policy 36
display screen equipment (DSE)
  definition xvi
  regulations 34
dispute resolution (DR)
  arbitration 172
  choice of method 165
  definition
  escalation to senior management
    167
  expert determination 167–169
  key factors 165
  litigation 170
  mediation 175
  methods 165
  negotiation 166
  reasons for need 164
distance contracts
  information requirements 95
  legislation 93
distance selling
  definition xvi
  regulations
    see Consumer Protection
    (Distance Selling)
    Regulations
Distance Selling Directive 1997
  93
  performance time limits 97
  see also Consumer Protection
    (Distance Selling) Regulations
distribution agreements, joint
  ventures 108
Distributor Take-back Scheme
  (DTS) 145, 150
domain names
  avoiding dispute 47
  cyber-squatting 46
  definition xvi
  intellectual property rights and
    47
  problems with 46
  registration 47
  trade marks and 46, 47
DSE Regulations 34
dual licensing 130, 136–137
due diligence
  asset transfer 72
  cloud computing 121–122, 123
  data protection issues 79
  definition xvi
  open source software projects
    138, 140–141

ecommerce
  cancellation rights 97–98
  Consumer Protection (Distance
    Selling) Regulations 2000 95
  consumer rights enforcement
    101
  contract formation 97
  country of origin principle 99
  Electronic Commerce Directive
    2000 93
  generally 92
  information requirements
    checklist 102
    Consumer Protection
      (Distance Selling)
      Regulations 2000 95
    Electronic Commerce (EC
      Directive) Regulations 2002
      93, 97
    generally 95
  jurisdiction 99
  marketing communications 100
  non-compliance with
    legislation 101
  performance time limits 107
  resources 101
  spam, restrictions on sending 100
  Stop Now Orders 101
  terminology 93
electrical and electronic equipment
  146
Electronic Commerce (EC Directive)
  Regulations 2002
  information requirements 94, 97
  information society service
    providers
      enforcement actions against
      101
      operating rules for 99
  marketing communications 100
  non-compliance 101
Electronic Commerce Directive
  2000 93
  contract formation by electronic
    means 97
  hosting/caching of material 101
  information society service
    providers 99
  marketing communications
    100
  see also Electronic Commerce
    (EC Directive) Regulations
email
  business
    confidentiality 37
    disclaimers 33
    specimen policy 37
  confidentiality 37
  disclaimers, in business 33
  employees' misuse, consequences
    for employers 28, 29
  information disclosure 33
  monitoring by employers 30
  private 31
    specimen restriction 37
  problems with 29
  storage 29
  unsolicited 84
    see also spam
  usage policies 33
    action plan 33
    establishing 32
    monitoring 30
    specimen 37

employees
  code ownership 142
  computer systems usage
    action plan 33
    monitoring by employers 30
    policy 32
  customer systems usage 36
  display screen use 34
  email
    monitoring by employers 30
    private 31
  hacking 32
  internet usage
    inappropriate material 37
    monitoring by employers 30
    policy considerations 32
    specimen restriction 37
  misuse of computer systems
    consequences for employers
      28–29
    specimen policy 38
  private email 31
    specimen restriction 37
  right to eye tests 34
employers
  computer usage policies 32
  consequences of staff misuse of
    computers 28–29
  monitoring of staff
    communications 29–30, 38–39
  provision of eye tests 34
Enforcement Notices, under Data
  Protection Act 1998 91
Enterprise Act 2002 114
entire agreement clause 2
Environment Agency (EA) 145, 149
Environmental Information
  Regulations 2004 153
equipment disposal
  collection v. disposal 152
  commercial issues 152
  financial responsibility 144, 149,
    151
  household equipment 148
    PCS financial responsibility
      149
    waste handling obligations
      151
  non-household equipment
    148
    PCS financial responsibility
      149
    waste handling obligations
      150
  see also Waste Electrical and
    Electronic Equipment (WEEE)
    Regulations
escalation clauses
  as dispute resolution method 167
  in service level agreements 10
escrow
  definition xv, 55
  importance for software users 56
  see also source code escrow
European economic interest
  grouping (EEIG) 111–112
exclusion clauses
  contra proferentem rule 23
  enforceability 22
  forms 21
  reasonableness test 24, 27
expert determination, as dispute
  resolution method 167–169
eye tests for screen users 34

facilities management (FM)
  contract xvi, 65
Fax Preference Service 84
First-tier Tribunal (Information
  Rights), FOIA appeals 157
fitness for purpose, implied term 14
force majeure
  as boilerplate term 2
  definition xv
framing
  definition xvi
  in trade mark infringement 48
Free Software Foundation (FSF)
  127
freedom of information
  contract clauses 162
  definition 153
  legislation
    see Freedom of Information
    Act (FOIA)
  procurement 161–162
  public interest test 158
  requests for information
    appeal to Information
      Commissioner's Office 157
    appropriate/cost limit 158–159
    process 157
    public authority actions 157
    refusal to respond 158
    time limits 155
    unclear requests 155
    withholding information 158
  Transparency Agenda 154
  withholding information 158
Freedom of Information Act (FOIA)
  2000
  appeals
    to Information Commissioner's
      Office 157
    to Information Tribunal 157
  dealing with 160–161
  exemptions 158–159
    absolute 158
    commercial prejudice 160
    confidential information 160
    qualified 159
  impact on private companies
    159–160
  public authorities
    obligations 155
    provision of information to 156
    status under 154
  request process 156–157
  see also freedom of information

GNU General Public Licence
  134, 135–136, 138

hacking, by employees 32
hardware
  authorised sales 41
  intellectual property rights and
    42
  maintenance
    contracts for 6
    types 6
  purchase
    contracts for 6
    retention of title 19
  repairs 42
  special conditions of sale 42
health and safety
  action plan 34–35
  advice 33–35

DSE Regulations 34
  legislation 34
Health and Safety at Work etc Act
  1974 33
home state regulation 99
hybrid clouds 119

implied terms 13–14
independent contractors, code
  ownership 142
Information Commissioner
  code of conduct for monitoring at
    work 30
  definition xvii
  enforcement role 91
  FOIA appeals 157
  function 74
  power to impose fines 74, 90
  website 74
information society services
  definition 93
  operating rules for providers 99
infrastructure as a service (IaaS) 117
  see also cloud computing
insurance, in consultancy service
  contracts 5
intellectual property rights (IPRs)
  advice 54
  databases and 45
  definition xvii
  domain names and 47
  guide to 54
  hardware and 42
  indemnity clauses 20
  infringement
    of third party IPRs 20
    on the web 49
  joint ventures 106
  open source software 139–140
  software and 44
  systems procurement contracts 20
  terminology 54
  types 40
  websites and 46
internet, the
  cloud computing and 121
  copyrights and 49
  staff usage
    action plan 33
    inappropriate material 37
    monitoring by employers 30
    policy considerations 32
    specimen restriction 37
    trade marks and 49

joint ventures
  agency agreements 108
  bolt on terms 108–109
  business plans 106
  case study 104
  competition law and 114–115
  definition xvii, 103
  distribution agreements 108
  establishing 107
  exit arrangements 107
  heads of agreement 105
  intellectual property ownership
    106
  IT projects and 104
  licensing deals 108
  management 106
  non-disclosure agreements 104–105
  operating agreements 112–113,
    115–116

potential issues 103
  royalty deals 108
  structures 112
  terms 115
jurisdiction
  business-to-business contracts 99
  consumer contracts 99
  ecommerce 99

key performance indicators (KPIs)
  68
keyword advertising, trade mark
  infringement and 49

lawyers, selection 2
legal persons 110
letters, information disclosure 33
letters of intent 3
licences
  open 142
  software
    see software licences
licensing deals, joint ventures 108
limited companies 111
limited liability partnerships (LLPs)
  110–111
limited partnerships 110
linking
  copyright infringement 49
  database right infringement 49
  definition xvii
  trade mark infringement 49
Linux 131
liquidated damages 20
list brokers, information from 80–81
litigation
  as dispute resolution method 170
  procedure 170

Mailing Preference Service 84
Management of Health and Safety
  at Work Regulations 1999 33
manuals, copyright in 50
market testing 70
marketing
  communications in ecommerce
    100
  data subjects rights to opt out 85
mediation, as dispute resolution
  method 174–175
metatags
  definition xvii
  use in trade mark infringement
    49
migration procedures, in SLAs 11
misuse of computer systems
  consequences for employers
    28–29
  examples 38
  specimen policy 38
monitoring, by employers
  code 30
  covert 30
  emails 29–30, 38–39
  internet use 30, 31–32, 38–39
  website access 32
moral right
  copyright and 50
  definition xvii

negotiation
  as dispute resolution method 166
  systems procurement contracts
    14

networks, staff usage policy 36
non-disclosure agreements (NDAs)
  definition xvii
  joint ventures 104–105
  with public authorities 162
Northern Ireland Environment
  Agency (NIEA) 145

Open Source Initiative (OSI) 127
open source software
  commercial development 133
    examples 131
    financial considerations 132
  communities and 131
  contracts 140
  copyright 127, 134
  costs 133
  development model 131
    advantages 132
  dual licensing 130, 136–137
  due diligence 138, 140–141
  examples 126
  licences 130, 137
    academic licences 134–135
    compatibility 136
    copyleft licences 134–136
    dual licensing 130, 136–137
    external use 139
    internal use 138–139
    patent licences 142
  meaning 127
  ownership 142
  patents and 142
  policies and procedures
    140–141
  practical issues 137
  quality 134
  utilising in business 133–134
  warranties 134, 139–140
output specification 66
outsourcing
  asset transfer 71
  definition xvii, 65
  design risk 67
  exit arrangements 73
  functions commonly outsourced
    66
  inputs v outputs 66
  key elements 65
  key performance indicators (PIs)
    68
  life cycle 73
  offshore 73
  performance indicators (PIs) 68
  performance points 68
  pricing and payment
    mechanisms 70
  ratchet mechanisms 68
  service delivery phase 72
  service description drafting 66
  service level agreements 69
  transition of services 72

partnership
  agreements 110
  data protection requirements
    78
  definition 109
  disclosure of information on
    letters 32
  limited 110
  limited liability 110–111
Partnership Act 1890 109
passing off xvii, 52–53

password protection, computer
usage policies 38
patents 40
  application procedure 51
  definition xvii
  duration 51
  matter patentable 51
  open source software and 142
  software 51
payment arrangements
  cloud computing 120
  consultancy services contracts 4
  hardware maintenance
    contracts 6
  outsourcing contracts 70
  software development contracts
    9
  software maintenance contracts
    8
  systems procurement contracts
    19
penalties 90–91
performance indicators (PIs) 68
performance points 68
personal data
  see data protection
platform as a service (PaaS) 117
  see also cloud computing
pre-contract correspondence 11
pricing structures, outsourcing
  contracts 70
Privacy and Electronic
  Communications (EC Directive)
  Regulations 2003
  cookies 84–85
  unsolicited email 84, 100
  unsolicited text messages 84, 100
private clouds 119
private companies
  dealing with FOIA 160–161
  impact of FOIA 159–160
    commercial issues 159–160
    privacy 160
    reputation 160
  public authorities and 164
    contractual requirement to
      locate information 155–156,
      161
    information subject to
      disclosure under FOIA 155
    see also freedom of
      information
procurement, FOIA issues 161–162
Producer Compliance Scheme (PCS)
  compulsory membership 149
  definition 146
project open book accounting
  (POBA) 69–70
proportionality, personal data
  security 87
public authorities
  obligations 155
  private companies and 154
    contractual requirement to
      locate information 155–156,
      161
    information subject to
      disclosure under FOIA 155
    provision of information 156
    see also freedom of information
  requests for information 156
  status under FOIA 154
public clouds 119
public domain, software in 130

quality of goods, implied term 14
quiet possession of goods, implied
  term 14

ratchet mechanism 68
reasonable care and skill, implied
  term 14
reasonableness test 24, 26–27
record keeping
  computer usage policy 37
  waste handling 151
Regulation of Investigatory Powers
  Act 2000 29
repetitive strain injury (RSI)
  action on plan on reducing 35
  definition xvii
  level of claims 33
reseller agreements 107
retention of title, hardware supply
  contracts 19
royalty deals, joint ventures 108

Safe Harbor (2000) 87
Scottish Environmental Protection
  Agency (SEPA) 145
security
  cloud computing 120, 124–125
  computer usage policies 37
  personal data 78–78, 86–87
service description drafting 66
service level agreements (SLAs)
  breach 10
  contracts for 11
  definition xviii
  elements 69
  escalation clauses 10
  form 10
  outsourcing 69
  termination 10
service provider, definition 93
service recipient, definition 93
software
  adapting 42, 43
  backup copies 43
  copyright in 42, 50, 56
  decompilation 43
  development
    see software development
  intellectual property rights and 44
  licences
    see software licences
  maintenance
    see software maintenance
  patenting of 51
  proof of ownership 63
  public domain 130
  supply contracts, special
    considerations 25
  usage policy 36
software as a service (SaaS)
  definition 117
  emergence 118
  see also cloud computing
software development
  contracts for 9
    special considerations 25
  copyright in product 9
  payment arrangements 9
  source code escrow and 9
  suppliers' warranties 9
  termination rights 18
software licences
  contracts for 7
  financial issues 132

non-compliance 44
open source software 127–129,
  130, 134–137
  academic licences 134–135
  compatibility 136
  copyleft licences 135–136
  dual licensing 130, 136–137
  external use 139
  internal use 138–139
    patent licences 142
  permitted uses under 25
  restrictions imposed by 25
  scope 43
  staff usage and 36
  term 25
  transferring 44
  types 25
software maintenance
  charging arrangements 7, 8
  contracts for 8
  exclusions 8
  IPR issues 43
  payment arrangements 8
  scope 8
  termination 8, 18
sole traders, disclosure of
  information on letters 32
source code
  complexity 59
  conversion to executable code
    56, 126
  definition xviii, 56
  deposit agreements
    see source code escrow
  open source software 126, 138
  security 56, 126
  storage issues 63
source code escrow
  advantages for software owners
    62–63
  agents 62
  agreements 61–62
  items to be lodged 61
  proof of ownership of software 63
  providing for in IT contracts 12
  release events 61
  requirement for 57–58
  software development and 9
  technical considerations 59
  user's duties 62
  verification 60
  when needed 56–57
spam
  definition xviii
  legal restrictions on sending 100
specification xviii
staff transfers, TUPE and 73
standard contracts, dangers of 15
statement of requirements 66
Stop Now Orders 101
suppliers
  cloud computing 121–122, 124
  suitability 3
  terms proposed by 3, 15
  warranties given by
    cloud computing services
      contracts 124
    software development
      contracts 9
    systems procurement
      contracts 20
systems procurement contracts
  acceptance testing 17
  breach 20

change control 18
client obligations 17
consequential loss liability 23
delivery arrangements 16–17
exclusion clauses
    contra proferentem rule 23
    enforceabilty 22
    forms of 21
    reasonableness test 24, 27
implied terms 13–14
intellectual property rights 20
negotiation process 13
obligations 15, 17
payment arrangements 18–19
remedies 20
specification 15–16
standard contracts, dangers of 15
supplier warranties 20
termination provisions 18
timetable 16

technical solution 66
Telecommunications (Lawful
  Business Practice) (Interception
  of Communications)
  Regulations 2000 30
Telephone Preference Service 84
termination rights
  consultancy services contracts
    5, 18
  hardware maintenance contracts
    18
  outsourcing contracts 73
  service level agreements 11
  software development contracts 18
  software maintenance contracts
    8, 18
  systems procurement contracts 18
terms, contractual
  boilerplate terms 2
  implied by law 13–14

joint ventures 105
  suppliers' proposed 3, 15
title to goods
  implied term 13
  retention of 19
trade marks 40
  application procedure 52
  definition xviii
  domain names and 46, 47
  duration 52
  framing, infringement caused by
    48
  infringement of 48–49, 52
  internet and 49
  keyword advertising,
    infringement caused by 49
  linking, infringement caused by
    49
  metatags, infringement caused
    by 49
  registrability 52
  websites 45
training, IT contracts 12
Transfer of Undertakings
  (Protection of Employment)
  Regulations 2006 (TUPE)
  xviii, 73
Transparency Agenda 154, 161

unsolicited communications,
  restrictions on sending 84
    see also spam
usage policies
  computers 33
  email 28–33
  specimen 39

Valpak 145, 150
Vehicle Certification Agency (VCA)
  146
viruses, staff action policy 36

warranties
  open source software 134,
    139–140
  suppliers'
    cloud computing services
      contracts 124
    software development
      contracts 9
    systems procurement
      contracts 20
  third party IPRs 20
Waste Electrical and Electronic
  Equipment (WEEE) Regulations
  2006
  consumers 145
  distributors
    definition 145
    obligations 150
  enforcement 145
  exemptions 146
  generally 144
  geographical limitations 147
  obligations under 150–151
  parties 146
  producers
    definition 145
    obligations 150
    registration number 150
  scope 148
    see also equipment disposal
websites
  copyright 45, 50
  framing 49
  intellectual property rights
    46
  keyword advertising 49
  linking 49
  metatags 49
  monitoring staff access 32
  ownership 45
  protection of rights 46